The Scottish Law of Evidence

Angela Mcfarlane

The Scottish Law of Evidence

A. B. Wilkinson, MA, LLB, Advocate
Professor of Private Law in the University of Dundee

London/Edinburgh
Butterworths/The Law Society of Scotland
1986

United Kingdom	Butterworth & Co (Publishers) Ltd, 88 Kingsway, LONDON WC2B 6AB and 61A North Castle Street, EDINBURGH EH2 3LJ
Australia	Butterworths Pty Ltd, SYDNEY, MELBOURNE, BRISBANE, ADELAIDE, PERTH, CANBERRA and HOBART
Canada	Butterworths. A division of Reed Inc., TORONTO and VANCOUVER
New Zealand	Butterworths of New Zealand Ltd, WELLINGTON and AUCKLAND
Singapore	Butterworth & Co (Asia) Pte Ltd, SINGAPORE
South Africa	Butterworth Publishers (Pty) Ltd, DURBAN and PRETORIA
USA	Butterworth Legal Publishers, ST PAUL, Minnesota, SEATTLE, Washington, BOSTON, Massachusetts, AUSTIN, Texas and D&S Publishers, CLEARWATER, Florida

British Library Cataloguing in Publication Data

Wilkinson, A. B.
The Scottish law of evidence.
1. Evidence (Law)—Scotland
I. Title
344.1107′6 KDC888

ISBN 0 406 26110 5

Typeset by Latimer Trend & Company Ltd, Plymouth
Printed and bound in Great Britain by
Biddles Ltd, Guildford and King's Lynn

Preface

The purpose of this book is to give an account, within modest compass, of the main features of the Scottish law of evidence. In this, perhaps more than in other branches, the law is often subject to the charge of being piecemeal and incoherent. An attempt has, therefore, been made at a systematic treatment which it is hoped will show that, despite some historical anomalies and modern inconsistencies, the law has, when viewed against the purposes which it is designed to serve, an overall rational structure. The needs of both practitioners and students have been kept in mind. The interests of both are, it is believed, served by a work which seeks to provide a modern guide in accessible form to the principles of the law and the authorities on major topics and which also gives consideration, although necessarily brief, to the rationale of the legal rules and to points of difficulty, obscurity or controversy.

Since this is a book on the Scottish law of evidence, particular attention has been paid to distinctively Scottish characteristics. A rigid isolation from neighbouring influences is, however, as inimical to an independent jurisprudence as is slavish imitation. Reference has therefore been made to English authorities and, if sparingly, to cases from other jurisdictions where they offered scope for comparison or were illustrative of applicable principles.

I am indebted to Mrs Sheila Summers for coping resourcefully with the typing of a difficult draft text, to my family for their tolerance and to the staff of Messrs Butterworths for their forbearance and help through a number of vicissitudes.

A. B. Wilkinson
July 1986

Contents

Table of statutes and statutory instruments

Table of cases

D

S

Bibliography

The following are the principal works to which reference is made:

The late Sir Rupert Cross and Colin Tapper *Cross on Evidence* (6th edn, 1985) London

William Gillespie Dickson *A Treatise on the Law of Evidence in Scotland* (3rd edn by P J Hamilton Grieson, 1887) Edinburgh

Sheriff I D Macphail *Research Paper on the Law of Evidence in Scotland* Scottish Law Commission, 1979

Allan Grierson Walker and Norman Macdonald Lockhart Walker *The Law of Evidence in Scotland* (1964) Edinburgh

CHAPTER 1

Nature and function of the law of evidence

DEFINITION

Evidence has been defined as 'that which tends to prove or disprove any conclusion', or again, 'information given in a legal investigation to establish the fact or point in issue'.[1] Those definitions are, however, capable of embracing argument and questions of law whereas evidence for legal purposes comprises only the information which tends to prove or disprove any matter of fact the truth of which is submitted to judicial investigation. Its main means are the testimony of witnesses which the tribunal charged with determining whether the facts have been proved hears, and documents and things which are produced to it and which it may inspect. The law of evidence is concerned with the regulation of these means and of their function in constituting proof.

RESTRICTIVE FACTORS

'From the beginning a student of evidence must accustom himself to dealing as wisely and as understandingly as possible with principles which impede freedom of proof. He is making a study of calculated and supposedly helpful obstructionism.'[2]

The obstructive character of the law of evidence does not distinguish it radically from other branches of law, for an element of obstruction is implicit in regulation. The extent to which freedom of proof is impeded may, however, be surprising. The limiting function which the law performs in the process of judicial proof is in contrast with the freedom with which truth may be pursued in other kinds of investigation. To some extent the restrictive rules are but formal expressions of more loosely conceived notions which might guide any enquiry and are

1 *Shorter Oxford English Dictionary.*
2 Maguire *Evidence, Common Sense and Common Law* p 1.

concerned with discriminating between the relevant and the irrelevant, the reliable and unreliable, in the ascertainment of truth. Not all the rules can, however, be seen in that way and they have their origin in characteristics of the judicial process which mark it off from other forms of investigation. Among the factors which influence the restrictive nature of evidentiary rules are:

1 the practical consideration of keeping the enquiry and its expense within manageable bounds and so confining it to matters most likely to be helpful and excluding more distant matters;
2 the necessity of reaching a decision which is final so far as the issue between the parties is concerned. This consideration applies to evidence for the purpose of many practical non-judicial decisions as well, but distinguishes judicial evidence from evidence for the purposes of historical or scientific enquiry where decision may be suspended or a provisional or hypothetical conclusion reached;
3 the seriousness of the decision. This may mean that elements of evidence have to be excluded, as giving rise to an unacceptably high risk of error, which might be admitted where the issues were less serious and higher risks could be accepted;
4 the adversary nature of litigation. In *Thomson v Glasgow Corpn*[3] Lord Justic-Clerk Thomson said:

> 'A litigation is in essence a trial of skill between opposing parties, conducted under recognised rules and the prize is the judge's decision. We have rejected inquisitorial methods and prefer to regard our judges as entirely independent. Like referees at boxing contests, they see that the rules are kept and count the points.'

That view has not met with universal approval and it may be objected that it stresses means at the expense of ends and concentrates on the form of the process to the neglect of substance. Adversary procedure unlike a sporting contest is not self-justifying. The passage serves, however, to put the features of adversary procedure in high relief, and those features may call for a degree of caution which need not be exercised in an inquisitorial procedure which is less at the mercy of the parties. The partiality of the account which each party will present imposes need for control of the form which evidence should take. In particular there is a need, on the one hand, to protect a party against unfair surprise by his adversary and, on the other, to allow for that element of fair surprise which may further the ascertainment of truth;

3 1961 SLT 237 at 246, 1962 SC (HL) 36 at 52.

5 jury trial. In the *Berkeley Peerage*[4] case, Lord Mansfield CJ said that hearsay evidence was admitted in Scotland and the reason for its admission was that jury trial was not in use there. He must have had civil cases alone in mind for jury trial was a commonplace of Scottish criminal practice. Nor was he accurate even in relation to civil litigation. The rule against hearsay is of considerable antiquity[5] in the law of Scotland and was certainly well recognised at the time Lord Mansfield spoke. His remarks do, however, point to the significance of the jury as an institution relevant to the development of the law of evidence. The rules are substantially influenced by considerations of what it would be safe, or unsafe, to leave to a jury and by the need to keep the mass of evidence within bounds sufficient to enable adequate directions to be given; and
6 the protection of interests deemed to be socially valuable: eg protection of the relationship of husband and wife, protection against self-incrimination, protection of the public interest.

HISTORICAL OUTLINE

Trial by combat, compurgation (the use of 'oath helpers' or wagers at law) and possibly ordeal,[6] were methods of dispute settlement known to medieval Scotland as to other countries but they pre-date the use of evidence and although a claim has recently been made that the first is still competent,[7] they have left little mark on the law. They gave way in the secular judicial system to the inquest (or visnet or assise of peers) which was the forerunner of the modern jury but which, in its original form, consisted of persons with local knowledge who were expected to return their verdict from that knowledge rather than from evidence adduced before them.[8] A relic of those origins was, until 1976, preserved in the form of oath administered to criminal juries: 'You fifteen swear

4 (1811) 4 Camp 401 at 414: 'In Scotland and in most continental countries, the judges determine about the facts in dispute as well as on the law; and they think that there is no danger in their listening to evidence of hearsay because when they come to consider of their judgment on the merits of the case they can trust themselves to disregard entirely the hearsay evidence, or give it any little weight which it seems to deserve. But in England, where the jury are the sole judges of the facts, hearsay evidence is properly excluded because no man can tell what effect it might have upon their minds.'
5 Balfour Prac 381, Stair IV 43 15, Burnett 600, Hume II 406. See Wilkinson *The Rule Against Hearsay in Scotland* 1982 Jur Rev 213.
6 DM Walker in *An Introduction to Scottish Legal History* Stair Society vol 20, ch XXII, pp 302–4.
7 The Times, 23 April 1985, p 3.
8 Walker ibid; Willock *The Jury in Scotland.*

. . . that you will truth speak and no truth conceal so far as you are to pass on this assize?'[9] As a tribunal in civil cases, any form of jury had, however, died out before the institution of the Court of Session in 1532. Much civil litigation in the medieval period was, however, handled not by the secular courts but by the courts of the Church administering Canon law. In these courts decisions were reached by judges on the basis of evidence. Documentary evidence was preferred in matters such as voluntary obligations which were susceptible of documentary proof and in its absence reliance was frequently put on the conscience of parties as evidenced by their oath. The testimony of witness was, however, also received. The Canon law and the civil law which was current in the secular courts of later medieval Scotland and became dominant after the Reformation, are the principal early sources of the Scottish law of evidence. The distrust of oral testimony and the consequent disqualification of large classes of witnesses which for long obtained,[10] the requirement of corroboration, the oath in litem, the oath in supplement, the oath of calumny, the oath of credulity, all of which were, for a long period, in use,[11] the obsolescent oath of verity,[12] the requirement that certain matters be proved by writ or oath, many presumptions and probably even the rule against hearsay[13] have Canon law or civil law roots. From the early nineteenth century onwards the main external source for the development of the Scottish rules of evidence has, however, been English law. The introduction of civil jury trial in 1816[14] and the jury court which existed between then and 1830 and followed English jury practice and rules of evidence were a formative influence. A climate of reform which in both countries owed much to Benthamite thinking, the sweeping away by nineteenth century statutes of many of the old impediments to proof, and particularly of the restrictions on the admission of witnesses, opened the way to parallel developments in both countries. Distinctive features, however, remain. The general requirement of corroboration is among those which are notable and important and in many areas there are differences on points of emphasis and detail. Some of the distinctive features, such as the exceptions to the rule against hearsay in the admission of statements by deceased persons and the evidentiary use of business books seem to represent an adherence to basic principle in the face of divergent trends elsewhere while others,

9 Renton and Brown *Criminal Procedure according to the Law of Scotland* (3rd edn) p 116.
10 Stair IV 43,7; Hume II 339 ff.
11 For the old forms of oath see Walker ibid, pp 311–14.
12 Walker ibid, pp 311 and 312. The oath of verity is given by a party when the cause or part of it is referred to his oath (see p 215 below). It is the French *serment decisoire* and is not to be confused with the witness's oath.
13 Wilkinson ibid.
14 Jury Trials (Scotland) Act 1815.

such as the rules on the inadmissibility of evidence irregularly obtained, owe more to independent indigenous development than to external sources.

CLASSIFICATION AND TERMINOLOGY

Questions of fact and law; province of court and jury

The law of evidence as that part of the law which is concerned with the regulation of proof, consists of rules bearing on the ascertainments of fact. Within those rules the reaching of a conclusion on what facts are proved, or not proved, is a function of human reason and experience entrusted to the jury or other tribunal of fact. A distinction is, therefore, to be made between questions of fact and questions of law, including the law of evidence. The former are questions to be determined by the jury; the latter are entirely within the province of the judge. The distinction is sometimes blurred where the substantive law prescribes a standard which includes, or refers to, matters within ordinary experience but the consequent difficulties of distinguishing between questions of fact and of law relate not to the ascertainment of fact but to the application of the substantive law to the facts ascertained and are not relevant in the present context. There are, however, some questions of fact in the sense at present under discussion which are not jury questions. These are questions of fact which have to be determined in order to enable a ruling to be given on the admissibility of evidence, or to enable a direction to be given on whether or not evidence which has been admitted should be disregarded. Thus, the relevance of evidence to a fact in issue is a question to be determined by ordinary experience aided in some cases by the findings of science and is not, in general, a question of law, but it must, nonetheless, be determined by the judge because irrelevant evidence is inadmissible. So too, questions of fact may have to be answered before a decision can be given on whether evidence has been irregularly recovered and so is inadmissible, or, on the admissibility of a confession, or on whether privilege attaches to a communication, and these are questions which the judge must determine.

Evidence and opinion; evidence and argument

Evidence is information derived from witnesses' perception of events or things and from inspection by the tribunal of fact of documents and things. It is, therefore, sometimes distinguished from opinion, which consists of inferences drawn from facts perceived. The drawing of inferences from facts is primarily a matter for the tribunal of fact and not for witnesses. The distinction between perceived facts and opinion is not, however, always exact as is discussed later,[15] and where the opinion of a witness is admissible it becomes, in effect, an item of evidence. Evidence is, however, to be distinguished from argument which consists of the reasons advanced for the acceptance or rejection of evidence or for the conclusions in law to be reached from it.

Relevance and admissibility

The primary rule of the law of evidence is that only relevant evidence is admissible and to that rule, all other rules are subsidiary. The relevance of evidence lies in its tendency to render more or less probable the existence or non-existence of a fact in issue. Not all relevant evidence is, however, admissible. The inadmissibility of relevant evidence is the subject matter of exclusionary rules which form a large part of the law of evidence. These rules are based on their supposed helpfulness in promoting the ascertainment of truth or on some of the other considerations outlined earlier in this chapter as affecting the restrictive character of evidentiary rules.

By admissibility of evidence, is meant that it is fit matter for consideration by the tribunal of fact, ie that it is relevant and is not affected by any exclusionary rule. Competency is virtually a synonym but may sometimes be the more convenient term to use when inadmissible evidence has been admitted and a question arises of whether it should be disregarded. Irrelevant evidence is never competent for consideration by the tribunal of fact and normally, where evidence struck at by an exclusionary rule is admitted, it remains incompetent and should be excluded from consideration, but sometimes the operation of personal bar[16] or like principles may render competent what was initially inadmissible.

Direct and circumstantial evidence

The terms 'direct' and 'circumstantial' describe a relationship between evidence and the facts in issue. Direct evidence consists of a witness's testimony of a fact in issue as immediately observed by himself or, where the terms of a document or the present state of a thing is in issue, direct evidence is afforded by production of the document or thing. Circumstantial evidence, on the other hand, is evidence of facts ('evidential facts') from which an inference may be drawn towards the existence or non-existence of a fact in issue. Both the direct evidence of witnesses and circumstantial evidence are subject to the hazards that the witness may be untruthful or faulty in his perception or recollection and circumstan-

15 Ch 4.
16 Ch 8 below.

tial evidence has the additional hazards attaching to the uncertainty of the inferences drawn. Circumstantial evidence is not, however, necessarily weaker. Its character and its possible strength were well described by Pollock CB in *R v Exall*:

> 'It has been said that circumstantial evidence is to be considered as a chain, and each piece of evidence is a link in the chain, but that is not so, for then, if any one link breaks, the chain would fall. It is more like the case of a rope comprised of several cords. One strand of the cord might be insufficient to sustain the weight, but three stranded together may be quite of sufficient strength. Thus it may be in circumstantial evidence—there may be a combination of circumstances, no one of which would raise a reasonable conviction or more than a mere suspicion; but the three taken together may create a conclusion of guilt with as much certainty as human affairs can require or admit of.'[17]

Primary and secondary evidence

Secondary evidence suggests by its nature the existence of other (primary) evidence from which it is derived. As a general rule, primary evidence is to be preferred to secondary but it is only in relation to documents and, to a lesser extent, to real evidence that that preference is expressed in a strict rule so as to exclude secondary evidence in the unexplained absence of the primary evidence.

Documentary evidence

It is seldom necessary to define documentary evidence or what constitutes a document, except for the purposes of certain statutes which carry their own definition,[18] but a document may be taken to include any written or printed matter expressed in words and also drawings, plans and maps. The specialties of documentary evidence arise mainly where documents are the means by which rights and obligations have been constituted or recorded.

Real evidence

Real evidence is evidence which consists not in what is stated to the tribunal of fact but what that tribunal observes of what is produced

17 (1866) 4 F and F 922 at 929.

18 Eg Criminal Evidence Act 1965 and Law Reform (Miscellaneous Provisions) (Scotland) Act 1966.

before it. Documents are not usually classified as real evidence because their significance normally rests in what they state and not in their appearance, but the physical characteristics of a document or the form of a signature on it is real evidence. The typical example of real evidence is a physical object produced to the jury. But the demeanour and physical appearances of witnesses or other persons present in court are real evidence as also is what is seen by the tribunal on a view of the locus. Some of the more problematic cases of real evidence are considered later.[19]

Testimony

Testimony is the account given by a witness in court or, where evidence is taken on commission, before the commissioner appointed by the court. It is given on oath or affirmation or, in the case of children and certain other witnesses, after an admonition to tell the truth. It is to be contrasted with hearsay which is a reported account of what someone has said and is generally inadmissible. Where, however, hearsay is admissible, it forms part of the testimony of the witness who speaks to it.

Facts in issue

The facts in issue are those facts which a party requires to prove if his contentions in law are to be sustained. They are determined by the application of the substantive law to the circumstances of the case. So they are the facts which, in a civil case, the pursuer requires to prove so that his pleas-in-law may be sustained and the action succeed, or which a defender requires to prove in order to establish a substantive defence. Similarly, in a criminal case, they are the facts which a prosecutor requires to prove if the libel is to be sustained or which an accused person must prove in any matter in respect of which the onus rests on him. They are, with the exception of matters proof of which is incumbent on the accused, ascertainable from the pleadings. They are alternatively described as *facta probanda*, crucial facts',[20] 'essential facts',[1] 'essential matter',[2] 'essential elements'[3] and 'material facts'.[4] In nearly every case there will be a number of facts in issue. In a criminal case both the factual elements constituting the criminal act and the identity of the accused as the perpetrator are in issue and must be proved.[5]

19 Chs 5 and 11.
20 *Farrell v Concannon* 1957 JC 12 at 19; *Lockwood v Walker* 1910 SC(J) 3 at 5.
1 *Bissett v Anderson* 1949 JC 106 at 110; *Stewart v Glasgow Corpn* 1958 SC 28 at 45.
2 *Gillespie v Macmillan* 1957 JC 31 at 39.
3 *McCourt v HM Advocate* 1913 SC (J) 6 at 8.
4 *McArthur v Stewart* 1955 JC 1.
5 *Mitchell v Macdonald* 1959 SLT (Notes) 74.

Evidential and procedural facts

Evidential facts are items of circumstantial evidence. They are facts which are not themselves in issue but from which inferences bearing on facts in issue can be drawn. They are alternatively described as *facta probationis* or *facta probantia*.

In criminal cases a category of procedural or incidental facts has been recognised.[6] The distinction between these facts and the facts in issue is not altogether satisfactory because they are facts which it is essential for the prosecutor to prove. They include the title of a private prosecutor,[7] the warning to be given before the medical examination of a person charged with driving under the influence of drink,[8] the ownership of stolen goods,[9] whether a house broken into had been secured,[10] and whether a lockfast place had been locked.[11] The distinction is mainly of importance for the doctrine of corroboration for which an understanding of the distinction between the facts in issue and evidential facts is also critical.[12]

Other categories of facts are facts which require to be proved in connection with the admissibility of evidence and facts bearing on credibility. The former may be regarded as a species of procedural or incidental fact.

Proof

Proof of a fact in issue is effected when the tribunal of fact is satisfied that it is established by evidence sufficient in law and sufficient in weight to discharge the onus of proof on the appropriate standard. What constitutes evidence sufficient in law and what the appropriate standard of proof is are questions of law. The weight of evidence is a question of fact. It comprehends the credibility and reliability of witnesses and the various factors which may bear on that, such as the demeanour of the witness, his opportunities for observation, the strength of his recollection, his prejudice or partiality, capability of understanding and possibilities of error. It also comprehends the extent to which circumstantial evidence may be open to a variety of explanations and the strength of inferences.

6 *Lees v Macdonald* (1893) 20 R (J) 55; *Farrell v Concannon* 1957 JC 12 at 19.
7 *Lees v Macdonald* above.
8 *Farrell v Concannon* above.
9 *Lees v Macdonald* above.
10 *HM Advocate v Davidson* (1841) 2 Swin 630.
11 *HM Advocate v Cameron* (1839) 2 Swin 447.
12 See ch 13 below.

BEST EVIDENCE RULE

In *Omychund v Barker* Lord Hardwicke said: 'The judges and sages of the law have laid it down that there is but one general rule of evidence, the best that the nature of the case will allow.'[13] From that formulation of 'the best evidence rule', it would seem to follow that evidence will be admitted, whatever its deficiencies, provided it is the best that the nature of the case will allow and that it will be excluded, whatever its merits, if it does not meet that test. There are clearly problems of what constitutes 'the best'. Dickson affirms the rule but mentions inter alia that it does not make it necessary to produce all the evidence which can be had,[14] that it does not exclude inferior evidence if primary in character, that where there are several primary sources of evidence, any one is admissible,[15] and that it does not exclude circumstantial evidence although direct evidence is available and not led.[16] 'The rule is directed to the specific character, not to the strength or amount of the proof. It excludes evidence, the substitutional nature of which implies that more original evidence can be obtained.'[17] Even under that limited description the best evidence rule is no longer a principle of general application. It may have influenced the development of specific rules such as the exceptions to the rule against hearsay and the admissibility of extrinsic evidence in relation to the terms of documents, but the specific rules now govern and do not yield to a consideration of what is the best evidence in the nature of the case. As a rule of admissibility, the main surviving applications of the rule are in the preference for primary evidence of the terms of documents and, subject to qualifications, of the condition of things. As a guide to the weighing of evidence it has, however, a wider scope and a new field for its application seems to have emerged in questions of dispensing with the requirement of corroboration in cases to which the Law Reform (Miscellaneous Provisions) (Scotland) Act 1968 applies.[18]

13 (1745) Willes 538 at 549–50.
14 Para 195.
15 Para 197.
16 Para 199.
17 Para 195.
18 S 9. See ch 13 below.

CHAPTER 2

Inadmissibility of evidence; irrelevancy; collateral fact

IRRELEVANCY

Irrelevant evidence inadmissible

> 'The first and the most general of the primary rules of evidence is this,—that the evidence led be confined to matters which are in dispute or under investigation.'[1]

From that principle it follows that evidence is admissible only if it is relevant to the facts on which the court or jury has to decide. If those facts are broadly defined as including not only the facts in issue in the proper sense but also procedural facts and facts bearing on credibility of witnesses and admissibility or reliability of evidence, there are no exceptions to the rule. The converse is not, however, true. Not all relevant evidence is admissibile. Evidence relevant to credibility may be elicited in cross-examination of the witness concerned but if the sole purpose of the evidence rests in its bearing on credibility it may not be the subject of evidence in causa.[2] And there is a wide range of exclusionary rules which operate to render relevant evidence inadmissible. These exclusionary rules form the subject matter of much of this and the subsequent chapters of this book. Any evidence to which no exclusionary rule applies is, if relevant, admissible.

1 Dickson, para 1. cf Thayer *Preliminary Treatise of Evidence at Common Law* p 266: 'Without an exception, nothing that is not logically relevant is admissible.

2 This is the basis of the rule that if a witness when cross-examined about his convictions for crimes of dishonesty denies them, the fact of conviction cannot be proved (*Dickie v HM Advocate* (1897) 24 R (J) 82; *Kennedy v HM Advocate* (1896) 23 R (J) 28). A witness's prior statements consistent with his evidence may, however, in some circumstances be proved, as under the Evidence (Scotland) Act 1852, s 3 may his prior inconsistent statements (see ch 3 below); and in *King v King* (1841) 4 D 124 evidence of a witness's prior expressions of hostility to a party was held to be admissible. The reason for the general exclusion of evidence bearing solely on credibility would seem to be to avoid encumbering the proof with a proliferation of issues remote from the main issues.

Nature of relevancy

Direct evidence of the facts in issue, is, by its nature, relevant. Problems of relevance arise in relation to circumstantial evidence, ie evidence of facts from which a conclusion on the facts in issue must be derived inferentially. One fact is relevant to another when

> 'they are so related to each other that according to the common course of events one, either taken by itself or in connection with other facts, proves or renders probable the past, present or future existence or non-existence of the other.'[3]

In the above test 'proves' is but a synonymn for a high degree of probability. The link of relevance is one of inferential probability. Fact 'a' is relevant to fact 'b' if, where 'a' exists, it is, according to the common course of events, probable that 'b' also exists. Commonly, however, the inference will depend on proof of a number of facts. It will be from the concurrence of facts 'a', 'c', 'd' and 'e' that an inference can be drawn as to the probable existence of fact 'b'. In such a situation the relevance of fact 'a' to fact 'b' may not be immediately evident but will appear only on proof of facts 'c', 'd', and 'e'. When, therefore, evidence of fact 'a' is tendered, the court will be unable at that stage to judge of its relevance. The problem has long been recognised and the solution is that the evidence must be accepted under reservation as to its relevancy. As Dickson says:

> 'The court therefore has to rely a good deal on the discretion and fairness of the counsel conducting the case, and they will rarely reject proof of facts, merely because at the time they appear to be irrelevant, if the counsel states on his professional responsibility that they are material. There is much greater risk of injustice from excluding than from admitting evidence objected to as irrelevant; and the court can always caution the jury against being misled by it, if it should turn out to be objectionable.'[4]

Relevance is sometimes said to be a question of logic but if so, it is of inductive rather than deductive logic. It may be that once the inference has been drawn its soundness can be tested by casting a syllogism,[5] but the syllogisms seem to be of rather a loose kind and to lack the character of leading to a necessary conclusion commonly associated with deductive logic. In any event, the real content of the process of inference comes not

3 Stephen *Digest of the Law of Evidence* (12th edn) art 1.
4 Para 1.
5 This procedure is suggested by Stephen (*General View of the Criminal Law* (1st edn) p 236). See *Cross on Evidence* (6th edn) p 50.

from any abstract logical criteria but from ordinary experience or, in some cases, from the empirical results of scientific investigation or technical experience.

'Legal relevancy'

The exclusion of irrelevant evidence is a matter of law in the obvious sense that the rule that irrelevant evidence is inadmissible is a rule of law. The content of the decision is a question of fact. It is for the judge to determine whether evidence is capable of giving rise to an inference bearing on a fact in issue and therefore relevant and admissible; for the jury to determine, if the evidence is admitted, whether the inference should be drawn. But the judge brings to his decision not rules of law but of ordinary experience aided, where the issue is technical, by the criteria of science spoken to by expert opinion, for rules of law cannot, generally, be laid down on the relevance of one fact to another. There is no legal prescription for determining the inferential probabilities of the almost infinite variety of facts which may arise in litigation.

There is, however, a view that there is a residual concept of 'legal relevance' to be applied, in certain situations, in place of ordinary relevance from which it is distinct. In part, that view is due to a confusion originating in Stephen's attempt, at one time influential but now generally discarded, to reduce all rules of evidence to questions of relevancy.[6] So some kinds of inadmissible evidence, particularly collateral evidence, are, it is said, 'deemed to be irrelevant'. That result is reached by rules of law not by science or experience. The law says, so the argument runs, that, with some exceptions, collateral evidence is irrelevant. The reasons for the exclusion of collateral evidence are discussed below and include, but are not exhausted by, considerations of relevancy. Whether or not one speaks of such evidence as being 'deemed to be irrelevant' is not of great practical importance but the usage tends to confuse rather than clarify issues. It is simpler just to say that such evidence is inadmissible because of a rule which excludes it.

The more substantial point in the argument about legal relevancy resolves itself into a question of whether decisions on relevancy serve as precedents for future cases. Thayer denied that they had any such function: 'The law has no orders for the reasoning faculty anymore than for the perceiving faculty—for the eyes and ears.'[7] Wigmore, supported by some American judicial dicta,[8] took the opposite view.

6 See *Cross* p 59.
7 14 Harvard LR 139. See also Montrose 'Basic Concepts of the Law of Evidence' (1954) 70 LQR 527 at 554 and 555.
8 *State v Lapage* 57 NH 288 per Cushing CJ: 'The subject of the relevancy of testimony has become . . . matter of precedence and authority'. See Montrose ibid.

> 'So long as courts continue to declare in judicial rulings what their notions of logic are, just so long must there be rules of law which must be observed. So if a court holds that fact X is relevant to fact Y that is a precedent for future cases in which facts of the class to which Y belongs are in issue and facts of the class to which X belongs are tendered in evidence.'[9]

It is thought that the dilemma is often avoided, and the absence of any clear rule on the matter explained, by the fact that issues of relevance rarely present themselves to appellate courts in a form which is sufficiently sharply defined or sufficiently open to generalisation to serve as a precedent. Future cases will usually yield some point on which a distinction can be made. In principle, Thayer's seems to be the better view. Precedents arise from the application of rules of law to facts. So far as the content of what constitutes relevancy is concerned that is not what happens in a judgment on relevancy. Nonetheless, where generalisation is possible, decisions on relevancy inevitably serve as precedents.[10] Whether the cases which follow those precedents fall into a category of 'legal relevancy' or under an exclusionary rule otherwise described is a purely semantic question.

Multiple relevancy

Evidence may be relevant for more than one purpose and admissible in relation to some purposes while inadmissible in relation to others. The most obvious examples are in the field of collateral evidence, where evidence of a party's previous actings may be relevant to 1 his disposition to act in a particular way and therefore the likelihood that he acted in that way on the occasion in issue and 2 his state of mind. It will generally be inadmissible for the first purpose but may be admissible for the second. The rule in such cases of multiple relevancy is that the evidence is admitted if it is competent evidence for any purpose. There is no balancing of considerations except that in a criminal trial the judge may, in his discretion, exclude collateral prosecution evidence if its

9 Wigmore *A Treatise on the Anglo-American System of Evidence* (3rd edn 1940) p 298.

10 The question is obscured by the occasional use in judicial dicta perhaps following *Stephen* of 'relevant' as a synonym for 'admissible'. Moreover in the Scottish cases decisions on the relevancy of pleadings often reflect views on the admissibility of evidence. In that context a decision that an averment is irrelevant may mean not that the fact averred has no relevance to the issue but that evidence of it would be inadmissible under an exclusionary rule. When, however, in *Oswald v Fairs* 1911 SC 257 Lord President Dunedin said 'the question being whether A said a certain thing to B, I do not think it is relevant evidence on that question to show that A said something of the same sort upon another occasion to C', it is clear that that was a judgment on relevancy which might serve as a precedent for future cases.

admission would be unduly prejudicial to the accused. The jury must, of course, be directed and the judge, if sitting alone, must direct himself that the evidence is to be disregarded for purposes for which it is not competent.

Insufficient relevancy

Probability is a question of degree. So questions may arise not only of whether evidence is altogether irrelevant but also of whether its relevancy is too remote or insufficient. Because evidence is relevant if it is capable of yielding an inference bearing on a fact in issue a judgment on relevancy involves some assessment of what a reasonable trier of fact might hold in terms of inferences to be drawn. Evidence whose relevance is purely conjectural or speculative is excluded. Beyond that, the degree of probability which attaches to the link between the *factum probans* and the *factum probandum* is a jury question. Nevertheless, there may be circumstances in which evidence should be excluded because its tendency to confuse or overburden the proof exceeds any probative value it may have.[11]

COLLATERAL FACT

Evidence of collateral facts is generally inadmissible where its relevance lies in its showing the likelihood of a recurrent pattern of conduct or events. The evidence principally struck at is (a) evidence of a person's character in the sense of his disposition or tendency to act in a particular way and his repuation in that respect and (b) evidence of facts similar to the facts in issue but occurring on other occasions. In the latter connection, the rule is mainly exemplified by, but is not confined to, similar actings of parties. Collateral evidence will be admissible where it is adduced for relevant purposes other than showing that the facts in issue were the result of a disposition, tendency or recurrent pattern and exceptionally where it does have that purpose. Its admissibility may be dependent on notice having been given.[12]

Reasons for exclusion

Although some decisions bear on relevancy, irrelevancy in the strict sense is not, it is thought, the main reason for the exclusion of collateral

11 That is one of the main reasons for the exclusion of collateral evidence (see *A v B* (1895) 22 R 402 per Lord President Robertson at 404 cited below) and the principle is, it is thought, capable of wider applications.

12 *C v M* 1923 SC 1, *HM Advocate v Joseph* 1929 JC 55, *HM Advocate v Tully* 1935 JC 8, *Griffen v HM Advocate* 1940 JC 1, but contra *Gallagher v Paton* 1909 SC (J) 50.

evidence. Human conduct has a tendency to repetition and a person's past actings may be highly relevant to his likely future conduct. If, as may sometimes happen, collateral evidence is irrelevant, it can be excluded on ordinary principles. The reasons for a special rule on collateral evidence seem to be twofold. First, the admission of such evidence might raise a variety of issues which would require to be explored at the expenditure of considerable time and cost and at the risk of diverting attention from more nearly central concerns. Litigation should concentrate on facts bearing proximately on the issues raised rather than explore byeways even if these should ultimately prove to be of some relevance.

> 'Courts of law are not bound to admit the ascertainment of every disputed fact which may contribute, however slightly or indirectly, towards the solution of the issue to be tried. Regard must be had to the limitations which time and human liability to confusion impose upon the conduct of all trials. Experience shows that it is better to sacrifice the aid which might be got from the more or less uncertain solution of collateral issues, than to spend a great amount of time, and confuse the jury with what, in the end, even supposing it to be certain, has only an indirect bearing on the matter in hand.'[13]

Second, collateral evidence is excluded because of its tendency to be prejudicial. The objection is not that it is irrelevant but that, if admitted, it will carry too much weight.

When character not collateral

Similar facts are, by definition, collateral but character is not always so. Thus, in an action of defamation, the character of the pursuer, in the sense of his reputation, is in issue and may be proved both in support of a claim of damages and in mitigation. Evidence must, however, be confined to general reputation, which is what is at stake, and must not embark on an exploration of particular incidents in the pursuer's life history. So, in *C v M*[14] the defender was held entitled to prove that the pursuer was well known as a person of loose and immoral character but not to lead evidence of specific acts of adultery. Where *veritas* is pleaded,

13 *A v B* (1895) 22 R 402 per Lord President Robertson at 404. See also *H v P* (1905) 8 F 232 at 234; *Houston v Aitken* 1912 SC 1037 at 1038 and *Swan v Bowie* 1948 SC 46 at 51.

14 1923 SC 1. Observations were made in that case that the pursuer might be cross-examined as to the specific acts as bearing both on character and credibility. In other cases such cross-examination had been regarded as restricted to credibility (*A v B* above, *H v P* (1905) 8 F 232 at 234). Notice must be given of such cross-examination (*C v M* 1923 SC 1 at 14; *H v P* above).

evidence may be led in support of the truth of the defamatory statement including any specific incidents which form part of its subject matter but not of other incidents which reflect on the pursuer's character.[15] So too, character may be proved, as not being collateral, where the possession of that character is integral to the commission of the crime as in the case of offences which can be committed only by a 'known or reputed thief' or offences in which previous convictions form part of the libel.

Actions of defamation are the only class of actions in which the pursuer's character is ordinarily in issue. In other actions of damages, questions of the pursuer's character may, however, arise incidentally. Thus evidence of the character has been admitted in order to show that the pursuer belonged to a class of persons whom a police constable was authorised to remove[16] and, in another case, to show that there were facts justifying a suspect's detention. So too in mitigation of damages evidence bearing on the pursuer's character has been admitted where it was relevant to a contention that loss sustained by a pursuer was partly due to his own intemperate habits.[17]

There are few, if any, exceptions to the general rule that a party's character is inadmissible where it is truly collateral. Thus in *A v B*[18] where the pursuer sued for damages for rape, she was not allowed to prove the defender's disposition, and in a series of old cases evidence of the defender's character was held to be inadmissible where the issues concerned assault, defamation, wrongous imprisonment, breach of contract and reduction of a will on the ground of fraud, facility and circumvention.[19]

Inadmissibility of similar facts in civil cases

'The question being whether A said a certain thing to B, I do not think it is relevant evidence on that question to show that A said something of the same sort upon another occasion to C.' In *Oswald v Fairs*[20] from which that quotation is taken, it was held that in order to establish representations made by the pursuer's wife to him the defender was not entitled to lead evidence that she had made similar representations to another person. In *Inglis v National Bank of Scotland*[1] where the pursuer claimed that he had been induced to pay a bill as a result of a false

15 *H v P* above
16 *Wallace v Mooney* (1885) 12 R 710.
17 *Butchart c Dundee and Arbroath Rly Co* (1859) 22 D 184.
18 (1895) 22 R 402.
19 *Haddoway v Goddard* (1816) 1 Mur 148 at 151; *Scott v McGavin* (1821) 2 Mur 484 at 493 (cf *Cooper v Macintosh* (1823) 3 Mur 357 at 359): *Simpson v Liddle* (1821) 2 Mur 579 at 580; *Aitchen v Fisher* (1821) 2 Mur 584 at 591; *Clark v Spence* (1825) 3 Mur 450.
20 1911 SC 257 per Lord President Dunedin at 265.
1 1909 SC 1038.

representation by the defenders' bank agent that it was still outstanding and averred that the agent had committed similar frauds on other parties, it was held that evidence of the other frauds was not evidence of the allged fraud in issue. And in *A v B*[2] the pursuer was precluded from leading evidence of the defender's attempts to rape two other women as relevant to the alleged rape on her. Evidence of similar actings of parties is, therefore, generally inadmissible. The same rule of inadmissibility applies to similar events which do not consist in the actings of persons. Thus, where the issue is whether an embankment had caused the silting of a harbour, evidence is not admissible that silting had occurred in other harbours where there were embankments.[3] Expert evidence based on the experience in other harbours would, however, be admissible.

Admissibility where link goes beyond similarity

Similar fact evidence is admissible where the link between the facts of which evidence is tendered and the facts in issue goes beyond mere similarity.

In *Hales v Kerr* where the plaintiff claimed damages for an infectious disease caused by the negligence of the defendant barber in using dirty appliances, it was held that he might lead evidence that other customers of the defendant had contracted the same disease in the previous month. Channell J said:

> 'It is not legitimate to charge a man with an act of negligence on a day in October and ask a jury to infer that he was negligent on that day because he was negligent every day in September. The defender may have mended his ways before the day in October. But where the issue is that the defender pursued a course of conduct which is dangerous to his neighbours it is a legitimate inference that having caused an injury on these occasions it has caused it in the plantiff's case.'[4]

The distinction between the course of conduct to which Channell J refers in the last sentence of that passage and the repeated acts of negligence to which he refers in the first may not be obvious but it seems to lie in the striking coincidence of the events from the standpoint of causation. It would be remarkable if several customers of the same barber had contracted a disease associated with hairdressing from different sources. It was a reasonable inference that they all had

2 (1895) 22 R 402.

3 *Folkes v Chadd* (1782) 3 Doug KB 157. Evidence was, however, admitted of harbours where there were no embankments because that tended to support expert evidence that the presence of the embankment was not the cause of the silting.

4 [1908] 2 KB 601.

contracted the disease from the same source and that the defendant was responsible for it.[5]

In *Knutzen v Mauritzen*[6] the pursuer averred that goods sold to him were of bad quality and that another parcel out of the same consignment, sold to a third party, was also bad. The averment was held relevant and so might be proved, since the two parcels came out of the same bulk. The link here was that the evidence of the condition of one part of the bulk was evidence of the condition of the bulk as a whole and so of another part. In *Morrison v Maclean's Trustees*, an action for reduction of three testamentary deeds, the jury was directed that if, in relation to one of the deeds, the witnesses had not seen the testator sign or heard him acknowledge his signature they might draw an inference from that as to whether there had been an irregularity in the execution of the other deeds.[7] The connecting link here seems to have been the testator's state of mind in relation to three deeds executed in similar circumstances over a short space of time.

More generally, where events are closely related in time, place and circumstances and flow from some common plan or course of conduct it is thought that in civil cases, as in criminal, evidence in relation to one may be used as evidence in relation to the other. Thus, evidence of adultery on one occasion may be used in proof of adultery on another[8] and that extends to earlier and condoned acts even with persons other than the paramour and to acts subsequent to the raising of the action which may be used retrospectively to cast light on the acts founded upon.[9] Adultery between the paramour and the third party may not, however, be used as casting light on the paramour's relationship with the defender. These cases have been explained as a relaxation of the general rule arising out of the duty of the court to protect the matrimonial bond against grievous injury but it is thought that the doctrine of *Moorov v HM Advocate*[10] puts them on a more satisfactory footing, the common link or nexus being the adoption, by the defender, of a course of conduct inconsistent with his duty to the pursuer. Similarly, in affiliation cases, evidence is admitted if acts of intercourse between the pursuer and defender, other than those to which the conception of the child may be

5 See *Cross* p 56.
6 (1918) 1 SLT 85.
7 (1862) 24 D 625 at 630.
8 *Whyte v Whyte* (1884) 11 R 712 at 711; *Wilson v Wilson* 1955 SLT (Notes) 81; *Dickson* para 1808.
9 *Collins v Collins* (1884) 11 R (HL) 19 at 29; *Robertson v Robertson* (1888) 15 R 1001 at 1003–4; *Nicol v Nicol* 1938 SLT 98; *Ross v Ross* 1928 SC 600 (retrospectan).
10 1930 JC 68. For the significance of *Moorov* for the admissibility of similar fact evidence see below. See also Walker and Walker *The Law of Evidence in Scotland* p 172 where, however, the matter is considered only in relation to corroboration.

attributed, as showing a continuing relationship from which the relationship between the parties at the time of the conception may be inferred.[11] Evidence of intercourse between the pursuer and other men, about the time of conception, is admitted for the rather different reason that it bears on the probabilities of paternity.[12]

Admissibility in relation to states of mind

The insanity of a party may be shown not only by his conduct at times material to the issue but also by conduct on previous occasions. In questions of malice and of whether conduct was intentional previous actings may be put in evidence for the purpose of showing the necessary malice or intent on the occasion in question. Where in an action of damages on the ground of negligence the defender's knowledge of the risk and so of the need to take a precaution is in issue, evidence of previous accidents may be led as instructing that knowledge. And in questions of liability for injury caused by an animal *mansuetae naturae* evidence of previous incidents is admissible as showing the owner's knowledge of the animal's vicious disposition. In *Gordon v Mackenzie* evidence of an incident after the one founded on was admitted to show, it seems, not the owner's knowledge but that the animal was of a vicious disposition and that the incident was not isolated.

Cases of the above kind are often and conveniently grouped together as instances of the admission of similar facts as evidence of a party's state of mind. The reasons for their admission are not, however, uniform. Where the question is one of insanity the relevance of evidence of past conduct indicating insanity lies in the tendency of such a state to continue. In questions of malice and intention the element of repetition is itself significant. Repeated acts directed against the same person suggest, in the absence of explanation, a course of malicious persecution, into which the occasion in issue may fit, rather than good faith. While one act may be the result of carelessness or mistake, repeated acts of the same kind, although open to explanation including the persistence of a mistaken belief, are more likely to be intentional. In questions of knowledge, on the other hand, the occurrence of a previous similar incident of which the defender must or should have known speaks directly to the defender's actual or constructive knowledge.

11 *Lawson v Eddie* (1861) 23 D 876; *Ross v Fraser* (1863) 1 M 783; *McDonald v Glass* (1883) 11 R 57; *Scott v Dawson* (1884) 11 R 518; *Buchanan v Finlayson* (1900) 3 F 245; *Havery v Brownlie* 1908 SC 424; *Florence v Smith* 1913 SC 978; *Roy v Pairman* 1958 SC 334. Generally only acts of intercourse prior to the time of conception are relevant (*Florence v Smith* at 985–6) but, exceptionally, later acts, if close in time, may be admitted (*Buchanan v Finlayson*, at 249 and 251).

12 *Butler v McLaren* 1909 SC 786; *Robertson v Hutchison* 1935 SC 708.

CHARACTER AND SIMILAR FACT IN CRIMINAL CASES

In criminal cases a sharp distinction is to be made between evidence of the accused's character and of similar facts when led in causa and the cross-examination of the accused on such matters. The former is governed entirely by common law and the latter entirely by statute. The common law rules on evidence of character and similar fact in causa are considered first.

Evidence for accused of his character

It is always open to the accused to lead evidence of his good character[13] or, if he thinks his interests may thereby be served, of a defect in character.[14] The admissibility of evidence of the accused's good character was accepted long before the accused became a competent witness in his own defence and its use is not restricted to supporting the accused's credibility if he should give evidence. It is evidence on the issue tendered with a view to casting doubt on the accused's guilt. It is, therefore, not properly collateral evidence because the accused's character thus becomes a matter which the jury should weigh on its own merits as relevant to their verdict.[15]

Evidence for prosecution of accused's character

The prosecutor may lead evidence of the accused's character only where the accused, whether by cross-examination of prosecution witnesses or by leading evidence, has put his character in issue.[16] The prosecutor may then lead evidence in rebuttal. An accused does not put his character in

13 *Dickson* para 15.

14 *Dickson* ibid, where the examples given are a cowardly disposition in crimes showing great boldness and stupidity in crimes for which ingenuity was required. Reference is also made to the case of *Burke* in which the fact that he carried on the trade of body-lifting was said to account for his having dead bodies in his house under suspicious circumstances. See *Burke* (1828) Syme 345.

15 'It has been put that evidence in favour of the character of a person on his trial raises a collateral issue. I can hardly think that it is a collateral issue in the proper sense of the term. It becomes one of the points on which the jury are to found their verdict.' (*R v Rowton* (1865) 34 LJMC 57 per Cockburn CJ at 60). Cf *R v Stannard* (1837) 7 C & P 673 at 674. 'The object of laying it before the jury is to induce them to believe, from the improbability that a person of good character should have conducted himself as alleged, that there is some mistake or misrepresentation in the evidence of the prosecution, and it is strictly evidence in the case.'

16 *Dickson* ibid. 'But the prosecutor is never permitted to attack the prisoner's character, unless the latter has set it up; and even then he very seldom goes beyond cross-examining the prisoner's witnesses on the point.'

issue by casting imputations on the character of prosecution witnesses although his doing so would, if he were to give evidence, expose him to cross-examination as to his character. So, in *R v Butterwasser*[17] a conviction was quashed where the Crown had led evidence designed to show the accused's bad character after he had made an attack on the character of a prosecution witness.

Meaning of character

It has been held in England that when it is open to the prosecution to lead evidence of the accused's bad character the only way in which they may do so, other than by cross-examination of the accused should he give evidence, is by witnesses speaking to the general reputation enjoyed by the accused.[18] The witnesses must not give their own opinion of the accused's true character, nor speak to specific incidents relevant to it. The corollary as was acknowledged in the same case, is that evidence of the same kind is the only means by which the accused can establish his character. That rule has the advantage that it avoids the exploration of a possibly large number of collateral issues which evidence of particular examples of conduct, or even of opinion, might raise. It has, however, the disadvantage that a witness may be obliged to give evidence of a reputation which he knows to be unjustified in fact.

Incidental reference to character

The strict limitation of the circumstances in which the prosecution may lead evidence of the accused's character does not exclude such evidence where it is necessarily incidental to otherwise competent evidence. So evidence may be received of an admissible confession by the accused, although it contains matter indicating his bad character[19] and evidence bearing on intention or motive or mental condition relevant to responsibility may be admissible although incidentally it reflects on the accused's character.[20]

Evidence of previous convictions

Evidence of the accused's previous convictions may be laid before the jury, or the court in a summary trial, where the accused has led evidence to prove his previous good character or where it is competent to lead evidence of such previous convictions as evidence in causa in support of

17 [1948] 1 KB 4, [1947] 2 All ER 415.
18 *R v Rowton* above.
19 *HM Advocate v McFadyen* 1926 JC 93. But see also *Lord Advocate's Reference no 1 of 1983* 1984 SLT 337 at 341.
20 *Gemmill v HM Advocate* 1979 SLT 217.

the substantive charge.[1] Otherwise it is incompetent to lay the accused's convictions before the jury or judge, or to refer to them in their presence before the verdict is returned and a breach of that rule may lead to any conviction obtained being quashed.[2] The Prevention of Crimes Act 1871, however, provides that for the purpose of proving guilty knowledge of reset the prosecutor, if he gives seven days' notice, may prove previous convictions inferring fraud or dishonesty obtained during the preceding five years, provided that he has first led evidence to establish that the accused was in possession of stolen property.[3] It is not necessarily fatal to conviction if a witness accidentally refers to the accused's previous convictions.[4]

Co-accused's character at instance of accused

In *R v Miller*[5] it was held that where the defence of one of a number of accused was that the offences had been committed by one of his co-accused, it was competent for him to ask a prosecution witness whether the offences stopped when that co-accused was sent to prison. That question can be defended on the view that the reflection on the co-accused's character implicit in it was necessarily and indicentally relevant to the accused's defence, ie whether the offences stopped when the co-accused was not in a position to commit them. It appears, however, from that case and from others, that the test of whether an accused can lead evidence of his co-accused's character is primarily one of relevance, or sufficiency of relevance, on which the nature of the defence has a strong bearing. In *R v Bracewell*[6] it was held, on a charge of murder, that the accused, Bracewell, could not cross-examine a prosecution witness about violent and uncontrolled attacks on her by his co-accused Lockwood because the matter was not then sufficiently relevant, but when Lockwood gave evidence contrasting his own coolness as an experienced burglar with Bracewell's inexperience and panicky nature, it then became open to Bracewell to cross-examine Lockwood about the violent incidents and, if these were denied, to lead evidence about them. The cross-examination of Lockwood could be justified independently

1 Criminal Procedure (Scotland) Act 1975 ss 160 and 375.

2 *Graham v HM Advocate* 1984 SLT 67. But disclosure may be necessary (*Gemmill* above) and in any event breach is not necessarily fatal to conviction (*Binks v HM Advocate* (1985 SLT 59; *Slane v HM Advocate* 1986 SLT 293).

3 S 19. *Watson v HM Advocate* (1984) 21 R (J) 26.

4 *Kepple v HM Advocate* 1936 JC 76; *Haslam v HM Advocate* 1936 JC 82 at 85; *Clark v Connell* 1952 JC 119. But cf *Newlands v HM Advocate* 1980 SLT (notes) 25.

5 [1952] 1 All ER 667, 36 Cr App R 169.

6 (1978) 68 Cr App R 44.

under statute but the leading of evidence in replication of a denial seems to have rested on the common law and on the view that Lockwood's evidence had rendered that evidence sufficiently relevant.

Similar fact evidence in criminal cases

The starting point for a consideration of similar fact evidence in criminal cases is the speech of Lord Herschell LC in *Makin v A-G for New South Wales*:

> 'It is undoubtedly not competent for the prosecution to adduce evidence tending to show that the accused had been guilty of criminal acts other than those covered by the indictment, for the purpose of leading to the conclusion that the accused is a person likely from his criminal conduct or character to have committed the offence for which he is being tried. On the other hand, the mere fact that the evidence adduced tends to show the commission of other crimes does not render it inadmissible if it be relevant to an issue before the jury, and it may be so relevant if it bears upon the question whether the acts alleged to constitute the crime charged in the indictment were designed or accidental, or to rebut a defence which would otherwise be open to the accused.'[7]

The first sentence in that passage sets forth the general exclusionary rule that evidence of the accused's criminal conduct on occasions other than those charged is not admissible for the purpose of showing that he had a disposition to commit the offence charged and was so likely to have done so. The rule, although, in that formulation expressed in relation to criminal acts, extends, it is thought, to acts which, although not themselves criminal, have no relevance other than to show the accused's criminal disposition. The second sentence explains the circumstances in which evidence of other criminal acts may, nonetheless, be admissible. It may seem to take all content out of the first sentence by saying that evidence of previous criminal conduct is admissible if it is relevant because evidence is never admissible unless it is relevant and evidence of previous criminal conduct would then be in no different position from other evidence. That, however, is clearly not what was meant, and, although the passage is no doubt not to be interpreted as if it were a statute, it is important to get some picture of its true meaning. A possible interpretation is that by 'if it be relevant' was meant 'if it be otherwise relevant', ie relevant in some way other than its tendency to show the accused's criminal disposition. There is, then, a sharp distinction between tendering similar fact evidence for the purpose of showing the

7 [1894] AC 57 at 65.

accused's criminal disposition which is always inadmissible, and tendering it for other purposes, which may be admissible. That interpretation has, it is submitted, cogency and may well have been what was meant at the time. It is, however, impossible to reconcile with subsequent authorities in which similar fact evidence has been admitted when its only relevance was to show the accused's disposition to commit crimes of the kind in question where that disposition had peculiar relevance or probative force.[8] It seems, therefore, that the second sentence is to be read as enfranchising similar fact evidence where 1 its purpose is not to show criminal disposition or 2 its tendency to show a criminal disposition has special relevance.

Similar fact evidence in questions of motive, guilty knowledge and intention

Where similar fact evidence or evidence of the accused's past criminal actings is admitted in questions of motive its admissibility is independent of any tendency it may have to show the accused's criminal disposition. The only significance of these cases in the present context is that they establish that evidence relevant to the accused's motive may be led, although it consists of the accused's criminal actings or other actings which reflect adversely on his character. The evidence is therefore within the first of the two categories suggested above covered by the second sentence of Lord Herschell's formula. Thus in *HM Advocate v Pritchard*[9] evidence of the accused's improper conduct with a domestic servant was admitted as relevant to his motive for the murder of his wife and in *HM Advocate v Merrett*[10] in which the accused was charged with murdering his mother, evidence was admitted as relevant to motive that he had forged her signature on cheques and that she must discover that.

Cases of the admission of similar fact evidence to show guilty knowledge and intention may be regarded in a similar if sometimes more ambiguous light. Often the similar facts will show, independently of any question of disposition, that the accused must have had the knowledge requisite to his guilt but in other cases the relevance of the similar fact evidence is more closely related to the accused's disposition in that,

8 *R v Bond* [1906] 2 KB 389; *R v Ball* [1911] AC 47; *R v Smith* (1915) 11 Cr App R 229; *Thompson v R* [1918] AC 221; *R v Sims* [1946] KB 531, [1946] 1 All ER 697; *R v Straffen* [1952] 2 QB 911, [1952] 2 All ER 657; *Harris v DPP* [1952] AC 694, [1952] 1 All ER 1044, *DPP v Boardman* [1975] AC 421. For cases in which similar fact evidence was held not to be admissible see *Noor Mohamed v R* [1949] AC 182, [1949] 1 All ER 365; *R v Combes* (1960) 45 Cr App R 36; *R v Wilson* [1973] 58 Cr App R 169; *R v Brown, Smith Woods & Flanagan* (1963) 47 Cr App R 205.

9 (1865) 5 Irv 88.

10 See *Notable British Trials.*

although not tendered for the purpose of establishing that the criminal acts in issue took place, its purpose is to show that they fitted into a pattern of conduct which is likely to have been intentional. In either event, such evidence is admissible. So, in cases of fraud, evidence of previous false representations may be led for the purpose of showing that the representations in issue were made in knowledge of their falsity and, therefore, with criminal intent. The reasons for the admission of such evidence and the limitations on its admissibility were indicated by Lord MacLaren in *Gallagher v Paton*:[11]

> 'When the question is whether the accused person made false statements, knowing the statements to be false, and for the purpose of obtaining money to which he was not entitled, I do not know of any better method of establishing the criminal intention than by proof that he had made similar false statements on the same day to other people and apparently with the same object. . . .
>
> . . . However, the evidence of like representations must be confined to those that were made about the same time, because, if the prosecution were allowed to prove statements made at an earlier period, this would only go to general character, and would not necessarily throw light on the particular act which is under consideration.'

Similar fact evidence where nexus

Makin has been little considered in Scotland but it was cited in *HM Advocate v Joseph*[12] in which in an obvious reference to the second sentence of Lord Herschell's formula Lord Murray said that it represented the law in Scotland as in England. In that case a fraud committed abroad had been libelled, although it could not form a substantive charge, for the purpose, it seems, of showing that the matters charged as having been committed in this country had been done with fraudulent intent. The opinion of Lord Murray has, however, a wider application for the admission of similar fact evidence. He said:

> 'Evidence in regard to another incident of a similar character may be admitted in proof of a crime charged notwithstanding that this evidence may incidentally show, or tend to show, the commission of another crime, provided there be some connection or 'nexus' which in the opinion of the court is sufficiently intimate between the two "incidents".'

These words foreshadow *Moorov v HM Advocate*[13] which, although

11 1909 SC (J) 50 at 55.
12 1929 JC 55.
13 1930 JC 68.

decided on a question of corroboration, has necessary implications for the admission of similar fact evidence. In *Moorov* it was held that evidence of a single witness on one charge might corroborate the evidence of single witnesses to each of several other charges if the charges were so interrelated in time, character and circumstances as to suggest an underlying unity or nexus. It is a necessary corollary that, if there is the required interrelation, evidence on one charge is admissible in relation to the other. If evidence is to be corroborative it must be admissible on the charge for which it is to provide corroboration.[14] It appears, therefore, that evidence of similar facts is admissible if it satisfies the requirements for corroboration laid down in *Moorov v HM Advocate*. In such cases the relevance of the evidence lies in its tendency to show the accused's disposition. That disposition is, however, to be understood not in the sense of a general criminal disposition, or even of a tendency to commit crimes of a particular but broad class, eg theft or assault, but of a disposition which has peculiar cogency as evidence in the circumstances of the case. The 'nexus' required by *Moorov* provides that cogency. It accords with the stress put on probative force in the leading English case of *DPP v Boardman* in which Lord Wilberforce said:

> 'The basic principle must be that the admission of similar fact evidence (of the kind now in question) is exceptional and requires a strong degree of probative force. This probative force is derived, if at all, from the circumstances that the facts testified to by the several witnesses bear to each other such a striking similarity that they must, when judged by experience and common sense, either all be true, or have arisen from a cause common to the witnesses or from pure coincidence.'[15]

CROSS-EXAMINATION OF ACCUSED ON CHARACTER, OTHER OFFENCES, ETC.

The Criminal Procedure (Scotland) Act 1975[16] contains the following provisions under which the accused who gives evidence on his own behalf:

(e) may be asked any question in cross-examination, notwithstanding that it would incriminate him as to the offence charged and
(f) shall not be asked, and if asked, shall not be required to answer any

14 The interrelation of the admissibility of similar fact evidence and corroboration is acknowledged in *DPP v Kilbourne* [1973] AC 729, [1973] 1 All ER 440 in which *Makin* is followed and *Moorov* cited with approval.
15 [1975] AC 421 at 444.
16 Ss 141 and 346.

question tending to show that he has committed, or been convicted of, or been charged with, any offence other than that with which he is then charged, or is of bad character, unless—

(i) the proof that he has committed or been convicted of such other offence is admissible evidence to show that he is guilty of the offence with which he is then charged; or

(ii) the accused or his counsel or solicitor has asked questions of the witnesses for the prosecution with a view to establishing the accused's good character, or the accused has given evidence of his own good character, or the nature or conduct of the defence is such as to involve imputations on the character of the prosecutor or of the witnesses for the prosecution; or

(iii) the accused has given evidence against any other person charged in the same proceedings.[17]

Effect of proviso (e)

The effect of proviso (e)—a necessary provision if cross-examination of the accused is to be effective—is that the accused if he gives evidence loses his privilege against self-incrimination in respect of the offence charged. That loss extends, however, only to questions tending to incriminate him directly. Unless proviso (f) can be brought into operation the accused remains protected against questions which would tend to incriminate him indirectly, such as questions of an incriminative character which bear solely on his credibility.[18]

Meaning of 'tending to show'; necessity of relevance

In *Jones v DPP*[19] it was held that 'tending to show' in proviso (f) meant 'tending to show for the first time'. That has large consequences because it means that if the accused in his evidence makes an incidental reference

17 It is enough to justify cross-examination on previous convictions, etc that the evidence given by one accused should by plain implication be evidence against another (*Burton v HM Advocate* 1979 SLT (Notes) 59). See also *Sandlan v HM Advocate* 1983 SLT 208.

18 That view is implicit in the speeches of the majority of the House of Lords (Lord Simmonds, Lord Reid and Lord Morris) in *Jones v DPP* below. Cross-examination of the accused is permitted under proviso (f) (i) where it would tend to incriminate him indirectly if it is to the effect that he has committed another offence, evidence of which is admissible to show that he is guilty of the offence with which he is charged (eg where similar fact evidence is admissible at common law) or if it is to the effect that he has been convicted of another offence in the rare instances in which such evidence is admissible. The accused cannot, however, be cross-examined under either proviso (e) or proviso (f) (i) as to an offence with which he has been charged and acquitted, although exceptionally such evidence may be relevant, or as to his bad character (*R v Cokar* [1960] 2 QB 207, [1960] 2 All ER 175). The contrary view taken in *R v Chitson* [1909] 2 KB 945 and *R v Kurasch* [1915] 2 KB 749 cannot, it is thought, be reconciled with the majority opinion in *Jones v DPP*.

19 [1962] AC 635, [1962] 1 All ER 569.

as may sometimes be necessary for his defence to his having previously been convicted, he becomes open to cross-examination on the whole range of matters for which proviso (f) provides. His only protection then is that the court may in its discretion refuse to permit the cross-examination if it would be unduly prejudicial.

The Act does not override the principle that all evidence must be relevant, and so cross-examination will not be permitted if it is irrelevant. Thus it will not usually be competent to cross-examine an accused person under proviso (f) as to a charge of which he was acquitted because that cannot in ordinary circumstances be relevant to his guilt.[20] But it may in special circumstances become relevant, eg where it shows relevant knowledge.[1] Character for the purpose of the proviso is indivisible and so, once the accused's character is in issue, his whole character may be the subject of cross-examination.[2] Character for this purpose embraces not only reputation but also actual disposition.[3]

Effect of proviso (f)

Proviso (f) (i) enables cross-examination of the accused on character, other offences, etc where evidence of these matters would be admissible against him at common law and also cross-examination as to convictions where the offence is one in which previous convictions form part of the libel.

Proviso (f) (ii) in its first limb appears to have a gap in that it makes no reference to evidence of good character which emerges from defence witnesses other than the accused.[4] The second limb of proviso (f) (ii) has been the subject of Scottish authority. In *O'Hara v HM Advocate*[5] it was held that the accused did not under this limb lose his statutory protection where the attack on the character of a prosecution witness was necessary to enable the accused fairly to establish his defence. The protection was lost only if there was an attack on the witness's general character. In that case which concerned inter alia assault on two police officers who gave evidence that they had been the victims of an unprovoked attack, there was cross-examination of one of them on

20 *Maxwell v DPP* [1935] AC 309.

1 *R v Cokar* above. In the circumstances of *R v Cokar* the evidence was inadmissible because it was not permitted by proviso (e) or proviso (f) (i) and proviso (f) (ii) or (iii) could not be invoked. Where, however, such evidence is relevant and the accused has thrown away his shield under proviso (f) (ii) or (iii) it may be admitted. 'Charged' means 'charged in court' (*Stirland v DPP* [1944] AC 315, [1944] 2 All ER 13).

2 *R v Winfield* [1939] 27 Cr App R 139; *Stirland v DPP* [1944] AC 315 per Lord Simon at 324, [1944] 2 All ER 13 at 18.

3 *R v Dunkley* [1927] 1 KB 323 per Lord Hewart CJ at 329; *Jones v DPP* [1962] AC 635, [1962] 1 All ER 569 per Lord Denning at 671 and 580 and Lord Devlin at 699 and 604.

4 Walker and Walker *The Law of Evidence in Scotland* para 358(C), p 383.

5 1948 JC 90.

behalf of the accused that he (the police officer) had been under the influence of drink at the time and was the aggressor. It was held that as that cross-examination was necessary to enable the accused to establish his defence he had not thereby thrown away his shield against cross-examination as to character and previous criminal acts. That decision involves reading into the Act words such as 'unnecessarily', or 'unjustifiably' and cannot be reconciled with the decision of the House of Lords in *R v Selvey*[6] but it reflects what may be a sound principle and is the authoritative interpretation of the Act so far as Scotland is concerned.[6a]

Judicial discretion in relation to proviso (f)

Where the requirements of proviso (f) are satisfied it remains for the court to determine in its discretion whether cross-examination should be allowed. That discretion is to be exercised with regard to the fundamental consideration that the trial should be fair and accordingly cross-examination may be prohibited where it would be unduly prejudicial.[7] There is, however, no discretion to exclude cross-examination by a co-accused when that becomes competent to him under proviso (f) (iii).[8]

CHARACTER OF VICTIM

The question of whether evidence may be led of the character or disposition of the victim or alleged victim of crime is largely one of relevance. Where it is relevant it is admissible. So where self-defence or provocation is in issue in cases of homicide or assault the accused may on giving notice lead evidence of the victim's violent or quarrelsome disposition as relevant to those issues.[9] He may not, however, lead evidence of specific acts of violence.[10] It is open to the prosecutor to lead evidence of the victim's disposition where relevant.[11] Questions about the victim's insobriety or other conduct at the time of the offence may be put without notice for these matters are not collateral.[12]

6 [1970] AC 304, [1968] 2 All ER 497.

6a An imputation of falsehood may be necessary to enable the accused fairly to establish his defence and does not deprive him of the protection of the statute. But to allege a conspiracy to fabricate evidence and defeat the ends of justice is an attack on general character which, even if necessary for the defence, opens the way to cross-examination of the accused as to his own character: *Templeton v MacLeod* 1986 SLT 149.

7 *O'Hara v HM Advocate* above per Lord Justice-Clerk Thomson at 99 and Lord Jamieson at 102.

8 *McCourtney v HM Advocate* 1978 SLT 10 at 13.

9 *Blair* (1836) Bell's Notes 294; Irving (1838) 2 Swin 109; *Fletcher* (1846) Ark 171.

10 *Irving* above, *Fletcher* above.

11 *Porteus* (1831) Bell's Notes 293.

12 *Falconer v Brown* (1893) 21 R (J) 1.

The common law was that in cases of rape the character of the victim in relation to sexual matters might be the subject of evidence as relevant to the question of consent[13] but the specific acts of intercourse could not be proved unless, if they were proximate in time, with the accused and perhaps, in the case of other men, if they were part of what was called the res gestae. The victim's association with prostitutes might also be proved but not that her friends were otherwise of bad character.[14] Such evidence might be countered by evidence on behalf of the crown of the victim's good character.[15] These common law rules are now superseded by statute. The Criminal Procedure (Scotland) Act 1975 as amended[16] provides that the court is not to admit or allow questioning designed to elicit evidence which shows or tends to show that the person against whom the offence is alleged to have been committed (a) is not of good character in relation to sexual matters, (b) is a prostitute or an associate of prostitutes or (c) has at any time engaged with any person in sexual behaviour not forming part of the subject matter of the charge. The prohibition applies to evidence in any charge of committing or attempting to commit rape, sodomy, assault with intent to rape, indecent assault (including lewd, indecent or libidinous practices) unlawful sexual intercourse with a mentally handicapped female patient, offences under the Sexual Offences (Scotland) Act 1976 consisting in procuring by threats unlawful sexual intercourse with a girl under 13 years, indecent behaviour towards a girl between 12 and 16, abduction of a girl under 18 and unlawful detention of a female, and homosexual offences under the Criminal Justice (Scotland) Act 1980. The prohibition does not, however, apply to questioning or evidence adduced by the crown and the court may on an application by the accused allow questioning or admit evidence of the prohibited kind if (a) it is designed to explain or rebut evidence adduced or to be adduced otherwise than by or on behalf of the accused or (b) it relates to sexual behaviour which took place on the same occasion as the behaviour forming the subject matter of the charge or is relevant to a defence of incrimination or (c) its exclusion would be contrary to the interests of justice. Where questioning or evidence is allowed or admitted, the court may as it thinks fit limit its extent.

CHARACTER OF WITNESS

A witness may be cross-examined on any matter bearing on his credibility including his character for honesty, his convictions for crimes of dishonesty and, subject to privilege, any criminal acts committed by

13 *Dickie v HM Advocate* (1897) 24 R (J) 82.
14 *Webster* (1847) Ark 269.
15 *McMillan* (1846) Ark 209.
16 Ss 141A and B and 346A and B as inserted by Law Reform (Miscellaneous Provisions) (Scotland) Act 1985 s 36.

him suggestive of his dishonesty or unreliability.[17] It is competent to cross-examine a witness in a criminal trial as to whether he is an accomplice of the accused because the evidence of accomplices is suspect.[18] There is also authority for the view that the evidence of prostitutes is suspect[19] and, if that is still the law, a witness may be questioned on whether she has that character, but it is doubtful if the authority would now be followed. If the witness denies the matter put to him in cross-examination, evidence cannot be led to disprove his denial. That is a feature of the general rule that evidence cannot be adduced solely for the purpose of reflecting on a witness's credibility. As an exception to that, evidence may, under statute, be led of a witness's statements which are inconsistent with the evidence he has given if he has been cross-examined about his making these statements and has denied it.[20] It is uncertain whether the general exclusion of evidence bearing on credibility applies to opinion evidene from suitably qualified persons. In two old cases, evidence was admitted from the mother of a child witness as to whether the child was truthful and whether she believed the child's story, but in another case questioning of a witness, not the mother of the children, to similar effect was refused.[1] There is English authority that psychiatric and other medical evidence is admissible for the purpose of impugning the reliability of testimony,[2] and also that a lay witness who is acquainted with another witness may give evidence of his opinion of the credibility of the latter based on personal knowledge of reputation.[3]

CHARACTER OF OTHER PERSONS

In some cases the character of persons who are not parties nor victims of crime nor witnesses may be relevant. Thus, it may be relevant to a charge of reset that persons frequenting the accused's premises were known thieves or persons dealing in stolen property, and, in a charge of brothel-keeping, it may be relevant that the premises were frequented by known prostitutes.[4] Where such evidence is relevant it is admissible,[5] but evidence of particular acts, unless connected with the charge, would not be admissible.

17 A witness may probably also be cross-examined about non-criminal conduct inferring dishonesty, but the admission of evidence that another person has criticised the witness for telling lies seems to be hearsay and inadmissible (see, however, *King v King* (1842) 4 D 590).

18 Ch 9 below.

19 *Tennant v Tennant* (1883) 10 R 1187. Cf *Webster*, n 14, above.

20 Ch 3 below.

1 *Maclean* (1829) Bell's Notes 294; *Buchan* (1833) Bell's Notes 246; *Galloway* (1836) 1 Swinton 232, Bell's Notes 254.

2 *Tohey v Metropolitan Police Commissioner* [1965] AC 595, [1965] 1 All ER 506.

3 *Mawson v Hartsink* (1802) 4 Esp 102. According to *Dickson* (2nd edn) para 1802, the law of England differs widely from the law of Scotland on this point.

4 *R v Richardon and Longman* [1969] 1 QB 299, [1968] 2 All ER 761.

5 *Gracie v Stuart* (1884) 11 R (J) 22; *Macpherson v Crisp* 1919 JC 1.

CHAPTER 3

Inadmissibility of evidence; hearsay

DEFINITION OF RULE

'Testimonies ex auditu prove not'.[1]

What a person sees or hears or apprehends by the senses of touch, taste or smell is, generally speaking, admissible if it is relevant to a fact or facts in issue. And usually the admissibility of the evidence is not affected by the nature of what has been seen or heard or otherwise apprehended, whether it be an inaminate object, human conduct, animal behaviour, the functioning of a mechanism or a natural phenomenon. Where, however, the object of evidence is the spoken or written word or its equivalent in expressive conduct, special problems arise. The reason for that is that language is the vehicle by which assertions of fact are made. It is at such assertions that the rule against hearsay strikes. The medium by which the assertion is conveyed is immaterial, whether speech, writing, sign or gesture, mime or diagrammatic representation. The rule against hearsay is designed to avoid what someone has asserted on an occasion other than that on which he is giving evidence being used as if it were evidence of the facts stated. In this sense hearsay is secondary evidence. If the point at issue is whether Y struck Z it is incompetent to prove the assault by means of evidence that Z (or anyone else for that matter) has said that Y struck him. The primary evidence, and the only evidence which should be used, is the testimony in court of Z or of any witness to the event, that Y struck Z. In other words, the rule against hearsay is designed to secure that proof proceeds on what witnesses say in the course of giving their testimony and not on reports of what they or other persons have said on other occasions. The rule excludes therefore, subject to exceptions, all forms of assertion other than those made by the witness of his own knowledge in giving his testimony. It does so, however, only where the assertion is tendered in evidence for the purpose of proving the fact asserted. At the trial of A for theft it is hearsay and inadmissible for a witness to testify that B said

1 Stair IV 43, 15.

that A stole the goods, for the purpose of proving A's guilt; but in an action for defamation by A against B it would not be hearsay for a witness to give that evidence for the purpose of proving that the defamatory statement was made. What has been said on other occasions is objectionable only where the statement is used as evidence of the fact stated.

> 'There is no general rule of evidence to the effect that a witness may not testify as to the words spoken by a person who is not produced as a witness. There is a general rule, subject to many exceptions, that evidence of the speaking of such words is inadmissible to prove the truth of the facts they assert.'[2]

That quotation points the contrast between hearsay statements and statements as original evidence and epitomises, although it does not fully state, the rule against hearsay. A complete formulation is:

> 'An assertion other than one made by a person while giving oral evidence is inadmissible as *evidence of any fact (or opinion) asserted.*'

The words in brackets are added because second-hand opinion is no less objectionable than second-hand evidence of fact.

The rule so formulated excludes evidence by the witness of his own previous assertions as well as those made by others. As the former would not ordinarily be called hearsay, the rule against hearsay can be said to have absorbed another and subsidiary rule against evidence of a witness's own previous assertions.[3] Such evidence would in any event usually be of little value but that would not always be so, eg where the witness had compiled a detailed written record of complicated facts. Any resultant disadvantages are in part compensated by enabling the witness to refresh his memory[4] from notes made by him at the time of an occurrence as well as by exceptions to the rule against hearsay.

STATEMENTS AS ORIGINAL EVIDENCE

Not all statements are assertive of existing fact or of opinion. An offer to contract although it may sometimes embody an assertion of fact need not qua offer make any assertion other, perhaps, than an implied assertion of intention for the future conditional on acceptance. So too, expressions of good wishes or of hope are typically non-assertive. Non-

2 *Cullen v Clarke* [1963] IR 368 per Kingsmill Moore J.
3 *Cross on Evidence* (6th edn, 1979) p 38.
4 Ch 10 below.

assertive statements or utterances and assertive statements tendered for a purpose other than proof of the fact asserted are, subject to relevancy, generally admissible. They are what Walker and Walker, who define hearsay as 'evidence of what another person has said',[5] call primary hearsay but are more commonly called original evidence. They are best regarded as falling outwith, rather than constituting an exception to, the rule against hearsay.

The classification of a statement as original evidence often presents no difficulty, eg the offer and acceptance where a contract is disputed, the defamatory words in an action of defamation, threats where duress is alleged. Whenever the making of a statement is in issue evidence that the statement was made, which necessarily includes a narration of its terms, is original evidence. The evidence is admissible in proof of the making of the statement whether or not the statement was assertive but it is incompetent to use any assertion contained in the statement as proof of the matter asserted. The general principle was laid down in *Subramaniam v Public Prosecutor*:

> 'Evidence of a statement . . . is hearsay and inadmissible when the object of the evidence is to establish the truth of what is contained in the statement. It is not hearsay and is admissible when it is proposed to establish by the evidence, not the truth of the statement, but the fact that it was made.'[6]

That principle assumes, however, the relevance of the fact that the statement was made and where that fact is not immediately in issue problems of the classification of evidence as original or hearsay may arise from a difficulty in distinguishing the relevance of the making of the statement from the relevance of any assertion it contains. It is sometimes said that a statement is admissible as original evidence where it is significant (ie relevant) that the statement was made. But that is not in itself enough. Circumstances may sometimes lend colour to the probability that an assertion is true and, in that sense, it may be significant that the statement was made in those circumstances but that

5 *Law of Evidence in Scotland* p 394. The definition is etymologically exact but at variance with common usage. It involves treating as hearsay matters such as the offer in a contract or the alleged defamatory statement in an action of defamation, which no one would describe as hearsay. The consequent description of original evidence as primary hearsay, and of hearsay evidence in the usual sense as secondary hearsay, creates a barrier to understanding in other jurisdictions where that terminology is not used. The definition of hearsay and of original evidence adopted in this book follows general Anglo/American as well as the older Scottish usage.

6 [1956] 1 WLR 965 at 969.

does not render it admissible in proof of the fact asserted: it remains hearsay and not original evidence. The relevance of the fact that the statement was made must be independent of whether any assertion made is true or false. *Maclaren v Macleod*[7] may be given as an example. The accused was charged with keeping a brothel and evidence was led of conversations which two witnesses had overheard in the premises which the accused had occupied. An objection was taken on the ground of hearsay, but the evidence was held to be competent because significance attached to the fact that the statements were made (ie that the conversation took place) quite independently of whether their contents were true or false. The fact that conversations of the kind alleged took place, cast some light—or so it was thought—on the nature of the premises and the purpose for which they were being used, even if what was said in the course of these conversations was quite untrue.

R v Rice,[8] in which an airline ticket was admitted as evidence that a person bearing the name inserted on the ticket had travelled on the flight for which the ticket was issued, illustrates the difficulty of distinguishing original evidence from hearsay. If the name on the ticket is regarded merely as an identifying label its admission was unobjectionable. If a ticket bearing an identifying mark can be shown to have been in the possession of X then evidence that the ticket was among the used tickets for a particular flight is prima facie evidence that X travelled on that flight. A number or specific symbol would be as good for that purpose as a name and where a name is used it is immaterial whether or not it is X's actual name. It may be only a slight extension of that line of reasoning to say that the presence of a name on a ticket is itself prima facie evidence that the ticket was issued to a person of that name and that from the used ticket an inference can be drawn that a person so named travelled. That may be the justification of the decision in *R v Rice*. A stricter analysis would, however, suggest that the presence of the name on the ticket is merely the record of an assertion by someone (the person who gave the name to the booking clerk) that a person of that name was expected to travel, that the whole process of inference rests on that extra-judicial assertion and that the evidence is therefore inadmissible as hearsay. The decision in *R v Rice* is difficult to reconcile with cases in which labels or marks on goods indicating the country of origin have been held to be inadmissible in proof of the fact asserted (ie of the fact that the goods did so originate).[9]

7 1913 SC (J) 61.
8 [1963] 1 QB 957, [1963] 1 All ER 832, [1963] 2 WLR 585.
9 *Patel v Comptroller of Customs* [1966] AC 356, [1965] 3 All ER 593; *Comptroller of Customs v Western Lectric Co Ltd* [1966] AC 367, [1965] 3 All ER 599.

IMPLIED ASSERTIONS

It is sometimes a question of difficulty whether an implied assertion offends against the hearsay rule. Clearly where an assertion is intended but is not explicit, evidence of the statement is objectionable if tendered for the purpose of proving the matter impliedly intended. Also, where an assertion has been made, evidence of it is hearsay and objectionable not only in proof of the fact actually asserted but also in proof of other facts necessarily implicit in it (eg evidence that 'B said that he saw X murdering Y' is inadmissible not only for the purpose of proving that X did murder Y but also in proof of the fact, implied in the statement, that X used violence to Y). Equally the rule is infringed by evidence which rests on a concealed assertion and which cannot therefore be of value unless the existence of that assertion and its reliability are assumed; eg where a witness gives evidence of the results of his inquiries and those results, however presented, consist in fact of a record, précis, version or interpretation of what he had been told. There is in such cases an implication, although it may not be recognised, that an assertion was made and the evidence is tendered in proof of the facts asserted and is therefore objectionable. It is where the statement or conduct from which the assertion is implied is not intended to be assertive that difficulties arise. In practice these difficulties are lessened by the fact that if the implied assertion is treated as hearsay it will nonetheless often be admissible under an exception to the rule, as, eg conduct by an accused person inferring guilt, under the exception for confessions, or an exclamation by a bystander at an occurrence from which his views as to the existence of some state of affairs is implied, under the exception for statements forming part of the res gestae. Is it, however, objectionable, where no such exception applies, to lead evidence of the fact that a ship's captain set sail along with his family in proof of the fact that the ship was seaworthy (an implied assertion that it was seaworthy) or of Smith's greeting 'Good morning, Brown' in proof of the fact that Brown was present when the greeting was uttered (an implied assertion to that effect)?[10] The evidence is, of course, admissible in proof of the captain's state of mind, in the former case, and of Smith's, in the latter, if that be in issue. Of that it is original evidence. Is it, however, admissible where the sole issue is the truth of the facts impliedly asserted? There are dicta in English authority[11] that such evidence is inadmissible and there is

10 See *Wright v Doe d Tatham* (1837) 7 Ad El 313 per Parke B at 387; *R v Gibson* (1887) 18 QBD 537.
11 *Wright v Doe d Tatham* above.

some force in that view. Where an assertion is explicit it is the belief of the maker of the assertion which is expressed and where an assertion is implied from actings or a non-assertive utterance it is equally on the belief of the actor or utterer that the significance of the evidence depends. There is some artificiality or arbitrariness in distinguishing radically between the two. But the view that evidence of non-assertive conduct or statements is hearsay whenever its evidentiary significance lies in an implied assertion is difficult to reconcile with *Ratten v R*[12] in which evidence was admitted of a phone call made by a woman, shortly before she was murdered asking for the police. In Scotland that evidence, if regarded as hearsay, would have been admissible under the exception for statements by deceased persons and it was, in fact, held to be admissible under the exception for res gestae statements. The Privy Council's primary ground of decision was, however, that it was original evidence. It was original in two respects: 1 to rebut evidence that the only phone call from the house had been one made by the accused and 2 as showing the victim's state of alarm from which the jury might infer that she was faced with an actual or impending emergency. In the latter respect it is difficult to see the significance of the evidence as lying in anything other than an assertion implied from the victim's conduct and utterance. It seems therefore that the fact that an assertion is implied does not deprive non-assertive conduct or statements of their character as original evidence. As indicated at the beginning of this paragraph an assertion may be implied where it is intended but not expressed or is necessarily implicit in or concealed by words themselves assertive. In those cases the implied assertion is hearsay. With those exceptions a question of hearsay arises only when the words spoken are relied upon as 'establishing some fact narrated by the words'.[13]

EXCEPTIONS TO THE RULE

The rule against hearsay is ancient and as a rule of Scots law is probably derived from Roman law.[14] Neither the exigencies of jury trial nor the requirements of adversary procedure are satisfactory explanations of its Scottish origins although both have probably been potent influences in its later development. Reasons for excluding hearsay include the fact that the maker of the statement is not subject to cross-examination and has not been put on oath or affirmation, that other safeguards which may attach to the giving of testimony in court are lacking and that the

12 [1972] AC 378, [1971] 3 All ER 801, [1971] 3 WLR 930.
13 *Ratten v R* [1972] AC 378 at 387, [1971] 3 All ER 801 at 805 per Lord Wilberforce.
14 See Wilkinson 'The Rule Against Hearsay in Scotland' 1982 Jur Rev 213.

risks of distortion, concoction and the effects of faulty recollection are particularly high. Not all these objections apply, however, with equal force to all forms of hearsay and if hearsay were never admitted much valuable evidence would be lost. Accordingly the rule against hearsay admits of a number of exceptions. Although these exceptions have developed in a somewhat piecemeal fashion and contain some anomalies they can, in the main, be justified by reference to one or other of the two rational principles on which Wigmore has explained exceptions to the rule: the necessity principle and the principle of circumstantial probability of trustworthiness. By the necessity principle Wigmore meant, to paraphrase him, that the admissions of evidence was justified on the ground of necessity when it came from a source which would otherwise be lost or when it was such that we could not expect to get evidence of the same value from the same or other sources. By circumstantial probability of trustworthiness he meant that the evidence was of a kind to which such a degree of probability of accuracy and trustworthiness attached as to make the reported statement an adequate substitute for evidence tested by cross-examination in the conventional manner.[15] The principal exceptions are discussed in the following pages.

1 Statements forming part of the res gestae

Evidence is admissible of a statement made contemporaneously with an action or event which is, or forms part of, the fact or facts in issue by a person present at that action or event. The res gestae may be defined as the whole circumstances immediately and directly connected with an occurrence which is part of the facts in issue. So, in *The Schwalbe*,[16] an exclamation by a pilot at the time of a collision 'the damned helm is still astarboard' was held to be admissible. Strict contemporaneity is not, however, essential. It is enough that the statement should be so clearly associated with the action or event in time, place and circumstances as substantially to form part of it.[17] *R v Bedingfield*[18] affords an example of a statement made after the event but closely connected with it. The victim, whose throat had been cut, staggered from the room in which she had been with the accused and gasped out certain words which were never proved but are alleged to have been 'Oh aunt, see what Bedingfield has done to me!' Evidence of that statement was excluded on the ground that it was not part of the res gestae. In *Ratten v R*,[19] however, it

15 *Evidence in Trials at Common Law I* p 204, paras 1421, 1422. See Wilkinson ibid.
16 [1861] 14 Moore PC 241, [1861] Lush 239, (1861) 4 LT 160.
17 *Leizor Teper v R* [1952] AC 480 per Lord Normand at 487.
18 (1879) 14 Cox CC 341.
19 [1972] AC 378, [1971] 3 All ER 801.

was held that *Bedingfield* was wrongly decided although the principle which the court laid down and purported to apply was sound, ie that a statement made after the event must be distinguished from statements forming part of the occurrence, the latter being part of the res gestae and the former not. In *Bedingfield* the evidence of the victim's statement should have been admitted as forming part of the occurrence and therefore part of the res gestae. The test is whether the statement was generated by the occurrence in such circumstances of spontaneity as to exclude the possibility of concoction. The boundaries of the occurrence are not to be defined narrowly and a statement which satisfies that test is to be regarded as falling within these boundaries rather than as made after the event.

> 'There is ample support for the principle that hearsay evidence may be admitted of the statement providing it is made in such conditions (always being those of approximate but not exact contemporaneity) of involvement or pressure as to exclude the possibility of concoction or distortion.'[20]

'Possibility' is here to be understood in a practical sense as the risk of concoction or distortion can seldom be absolutely excluded.

Res gestae statements are not confined to the utterances of a party, but may be the words of any witness and, despite any inference that might be drawn from dicta about their being real evidence,[1] they are admitted for the purpose of proving the truth of the matters asserted and not merely for the sake of any significance resting in the fact that they were made.[2] They constitute therefore an exception to the rule against hearsay. Sometimes, however, a statement falling within this exception may also have the character of original evidence as in *Ratten*.

20 *Ratten v R* [1972] AC 378 at 391 per Lord Wilberforce.

1 *O'Hara v Central SMT* 1941 SC 363 per Lord Moncrieff at 390; *Leizor Teper v R* [1952] AC 480 at 487 per Lord Normand. The description is vivid but, perhaps, unguarded.

2 That res gestae statements are admitted as an exception to the rule against hearsay and not merely for any significance they have as original evidence is put beyond doubt by *Ratten v R* in which it was held that the statement in question was admissible both as original evidence and, under an exception to the hearsay rule, as a res gestae statement. But the matter had, in any event, always been clear in principle. Statements admissible as original evidence, ie independently of the truth or falsity of any fact asserted, will often be part of the res gestae but their admissibility is not determined by that. They are admissible provided they are relevant whenever and in whatever circumstances they are uttered. There is no need for a category of res gestae statements to cover their admissibility. The point is driven home by the fact that in many of the cases in which statements have been admitted as part of the res gestae they have been admitted as evidence of the fact asserted and, if regarded independently of their truth or falsity, would have been of little or no relevance (eg *The Schwalbe*).

2 Statements regarding physical or mental condition

Evidence is admissible of statements regarding the physical or mental condition of the maker in the sense of physical sensations experienced or the content of the mind at the time the statement was made.[3] Such statements are admitted as being the ordinary indications of state of mind or physical sensation. In many cases physical symptoms and sufferings and the content of the mind cannot otherwise be ascertained.

3 Statements against interest; general

Evidence is admissible of a statement against interest made by a party to the cause in which the evidence is tendered, including an accused person in a criminal case. Subject to certain special protections in the case of accused persons, such statements are generally admissible whether made before, during or after the transaction or event in issue. This exception therefore comprehends, but goes beyond, the admissibility of evidence of extra-judicial admissions and confessions which, by their nature, are made after the event. It is based on the view that what someone says to his prejudice is likely to be true and therefore free from the disadvantages which often attach, from the standpoint of reliability, to hearsay evidence. It is, however, only statements by parties, or by persons who stand in such a relationship to a party that statements made by them are to be vicariously imputed to the party, which are admissible.

Jackson v Glasgow Corpn[4] illustrates the restriction of the exception to statements made by parties. In that case, damages were claimed in respect of injuries sustained by the pursuer in a collision between a car driven by her husband and a bus driven by an employee of the defenders. The defenders blamed the husband and said he had admitted liability in an action brought at their instance against him. It was held that evidence of statements made by him was incompetent unless he was examined as a witness. The rule permitting a party's previous statement to be proven was, it was said, to prevent his escaping liability for a wrong

3 This exception is part of, or akin to the res gestae exception. It is affirmed by *Dickson* (paras 249 ff) and so far as admission of statements indicative of a particular disposition towards a party is concerned, it is borne out by *King v King* (1841) 4 D 124 and *Rose v Junor* (1846) 9 D 12. With those exceptions, there is little Scottish authority in point and there is some, if slender, authority, against admitting evidence of statements indicative that the maker of the statement was suffering physical pain (*Hall v Otto* (1818) 1 Mur 444). It is thought, however, that the admission of evidence of statements showing the maker's state of mind (eg knowledge, feeling or disposition) and physical sensations accords with practice. It is well recognised in England (see *Cross* pp 590–7). The statement must refer to the maker's contemporary and not his past state, although, as in the case of the res gestae exception generally, the question of what constitutes contemporaneity is to some extent a question of degree.

4 1956 SC 354.

which he had previously admitted and was not designed to relieve other parties of liability. So, a party who has made a damaging admission may escape its consequences if an action to which he is not a party is treated as the leading case. In *Wilson v Jacobs*[5] three separate actions, the merits of which were identical, had been raised against the defender, Jacobs. It was agreed that one case should be taken as the leading case, but the actions were not conjoined. Objection was successfully taken to evidence by a witness in the leading case about a statement made to him by the pursuer in the second action. If, however, the question had been asked of a witness in the second action, the evidence would then have been admissible as evidence of a statement against interest by a party.

Except where an employee has authority to make statements or admissions on behalf of his employer, statements made by an employee are not vicariously imputed to his employer. Where, therefore, an employer is sued on the ground of his liability for an employee's fault, an admission of fault by the employee will not be admissible evidence. So, where the pursuer averred that a fire had been caused by the negligence of the defender's employee it was held inadmissible to lead evidence of an extra-judicial statement made by the employee, admitting that the fire had been caused by his running a blowlamp along pipes in an attempt to thaw them.[6] In that case the statement, although made immediately after the fire, was too late to form part of the res gestae but an employee's statements are of course admissible where they are part of the res gestae or otherwise properly come within an exception to the rule against hearsay.

4 Vicarious statements against interest

Where an employee has authority to make statements against interest and admission on behalf of his employer, then such statements may be vicariously imputed to the employer (eg an employee in a shop granting a receipt on behalf of the employer). On similar principles a statement made by an agent against the interests of his principal may, if made during the agency and relating to matters within the scope of the agent's authority, be imputed to his principal[7] and a statement made by a bankrupt before sequestration may, if there was no collusion, be

5 1954 SLT 215.

6 *Scott v Cormack Heating Engineers* 1942 SC 159.

7 *Dickson* paras 358 and 359. *Mitchell v Berwick* (1845) 7 D 382 at 384; *Aitchison v Robertson* (1846) 9 D 15; *McLean & Hope v Fleming* (1871) 9 M (HL) 38 at 41. Cf *Dryburgh v Macpherson* 1944 SLT 116; *Fisher v Fisher* 1952 SC 347 at 351; *Industrial Distributions (Central Scotland) Ltd v Quinn* 1984 SLT 240 (admission by directors as agents of company, admissible against company).

imputed against his trustee in bankruptcy.[8] A statement made by a deceased person contrary to his interest may be imputed against his executor.[9] A statement made against his interest by a cedent may be imputed against his assignee, and a statement against interest by a predecessor in title may, in some circumstances at least, be imputed against the present titleholder.[10]

5 Statements against interest in cases of concert

Where an accused person is charged with doing a criminal act along with others anything said or done by any of those with whom he acted in concert, is admissible in evidence against him, provided it was said or done in furtherance of the common object. So, where a group has acted in concert to accomplish a criminal object, the statement of one of them made in furtherance of the common object is admissible against the others and it is so admissible although the others were not present when the statement was made and had no knowledge of it. It is essential that the statement be made for the purpose of furthering the crime. It is not admissible if it is merely narrative by one of the parties to the criminal act stating what he has done. In general, therefore, the exception applies to statements made before, or contemporary with, the commission of the crime and not to confessions made after the event. The main problem which has arisen is whether there must be evidence of concert before statements can be admitted on this ground, and if so, whether there must be full legal evidence or merely prima facie evidence. The correct view seems to be that the evidence of the statements may be admitted before there is evidence of concert but that the jury should be directed to exclude the evidence of the statements from its consideration if concert is not proved. The statement should, of course, be excluded only in a question with anyone other than the maker of the statement. The statement will be good evidence against its maker if he is one of the accused. So, in *Young v HM Advocate*,[11] where a number of accused were tried together on a charge of acting in concert to defraud, documents executed by some of the accused, outwith the presence of the others, were admitted because a common purpose had been libelled. It was held that the court had been right in admitting the documents provisionally, but when there proved to be insufficient evidence of concert, the trial judge should have directed the jury to ignore the documents in a

8 *Dickson* para 357.
9 *Dickson* para 356.
10 That is the principle of the examples to which notes 8 and 9 above refer. The admission to be imputable to the successor must have been made before the transfer of title and must relate to the interest transferred.
11 1932 JC 63.

question with any of the accused other than those who had executed them.

6 Statements against interest by accused person

The general admissibility of statements against interest by parties suffers some qualification designed for the protection of accused persons where the statement of which evidence is tendered is the extra-judicial statement of the accused. It is necessary, for this purpose, to distinguish between statements made to the police and others in official positions similar to the police or to a prosecutor or to the judiciary (official persons), on the one hand, and to persons not in any of those categories (non-official persons), on the other. Prison warders[12] and probably a police doctor examining a person charged with an offence of driving under the influence of drink or drugs[13] are to be classified as in a similar position to the police, but not a police doctor who does not have an official relationship with the accused, as where he is examining the body of a deceased person.[14]

7 Statements by accused to non-official persons

Statements against interest made to non-official persons are admissible in criminal trials on much the same principles as they are admissible in civil actions. It is, accordingly sometimes said that it is irrelevant to the question of admissibility how the statement has been obtained and that it is admissible even if it has been obtained by threats, undue influence or inducement. The means of obtaining the statement is relevant only to weight and interpretation, not to admissibility. That view corresponds with what is probably the rule in civil cases, that the circumstances in which a statement against interest is obtained do not affect its admissibility although they may affect the interpretation to be put on it or the weight to be given to it. The better view, however, seems to be that there is here a divergence between the civil and criminal rules. In *HM Advocate v Robertson*,[15] a statement which the accused person had made regarding the commission by him of the crime of incest was held inadmissible because it had been made under threat to an inspector of the poor who had exerted undue influence to obtain it. In *HM Advocate v Graham*[16] 'substantially to offer a reward for a confession of guilt' was described as

12 *HM Advocate v Proudfoot* (1882) 9 R (J) 19.
13 Conceded, not decided, in *Reid v Nixon* 1948 JC 68—see per Lord Justice-Clerk Cooper at 72.
14 *HM Advocate v Duff* (1910) 6 Adam 248.
15 (1853) 1 Irv 219.
16 (1876) 3 Coup 217.

being wholly inconsistent with the principles of criminal procedure,[17] although the relevance of that case for present purposes is coloured by the fact that the offer had been made by a town councillor who had been baillie and who might therefore be thought to be vested with a quasi-official character. The probable rule is that evidence of confessions made to non-official persons is excluded if there is anything indicative of inducement or threat. That is consistent with the general rule of protecting the accused against all unfair means of abstracting a confession from him[17] The mere fact that the statement was obtained by questioning will not, however, render it inadmissible.[18]

8 Statements by accused to official persons

There is no doubt that evidence of statements made to official persons is inadmissible if the statement was made as a result of threats, promises or undue influence. Even, however, where there is no element of that kind, a statement made to an official person may be inadmissible because it fails to satisfy the special safeguards for the protection of the accused person. That is so, at any rate, so far as statements made to the police are concerned and it is with such statements that the cases have been mainly concerned.

Whether a statement made to the police will be admissible depends (threats, promises and undue influences apart) very largely on the stage which police investigations have reached and the degree of suspicion, if any, which has centred on the accused. In *Bell v HM Advocate*[19] the categories distinguished were 1 a person charged with crime and in custody awaiting trial, 2 a person detained on suspicion and 3 a person neither detained nor charged but who is merely being questioned by the police in the ordinary course of their investigations. In *HM Advocate v Aitken*[20] Lord Anderson had said 'the court ought to be more zealous to safeguard the rights of a prisoner in a case where a charge has not yet been made but where the prisoner has merely been detained by the police on suspicion' and the critical distinction in subsequent cases has been directed to the time when suspicion centred on the accused. Before that time the person who is ultimately accused of the crime is in no different position so far as need for protection is concerned from anyone else interviewed by the police.

> 'It would unduly hamper the investigation of crime if the threat of inadmissibility were to tie the hands of the police in asking

17 See *HM Advocate v Campbell* 1964 JC 80; *HM Advocate v Friel* 1978 SLT (Notes) 21.
18 *Morrison v Burrell* 1947 JC 40.
19 1935 JC 61.
20 1926 JC 83.

> questions. It would help to defeat the ends of justice if what the person so questioned said in answer to ordinary legitimate questions were not admissible in evidence against him.'[1]

So, at the stage of initial investigation the police may question anyone with a view to acquiring information which may lead to the detection of the criminal and anything said in answer to such questions by a person subsequently accused will be admissible in evidence against him. But when the stage has been reached at which suspicion, or more than suspicion, has centred upon someone as the likely perpetrator of the crime, 'further interrogation of that person becomes very dangerous, and if carried too far, eg to the point of extracting a confession by what amounts to cross-examination, the evidence of that confession will almost certainly be excluded'.

In *Chalmers v HM Advocate*[2] a youth under suspicion of murder and robbery was interrogated and made a statement. Thereafter, he was led by the police to a field and there pointed out a place where a purse which had once belonged to the murdered man was lying. These actings were clearly of an assertive character, the equivalent of an incriminating statement, and it was held by a full bench that in these circumstances there was no valid distinction in a question of admissibility between actings and statements and that the evidence of the actings was inadmissible as unfair to the accused. Two principles have to be reconciled: 1 that no accused person is bound to incriminate himself and need not submit himself as a witness and 2 that what an accused persons has said, provided it was said freely and voluntarily, is admissible evidence against him.[2] What was done in *Chalmers* offended against these principles because the accused was made to incriminate himself as a consequence of statements and their equivalents in actings which were neither free nor voluntary. Once the stage of suspicion is reached

> 'the suspect is in the position that thereafter the only evidence admissible against him is his own voluntary statement. A voluntary statement is one which is given freely, not in response to pressure and inducement and not elicited by cross-examination. This does not mean that if a person elects to give a statement it becomes inadmissible because he is asked some questions to clear his account of the matter up, but such questions as he is asked must not go beyond elucidation.'[2]

It is important to keep in mind that the point of time at which the axe falls is not necessarily related to the person's being in custody or

1 *Chalmers v HM Advocate* 1954 JC 66 per Lord Justice-Clerk Thomson at 81.
2 Note, 1 above.

detention of some sort. 'The fact that he is detained may point to his being under suspicion but he may come under suspicion without having been detained.'[2] Even a question not intended for the accused but understood by him to be directed to him may have the effect that the reply is regarded as not having been given freely and voluntarily as in *HM Advocate v Lieser*,[3] where one police officer addressing another said 'was there a razor found among his property?' and the accused made a statement which appeared to be a reply to that question. It was held that as the accused might have thought that the question was addressed to him, his statement was inadmissible. There has, however, in recent years been some retreat from the conservative attitude to the admission of evidence obtained by questioning which *Chalmers*, at least if rigidly applied, and perhaps *Lieser*, reflect. Suspicion, it has been said, is a matter of degree and in any event *Chalmers* does not exclude 'fair and proper' questioning.[4] It is 'interrogation' that is struck at[5] and interrogation is to be understood in the sense only of improper forms of questioning tainted with an element of bullying or pressure designed to break the will of the suspect or force from him a confession against his will.[6] There are, of course, factors other than questioning which may take a statement out of the free and voluntary category, such as any attempt to trap the accused into making a statement or any threat, bribe or promise. When an accused person is under suspicion he should be cautioned that he is not required to answer any question or to make any statement and that anything he says may be used in evidence. The absence of such a caution may result in any statement made in the course of a police interview being regarded as not free and voluntary and so inadmissible.[7] The wrongful refusal to an accused person of access to a solicitor, to which he is entitled once he has been arrested,[8]

3 1926 JC 88.
4 *Miln v Cullen* 1967 JC 21.
5 *Jones v Milne* 1975 SLT 2.
6 *Lord Advocate's Reference No 1 of 1983*, 1984 SLT 337. Cf *Brown v HM Advocate* 1966 SLT 105; *Hartley v HM Advocate* 1979 SLT 26; *HM Advocate v Mair* 1982 SLT 471; *Tonge v HM Advocate* 1982 SLT 506.
7 *HM Advocate v Von* 1979 SLT (Notes) 62; *HM Advocate v Docherty* 1981 JC 6; *Tonge v HM Advocate* 1982 SLT 506. A reply to a charge which had not been accompanied by a caution would probably be regarded as inadmissible against the accused because the accused might have understood himself to be under some obligation or compulsion to reply. If, however, in other circumstances, a person under arrest but not being interviewed, volunteers a statement, the absence of any prior caution does not necessarily make the statement inadmissible. The question is whether it was free and voluntary in the circumstances (see *Hodgeson v Macpherson* 1913 SC (J) 68; *Costello v Macpherson* 1922 JC 9). See also *Walkingshaw v McIntyre* 1985 SCCR (Sh Crt) 389.
8 Criminal Procedure (Scotland) Act 1975 ss 19 and 305.

may also have that result.[9]

The ultimate test in the admission of confessions and other statements against interest by accused persons is fairness to the accused.[10] In judging fairness, three matters require to be taken into account: 1 the nature of the charge; 2 the physical and mental capacity of the accused; and 3 the circumstances in which the statement was made.[11] In *McSwiggan*,[12] where a man of low mentality was charged with the crime of incest as a result of which the woman with whom he had incestuous relations became pregnant, and the accused insisted on making a statement explaining the precautions that he had taken to avoid pregnancy, it was held that as he clearly did not appreciate that the offence consisted in the incestuous relationship and not in causing the pregnancy, that the statement was inadmissible. More recent decisions have, however, stressed that fairness is bilateral, ie public interest in ascertainment of truth and in the detection and suppression of crime are also to be taken into account.[13]

9 Statements made in the presence of a party to a civil action or of an accused person in circumstances in which a reply or other reaction was to be expected

An admission or confession need not be express but may in some circumstances, be implied from a party's silence or guilty conduct in the face of an allegation against him; and generally where something is said affecting a person's interests he may be taken as accepting it if he does not respond when he has the opportunity to do so. Accordingly, statements made in the presence of a party to an action (including an accused person) are admissible if they contain an allegation against that party or contain matter affecting his interest and are made in circumstances in which a reply or other reaction is to be expected. The purpose of admitting such statements is to enable an inference of acceptance of what is said to be drawn from the party's silence or from his conduct in response; nothing turns on the making of the statement in itself, or on the contents of the statement, apart from the party's silence or other reaction.

9 The absence of a solicitor, where the accused has not asked for one, does not, however, affect admissibility (*HM Advocate v Cunningham* 1939 JC 61) nor, it is thought, is there any objection to the admissibility of a statement which a person in custody chooses to make pending the arrival of his solicitor. Failure to inform the person in custody of his right is not fatal (*HM Advocate v Fox* 1947 JC 30).

10 *Rigg v HM Advocate* 1946 JC 1.

11 *HM Advocate v Aitken* 1926 JC 83 per Lord Anderson.

12 1937 JC 50. Cf *HM Advocate v Gilgannon* 1983 SCCR 10 (statement by mentally subnormal person inadmissible).

13 *Miln v Cullen* 1967 JC 21. See also *Hartley v HM Advocate* 1979 SLT 26 per Lord Avonside at 28.

In the case of statements made in the presence of an accused person, similar safeguards apply to those which have already been noticed in connection with an accused person's confession. Just as a confession obtained by interrogation of an accused person after suspicion has centred on him is inadmissible so no adverse inference can legitimately be drawn from silence in the face of such interrogation. Moreover, although a confession freely given when an accused person is charged with an offence is admissible in evidence, and it would seem that guilty conduct in the fact of such a charge would also be admissible, no inference can be drawn adverse to the accused from his silence when charged.[14] The reason for that is that he is entitled to reserve his defence. Apart from these specialities it is a question of fact whether an adverse inference is to be drawn.

The general rule is that if the party would have been expected to repudiate the statement if untrue, then an inference that he admits it to be true may be drawn from his failure to repudiate. Where allegations are of a kind which it is customary, prudent or dignified to ignore, no adverse inference can be drawn from silence in the face of them. That will be particularly so where the allegations are in writing as correspondence of that kind is often ignored.[15] Where a verbal allegation is made to one's face, it is, however, more common to repudiate. Accordingly, an adverse inference may be drawn rather more easily from silence in the face of verbal allegations then from failure to reply to written allegations.[16] In the case of business communications, whether verbal or written, it is to be expected that, in the ordinary course, anything which is not accepted will be repudiated and accordingly acceptance of the terms of business communications may ordinarily be inferred from failure to reply.[17] In England silence in the face of an informal accusation of crime has been held to be some evidence of guilt.[18] In that connection it has been said to be important that the person who makes the allegation and the person who remains silent in the face of it should have been speaking 'on even terms'.[19]

10 Statements by deceased person, the insane and prisoners of war

Statements made prior to the time of trial or proof by persons who, by that time, are dead, insane or prisoners of war, are generally considered

14 *Robertson v Maxwell* 1951 JC 11 at 14.
15 *Wiedemann v Walpole* [1891] 2 QB 534.
16 *Bessela v Stern* (1877) 2 CPD 265.
17 *Smith v Maxwell* (1833) 1 S 323 per Lord Cringletie at 324; *Dowling v Henderson & Son* (1890) 17 R 921.
18 *R v Cramp* (1880) 14 Cox CC 390; *Parkes v R* [1976] 3 All ER 380.
19 *R v Mitchell* (1892) 17 Cox CC 503 per Cave J.

to be admissible[20] although only in the case of the first of these categories (deceased persons) can the law be said to be well settled.[1] It is necessary for admissibility that the maker of the statement would have been competent as a witness had he survived (or been free, or sane)[2] and that the statement should not have been made with a view to litigation or for the purpose of asserting a right or preserving evidence of a right of the maker of the statement.[3] The reason for excluding statements so made seems to be that they may have been tainted by interest or obtained by means giving rise to partially or, in the circumstances in which they were made, may not truly reflect what was in the maker's mind.[4] Where these risks can be excluded or are small evidence of the statement will be admitted. Thus, statements made on precognition or with a view to the commencement of legal proceedings, statements akin to precognition and averments in previous litigation are generally inadmissible,[5] although in one case a verbal account of what was said by the deceased while being precognosed was admitted and, in another, a precognition incorporated in a dying deposition was admitted.[6] Written statements given, without prompting or questioning, to insurers and oral statements made to the police have been admitted as have letters.[7] Moreover the exclusion of statements made with a view to litigation does not extend to evidence actually given in a trial or proof in a previous action or on commission[8] nor to dying depositions or declarations in a criminal case.[9]

20 *HM Advocate v Monson* (1893) 1 Adam 114, (1893) 21 R (J) 5.
1 *Dickson* paras 266–73. There is old authority for admitting statements by prisoners of war (*Cleland's Creditors* (1708) Mor 12634). The fact of death, etc must be established before the evidence will be admitted but prima facie proof will suffice and it seems hearsay may be admitted for that purpose (*Dickson* para 269).
2 *Dickson* para 267: 'Hearsay of a deceased person ... will be excluded if he was inadmissible as a witness when he made the statement'. If, however, the deceased person's statement is regarded as a substitute for his testimony, it seems to be more logical to refer the question of his competency as a witness to the time when evidence of the statement is tendered rather than to the time when the statement was made.
3 *Graham v Western Bank* (1865) 3M 617; *Tennant v Tennant* (1890) 17 R 1205 at 1225.
4 *Dickson* para 266. *Geils v Geils* (1855) 17 D 397 per Lord President McNeill at 404; *Dickson* para 271.
5 *Macdonald v Union Bank* (1864) 2 M 963; *Stevenson v Stevenson* (1893) 31 SLR 129; *Young v National Coal Board* 1960 SC 6; *Graham v Western Bank* above; *Traynor's Exx v Bairds & Scottish Steel Ltd* 1957 SC 311; *Tennant v Tennant* above; *Miller v Jackson* 1972 SLT (Notes) 31; *Cullen's Trustee v Johnston* (1865) 3 M 935; *Thomson v Jameson* 1886 SLT 72.
6 *Stephens* (1839) 2 Sw 348; *Wards* (1869) 1 Coup 186; *Petersen and Diluca* (1874) 2 Coup 557; *Dickson* para 271. These cases support the view that evidence of what has actually been said on precognition is admissible although the partial and reconstructed account usually contained in the written precognition is not. See ch 8 below.
7 *Moffat v Hunter* 1974 SLT (Sh Ct) 42; *HM Advocate v Irving* 1978 SLT 58; *McAlister v McAlister* (1833) 12 S 198; *Tennant v Tennant* (1890) 17R 1205.
8 *Coutts v Wear* (1914) 2 SLT 86; *Hogg v Frew* 1951 SLT 397.
9 *Dickson* paras 1754–6. Macdonald *Criminal Law* (5th edn) p 330; *Stewart* (1855) 2 Irv 166.

The wide scope which Scots law allows for the admission of statements by deceased persons contrasts with the much more restricted scope of the English common law rule.[10] Wigmore's comment on the latter is instructive:

> 'There was a time, in the early 1800s, when it came near to being settled that a general exception should exist for all statements of deceased persons who had competent knowledge and no apparent interest to deceive; but this tendency was of short-lived duration and was decisively negatived. Nevertheless, such an exception to the Hearsay rule, commends itself as a just addition to the present sharply defined exceptions, and represents undoubtedly the enlightened policy of the future.'[11]

The law of Scotland is in this respect close to what Wigmore regarded as the optimum. Whether the rule admitting statements by deceased and insane persons and by prisoners of war should be extended to cover statements made by persons who are permanently disabled by illness at the time of trial or proof was canvassed but left undecided in *McKie v Western SMT*.[12] The logical case for such an expansion is strong provided it is impossible for the person concerned to attend court or give evidence on commission.

11 Reputation in cases of marriage, legitimacy, pedigree and ancient rights

Evidence of reputation is admissible in proof of marriage and may when taken along with evidence of cohabitation amount to full proof.[13] This evidentiary use of reputation is distinct from the constitution of marriage by cohabitation with habit and rebute although it rests on a similar basis and may have similar origins. Evidence of reputations is also admissible in questions of legitimacy[14] and similarly evidence of family tradition may be admitted in questions of pedigree.[15] In pedigree cases it is only evidence of tradition emanating from persons with special means of knowledge which is admissible but it is not necessary that these persons be members of the family. They may include friends or

10 Now modified for civil cases by the Civil Evidence Act 1968.
11 *Evidence in Trials at Common Law I* p 204, paras 1421–2. Cf *Cross* p 562: 'As a minimal step in law reform, the statements of all deceased persons on every relevant matter should be made admissible in all criminal cases'.
12 1952 SC 206.
13 *De Thoren v Wall* (1876) 3 R (HL) 28; Clive *Law of Husband and Wife in Scotland* (2nd edn) p 487.
14 *Brooke's Exx v James* 1971 SC (HL) 77.
15 *Alexander v Officers of State* (1868) 6 M (HL) 54 per Lord Chelmsford at 62.

confidential servants.[16] There is a certain overlap between this rule and the general admission of the evidence of statements by deceased persons and also, given that overlap, a certain inconsistency in making the requirement of special means of knowledge. There is also an inconsistency between requiring such special means of knowledge in pedigree cases and not requiring it in legitimacy cases. In legitimacy cases, by contrast, some weight is attached to the element of *public* reputation. Yet questions of pedigree and legitimacy are closely interrelated.

On principles similar to the above reputable histories and like records are admissible in questions of ancient rights.[17]

12 Documentary evidence admissible under statute

The Criminal Evidence Act 1965[18] (for criminal cases) and the Law Reform (Miscellaneous Provisions) (Scotland) Act 1966[19] (for civil cases) respectively provide that in any proceedings where direct oral evidence of a fact would be admissible, certain statements contained in documents and tending to establish such facts, shall, on production of the document, be admissible. The conditions for admission in criminal cases are:

(a) the document must be, or form part of, a record compiled in the course of a trade or business;
(b) the document must be compiled from information supplied (whether directly or indirectly) by persons who have, or may reasonably be supposed to have, personal knowledge of the matters dealt with in the information; and
(c) the person who has supplied the information recorded in the statement in question must fall into one of the following categories:
  (i) he must be dead by the time of trial, or
  (ii) he must be beyond the seas, or
  (iii) he must be unfit by reason of his bodily or mental condition to attend as a witness, or
  (iv) it must be impossible, with reasonable diligence, to identify or find him, or
  (v) it must be beyond reasonable expectation (having regard to the time which has elapsed since he supplied the information and to all the circumstances) that he should have any recollection of the matters dealt with in the information he supplied.

The first of the five categories in (c) above makes no innovation so far as the law of Scotland is concerned but the others constitute important

16 *Macpherson v Reid's Trustees* (1876) 4 R 132.
17 Stair IV 43, 16; Erskine IV ii, 7.
18 S 1.
19 S 7.

extensions. In determining any question of admissibility under the Act the court may have regard to the form or content of the document and draw any reasonable inference therefrom. It may also act on a medical certificate. The Criminal Evidence Act 1965 was passed to obviate the consequences of the decision of the House of Lords in *Myers v DPP*[20] in which it had been held that car manufacturer's records which had been compiled by various workmen but were spoken to by the persons in charge of the records were inadmissible. The 1965 Act therefore referred to 'records compiled in the course of a trade or business' with a view to the particular mischief it was designed to remedy.[1] The only difference between it and the Law Reform (Miscellaneous Provisions) (Scotland) Act 1966 is that the latter Act was modelled on the language of the existing English legislation (then the Evidence Act 1938), which speaks of records compiled not 'in the course of a trade or business' but 'in the performance of a duty to record information supplied'. The 1966 Act contains no definition of a duty to record information but it is thought that it extends beyond a legally enforceable duty.

Some statutes make special provision for the admission in evidence of certain statements. These specific statutory exceptions mainly relate to statements of which a record is kept for the purposes of the statute in question and are usually with a view to making evidence available for those purposes but sometimes the provision is so worded as to make evidence of the kind in question generally available. A detailed consideration falls outwith the scope of this book. Examples are found in the Merchant Shipping Acts 1894 and 1970[2] and the Education (Scotland) Act 1980.[3]

13 Public records

The contents of records kept under statutory or other public authority are admissible in evidence so far as they fall within the purpose of the record. Thus, an entry in the Register of Births is evidence of the place and time of birth although further evidence will be necessary to link the entry with the person whose date or place of birth is in issue.[4]

14 Statements admitted out of considerations of fairness

A statement may be admissible in evidence if considerations of fairness require that that be done in view of the admission of evidence of other

20 [1965] AC 1001, [1964] 1 All ER 877, [1964] 3 WLR 145.
1 For case on inadmissible records, see *R v Sealby* [1965] 1 All ER 701 (car logbook); *R v Gwilliam* [1968] 1 WLR 1839 (government records).
2 Ch 11 below.
3 S 86.
4 See p 172.

statements. The sole authority for this is *O'Hara v Central SMT*[5] in which, as a result of the admission of a res gestae statement it was thought to be fair to admit a subsequent statement. The limits of this doctrine and what considerations enter into a judgment of fairness in this context are not clear.

15 Prior identification

In *Muldoon v Herron*[6] it was held that the accused were sufficiently identified although neither of the witnesses who had been adduced to identify them did, in fact, identify them in court and one of these witnesses actually said that the accused were not among those implicated. The identifying evidence came from police officers who spoke to the fact that the witnesses concerned had identified the accused shortly after the event in issue. The reasons of expediency for admitting such evidence were strong. As a result of intimidation, witnesses who were prepared to make an identification soon after the crime may fear to give evidence implicating the accused at the trial. In any event, an identification made shortly after the event, will usually be more reliable than an identification made much later in court.

The opinions in *Muldoon v Herron* attempt, however, to classify the identification as 'real' or 'primary' evidence. But to say that someone identifies a person is no more than a compact way of saying that the person identifying says that the person identified is the same person as he (the person identifying) saw on some other occasion, usually the occasion of the crime or an occasion connected with the commission of the crime. Its essence is a comparison made by the witness. Where witness X makes the identification in court, then that evidence is direct evidence. He is saying that it is the accused person whom he saw, eg at the scene of the crime. Where, however, evidence is given by witness Y that witness X made an identification on a previous occasion Y is, in effect saying that X made, on the previous occasion, a statement to the effect that the person whom he saw on that occasion (eg an identification parade) was the same person as he had seen on a still earlier occasion (eg at the commission of the crime). Evidence of a prior identification is, therefore, evidence of statements made on a previous occasion and is no different in principle, from other instances of reported statements. It makes no difference that the previous identification may have been by pointing to the person identified rather than by words. The gesture of pointing is, as assertive conduct, the equivalent of a statement. The admission of evidence of identification of the kind in issue in *Muldoon v*

5 1941 SC 363 per Lord Fleming at 386 and Lord Carmont at 394.
6 1970 JC 30. There is also earlier authority: *Thomas Wight* 22 February briefly reported in *Bell's Notes on Hume* p 288.

Herron must therefore, despite dicta to the contrary, be taken to constitute an exception to the rule against hearsay.[7] Once that is accepted the question arises of whether there is any logical justification for distinguishing between evidence of identification on a previous occasion and evidence of other statements relevant to the issue made on previous occasions. The difficulty becomes acute when in the one statement a witness has both identified the perpetrator of a crime and described its commission in terms which make the one inextricable from the other.

The decision in *Muldoon* bears to be restricted to identifications made to the police but it is doubtful if in fairness, or in principle, it can be so restricted. It appears that the doctrine in *Muldoon* can be invoked only where the person alleged to have made the identification on the previous occasion gives evidence and either denies, or cannot remember, having identified the accused.

16 Entries in business books regularly kept

Entries in business books may be evidence against the person by whom, or on whose behalf, the business books were kept. As such, they are admissible where that person is a party to an action as statements against his interest on principles which have already been discussed. Entries in business books regularly kept are, however, also admissible as evidence in favour of the person by whom, or on whose behalf, the books were kept. It is with their admissibility in that connection that we are here concerned. The principle is an historical survival from the period before 1853 when parties were not competent witnesses. The rule which excluded parties as witnesses bore hardly on merchants suing for their accounts and accordingly a practice was introduced of allowing a merchant to produce his account book as evidence of the defender's indebtedness and that account book, together with the merchant's oath in supplement could constitute sufficient proof of the matter in issue. The earliest authority for this is *Wood v Kello*[8] in 1672, although Stair, writing shortly after that, seems to have rejected the principle. He says 'count-books are probative against those who made them; but they prove not for them'. Erskine, however, founding on *Wood v Kello*, says:

> 'no merchant's books can be full evidence in his own favour; but if they be regularly kept, and contain his whole transactions, they

7 The corresponding English case, *R v Osbourne, R v Virtue* [1973] QB 678, [1973] 1 All ER 649 is recognised as raising hearsay problems. See *Cross* p 48.

8 IV ii, 4.

> ought to afford at least a semiplena probatio; and therefore, if they be supported by one witness, and articles which admit of parole evidence, they will be received as legal proof, provided the merchant himself, if required, make oath in supplement that the transaction is there fairly stated.'

The requirement of evidence from another source seems, however, to have fallen out of use. In *Grant v Johnston*[9] a justification of the principle was offered by Lord Medwin who said:

> 'If regularly kept, bank's or merchant's books are admitted to supplement or support proof in such matters, as from their minuteness and multiplicity, it cannot be the testimony of witnesses, unaided by reference to them, be expected to supply the requisite evidence.'

That is an intelligible justification although it is not the original reason for the rule.[10]

STATEMENTS BEARING ON CREDIBILITY

The rule against hearsay excludes, as has been seen, evidence of extra-judicial statements tendered in proof of the matter asserted and that exclusion applies whether or not the maker of the statement is a witness. A similar rule excludes evidence of extra-judicial statements by whomsoever made when tendered solely for the purpose of their bearing on the credibility of a witness or of an account given by a party to the proceedings or the victim of a criminal act. So far as witness's credibility is concerned that is an application of the rule that evidence of any kind may not be adduced solely for the purpose of supporting or impugning a witness's credibility, although evidence otherwise relevant may of course be used for that purpose and the witness may be cross-examined generally on his credibility. There appears, however, to be four exceptions to the exclusion of evidence of extra-judicial statements bearing on credibility. There is a degree of overlap, between the first three of those exceptions. In the case of all of them the evidence is admitted solely for its bearing on credibility and, unless its admission can be justified on

9 (1845) 7 D 390 at 393.

10 Wigmore notes that an exception for the regularly kept business books of a party was known to English law until 1609 when it was abolished by statute and that English and American jurisdictions have made good the loss of that exception in piecemeal fashion (*Evidence in Trials at Common Law I* pp 347–51, paras 1518–19. The civil law had a similar rule (Voet *Commentary on the Pandects* XXII, 4, 12 (Gane's transl vol 3, pp 751–2)).

other grounds, is to be disregarded as evidence in causa. In the case of statements consistent with the witnesses's evidence the distinction is not usually of practical importance although it excludes any question there might be of using the extra-judicial statement as corroboration; in the case of statements inconsistent with the witness's evidence the result is that acceptance of the statement may lead to the rejection of the witness's evidence but the statement itself has no standing as evidence and cannot be used in proof of any matter asserted in it. The four exceptions are:

1 Prior consistent statements by a witness

Evidence is admissible of a previous statement made by a witness for the purpose of showing his consistency and therefore negativing fabrication. In *Barr v Barr*[11] Lord President Normand said 'Evidence that A made a statement to C may be useful as showing that A's evidence in causa was true evidence, and may be useful to set up his credibility' and in *Gibson v National Cash Register Co*[12] a letter and telegram sent by a witness were held to have been properly admitted for the purpose of supporting his credibility. The admissibility of evidence of such prior statements by a witness is also supported by the Outer House case of *Burns v Colin McAndrew & Partners Ltd.*[13] In England (apart from the specialties introduced by the Civil Evidence Act 1968) and also in some jurisdictions influenced by English common law it is a prerequisite for the admission of a previous consistent statement that the witness should have been challenged in cross-examination with fabricating his evidence; and it is not sufficient that it has been suggested merely that his evidence is untruthful or inconsistent.[14] But of the Scottish authorities only *Burns v Colin McAndrew & Partners* mentions that qualification.

2 Prior consistent statements by a party

Statements previously made by an accused person in a criminal trial, and perhaps also by a party to a civil action, are admissible for the purpose of showing that the party has consistently given the same account of the matter in issue. The English and Commonwealth

11 1939 SC 696 at 699.
12 1925 SC 500.
13 1963 SLT (Notes) 71.
14 *Flanagan v Fahy* [1918] 2 IR 361; *Fox v General Medical Council* [1960] 3 All ER 225, [1960] 1 WLR 1017; *The Nominal Defendant v Clements* (1961) 104 CLR 476 per Dixon CJ at 479; *R v Oyesiku* (1971) 56 Cr App R 240 but cf *Ahmed v Brumfitt* (1967) 112 Sol Jo 32.

authorities do not distinguish between witnesses who are parties and those who are not and apply to a party's statement only where the party is witness. They again support the view that to render the evidence admissible there must be a charge of recent fabrication. The Scottish authorities do not explicitly make that requirement and, although some are later, seem to have their origin in the time when parties, including accused persons, were not competent as witnesses. It seems, therefore, that evidence of this kind can be led to show the consistency of a party's contention, even if the party does not himself give evidence.

The older authorities[15] vouch that where the accused had emitted a judicial declaration he might found on that declaration as 'a circumstance in his favour' and that evidence of statements made by the accused between the alleged commission of the crime and the emission of the declaration might be led in support of the declaration if consistent with it. The precise evidentiary status of the declaration and the statements in support is not clear but in practical terms it is sufficient that as a circumstance in favour of the defence they might be used to cast doubt on the case for the prosecution. It does not seem to have been contemplated in the earlier cases that the accused's extra-judicial statement could be put in evidence where he had elected not to emit a declaration but in *Brown v HM Advocate*[16] it was held that the accused's reply to caution and charge might he used as evidence in his favour and, in support of that, reliance was placed on a passage from *Alison* that:

> 'the principle of law and the rule of common sense is, that every deed done, and every word spoken by the prisoner subsequent to the date of the crime charged against him, is the fit subject for the consideration of the jury, and that if duly proved, it must enter into the composition of their verdict.[17]

It is, however, reasonably clear that *Alison*, although ambiguous, is to be understood in context as referring to the use of deeds and words as evidence against the accused. In any other sense the passage is inconsistent with *Hume*, also cited with approval in *Brown*: 'There are obvious reasons why a pannel's denial of his guilt, or his statements, in conversation afterwards, of his defences against the charge, or his narrative of the way in which the thing happened, cannot be admitted as evidence on his behalf'.[18] The unlimited admission of exculpatory extra-judicial statements made by the accused subsequent to the alleged occurrence of the crime would go beyond what the authorities before

15 *HM Advocate v Forrest* (1837) 1 Sw 404; *HM Advocate v Pye* (1838) 2 Sw 187.
16 1964 JC 10, 1964 SLT 53.
17 Alison II 555.
18 Hume II 401.

Brown vouched and is not necessary for the decision in that case. The result of *Brown* when read along with the earlier authorities would seem to be that any reply made by an accused person to caution and charge, any declaration emitted by him and the record of his judicial examination may be used in evidence in his favour as well as against him and that any statement made by him prior to these events may also be admitted as showing consistency.[19] In *Brown* some stress was laid on the fact that evidence of the reply to caution and charge had been elicited by the Crown but it is doubtful if that was intended to be a condition precedent of admission of evidence of that kind or could, consistently with the principles of fairness underlying criminal procedure, be so construed.

In relation to civil litigation it has been said on high authority that 'in the ordinary case the defender or pursuer of any action may have any matter which he has stated made the subject of evidence'.[20] These words were, however, spoken in relation to evidence of a statement of the defenders' manager (which seems to have been treated on the basis that it could be imputed to the defenders) which was excluded, because it was a statement of opinion and not of observed fact, but which, it seems, would, if it had been admitted, have had a tendency against, rather than in favour of, the defenders' interest. It is, it is submitted, not authority for any general doctrine allowing the admission of self-serving statements by parties in civil cases.

In modern conditions it is difficult to justify the admission of self-serving statements by parties, whether in a civil or a criminal case, unless, where the party testifies as a witness, on the principles applicable to witnesses generally or unless one of the exceptions to the rule against hearsay applies.

3 De recenti statements

In *Morton v HM Advocate*[21] it was said that in cases of assaults and sexual offences against women and children, evidence of the victims *de recenti* statements was admissible for the purpose only of supporting the victim's credibility. In order to qualify in a *de recenti* statement, the statement must have been made shortly after the event and no later than the first opportunity which the victim had of making a disclosure to a natural confidant. The purpose of these restrictions is to reduce the risk of concoction. In *Anderson v McFarlane*[1] evidence was admitted of what a girl had told her mother about an alleged assault, although the statement to the mother was made some three days after the assault. The

19 See now *Hendry v HM Advocate* [1986] 2 CL 626.
20 *Apthorpe v Edinburgh Street Tramways* (1882) 10 R 344 per Lord President Inglis at 351.
21 1938 JC 50 at 53.
1 (1899) 1 F (J) 36.

reason for admission was that before then she had had no opportunity of speaking to a natural confidant. On the other hand, statements made even quite a short time after the event may be rejected if, in the interval, there has been an opportunity of speaking to a natural confidant which has been neglected.[2] This ground for the admission of evidence of statements and the restrictions which surround it are difficult to reconcile with 1 and 2 above. The ratio of *Morton v HM Advocate* is concerned with the restriction of the use of *de recenti* statements to purposes of credibility as distinct from corroboration so as to afford full legal proof. What is said about the class of case to which the admission of *de recenti* statements is restricted is strictly obiter. The dicta to that effect are nonetheless of high authority. It is difficult to understand the elaborate consideration given to *de recenti* statements in *Morton v HM Advocate*, if prior consistent statements by a witness were in any event generally admissible. For once the use of *de recenti* statements is restricted to supporting the victim's credibility, it is clear both that the victim must be a witness before his *de recenti* stastements can be used and that these statements cannot in any sense form a substitute for, or have any status apart from, his evidence. *De recenti* statements, so considered, perform a function in relation to the evidence of the victim as witness precisely the same as, on the authorities considered above, is performed in any event by the prior consistent statement of any witness. If that is right, the rule on *de recenti* statements is redundant. The point of distinction may be that the *de recenti* statement of the woman or child victim of an assault or sexual offence is admissible whether or not a charge of fabrication is made, whereas the prior statements of other witnesses, including victims in other types of case, are admissible only if fabrication is alleged; but that is a narrow and unsettled point and the absence of any acknowledgment of it in *Morton* is striking.

4 Prior inconsistent statements by a witness

Section 3 of the Evidence (Scotland) Act 1852 provides:

> 'It. shall be competent to examine any witness who may be adduced in any action or proceeding, as to whether he has on any specified occasion made a statement on any matter pertinent to the issue different from the evidence given by him in such action or proceedings; and it shall be competent in the course of such action or proceeding to adduce evidence to prove that such witnesses made such different statements on the occasion specified.'

That provision still governs civil proceedings. So far as criminal

2 See *Hill v Fletcher* (1847) 10 D 7.

proceedings are concerned it has been replaced by the Criminal Procedure (Scotland) Act 1975 ss 147 and 349 which are, however, in similar terms. In order to make a statement admissible under this head the witness must first be cross-examined to the effect that he has previously made an inconsistent statement and, if he denies that, the way is then open to the party alleging the inconsistency to lead evidence of the inconsistency. Without such a basis of foundation in cross-examination (or, exceptionally, in examination in chief of a witness who unexpectedly gives evidence adverse to the party adducing him) evidence of the statement is inadmissible.[3] Despite the generality of the statutory provisions they do not admit of evidence being given of an inconsistent statement where that statement has been made on precognition.[4]

3 *Wilson v Jacobs* 1934 SLT 215.
4 Ch 7 below. *Kerr v HM Advocate* 1958 JC 14 especially per Lord Justice-Clerk Thomson at 19.

CHAPTER 4

Inadmissibility of evidence; opinion

PERCEIVED FACTS AND OPINION

The general rule is that a witness must confine his evidence to what he has seen or heard or otherwise perceived by his senses and must not express opinion. But the line between perception and opinion is not always easy to draw. The sense data presented to the mind cannot be transmitted without an element of mental construction. All evidence consists not of crude sense data but of the mind's construction upon them. If a witness says that he saw an old building or a drunk man, he is introducing an element of mental construction, of opinion, into what he says that he saw. Essentially, if less obviously, that is true even if all he says is that he saw a building or a man. In all testimony not only the perceptive, but also the constructive functions of the mind are at work. What a witness says that he saw is the result of conclusions drawn from the sense impressions made on his mind. Sometimes the conclusion will be mistaken, not because of any defect of vision (although that, too, may occur) but because the witness's mind, even unconsciously, 'jumped to the wrong conclusion'. In the last analysis, the distinction which the law seeks to make between evidence of facts perceived and opinion evidence may be unreal. What lies behind the distinction is, however, an attempt to separate the immediate fruits of perception from opinion formed by reflection after the event.

Impression and reflection

To impressions formed at the time, the witness may speak as integral to any account of his perceptions. Thus he may say not only that he saw a building or a man, but that he saw an old building or a drunk man, if these be the impressions formed at the time and they are relevant to the issue. Examples of the admission of such impression evidence are numerous—on questions of age, sobriety, sanity, the state of a person's health, his emotional or physical condition, the speed of vehicles, temperature, weather. Perhaps the strongest example is evidence of identification, whether of persons, or things, or handwriting. Identification involves a comparison between two sets of phenomena and an affirmation of their identity. Sometimes the witness will be able to make that affirmation so spontaneously and with such confidence that it is tempting to describe the identification as bare fact, but in cases of uncertainty the essentially opinion character of the evidence is apparent. Except, however, where the identification is by experts using scientific criteria, the opinion is nearly always based on impression and not on conscious reflection on data.

The reason for the admission of impression evidence is that it has a value of its own for which there can be no substitute. Without it, the tribunal of fact would be deprived of material which may often be of the greatest importance for the determination of the issues before it. The reflections of the ordinary witness do not, however, have the same value. Given the data which he has observed, the tribunal of fact is usually as well placed as is he to interpret them. The witness's reflections are, therefore, of no assistance. In some cases, however, it may be difficult to distinguish impression from reflection, and in others, the witness may have advantages derived from his observation of the facts, or from his familiarity with the circumstances, such as to give peculiar value to any inferences he has drawn. Although the matter is not clear on reported decision, evidence which consists at least in part of reflected opinion is often admitted in such cases.

EXPERT OPINION

The general exclusion of evidence of reflective opinion does not apply to the expert witness, ie a witness expert in some specialised skill or branch of knowledge necessary for the ascertainment or understanding of facts in issue.[1] Such witnesses may give opinion evidence. Indeed, their evidence will necessarily be of an opinion nature and it is for the value which may be attached to their opinion that they are brought as witnesses. There is no definition of what constitutes an expert. The value of his evidence may, of course, depend inter alia on his qualifications and experience, but formal qualifications are not essential. Anyone will be admitted as an expert who has devoted time and attention to the special branch of knowledge concerned, has had practical experience of it, where appropriate, and has acquired a reputation of being skilled in it.[2] Usually the skill will have been acquired in the course of a profession or trade, but an amateur who has acquired comparable skills is not debarred.[3] The field of expertise must be a recognised one which rests on

1 *Dickson* para 397.
2 *Dickson* para 398.
3 *R v Silverlock* [1894] 2 QB 766 (solicitor with amateur expertise in handwriting).

a scientific or on a sound practical base, because otherwise there is no means by which the value of the evidence can be assessed. Sometimes a witness may be treated, at least temporarily, as an expert and his opinion evidence received because of his familiarity with a particular set of facts, although he has no general expertise. In England the evidence of a drug addict has been admitted for the purpose of identifying a drug.[4] It seems that ultimately the question of whether a witness can be treated as an expert so as to enable evidence of his opinion to be received depends on whether he has acquired a skill not within the ordinary competence of the tribunal of fact, the use of which can assist the tribunal in the interpretation of the evidence of fact before it. Experience of driving motor vehicles does not qualify a witness to express an expert opinion on the capabilities of a driver.[5] That may be justified on the view, either that driving experience is such a commonplace that the opinion of the witness is of no more value than the opinion which the tribunal of fact might itself form independently, or that driving skill does not necessarily confer any skill in assessment of capability.

Factual basis for opinion

An expert witness does not need to know, and ordinarily will not know, the facts of the case from his own knowledge. Accordingly his knowledge of the facts has to be obtained from information supplied to him, and from his inspection of the documentary and real evidence. It may be supplemented by his presence in court during the testimony of witnesses to fact.[6] He must, therefore, be asked in giving his evidence to assume a certain version or versions of fact. If any of a number of versions will serve the party adducing the expert equally well and form a satisfactory basis for the expert's opinion they should all be put to him lest, if only one be put, the opinion be undermined by failure to prove its basis in fact. The assumptions of fact should be clearly distinguished from the opinion, and it will often be in the cross-examiner's interest to do so because if he can then show that the facts assumed are insufficient to support the opinion, or are not proved by sufficient evidence, or are disproved, or have been misunderstood by the expert, or can be explained in a sense different from which he understood them, the value of the opinion will thereby be reduced or nullified. That evidence is required to establish the basis of an expert opinion, or to disprove its basis, will be sufficient ground for the admission of evidence which might otherwise be regarded as irrelevant or insufficiently relevant.

4 *R v Chatwood* [1980] 1 All ER 467, [1980] 1 WLR 874. Cf *Hope's and Lavery v HM Advocate* 1960 JC 104 (stenographer interpreting tape recording).

5 *R v Davis* [1962] 3 All ER 97, [1962] WLR 1111.

6 Ch 9 below.

Where expert also witness to fact

Expert witnesses may sometimes also be witnesses to fact as, for example, where a medical witness has examined a party whose physical or mental condition is in issue, with a view to forming an opinion on it. In such cases the evidence of the facts observed should so far as possible, be distinguished from the evidence of the opinion formed from these facts.[7] Unless the observation of the facts itself required special skill, the evidence of a lay witness, who also observed them, will be admissible in disproof of the evidence of fact but not of opinion.[8] Problems of hearsay may sometimes arise in this connection. A medical witness may often include in his evidence an account of what the person examined has told him about his symptoms, because that account may form the basis on which the expert has formed his opinion. If the account given was one of symptoms from which the person examined was then suffering, it will probably be admissible under one of the exceptions to the rule against hearsay as evidence of the existence of the symptoms. If, however, it was an account of symptoms which had been suffered in the past, evidence of it is inadmissible hearsay so far as proof of the existence of the symptoms is concerned.[8] It may nonetheless be admitted as showing the basis on which the expert proceeded to form his opinion, ie as showing the assumptions underlying the opinion, but if the opinion is to stand that basis must be established *aliunde*.

FUNCTION OF EXPERT

Encroachment on function of court or jury

The function and duty of an expert witness is:

> 'to furnish the judge and jury with the necessary scientific criteria for testing the accuracy of their conclusions, so as to enable the judge or jury to form their own independent judgment by the application of these criteria to the facts proved in evidence.'[9]

The point that Lord President Cooper was concerned to make is sometimes overlooked. The function of the expert is not to present ready-made conclusions but to provide the tribunal of fact with material on which it can reach its own conclusions. The decision on the various issues in the case, including the issues of fact in the resolution of which

7 See *Seyfang v G D Searle* [1973] 1 QB 148 per Cooke J at 151.
8 *Sutton v Prenter* [1963] Qd R 401. See *Cross on Evidence* (6th edn) p 441.
9 *Davie v Edinburgh Corpn* 1953 SC 34 per Lord President Cooper at 40.

the expert may assist, is for the judge or jury. The expert must not usurp their function. On the basis of that perception, it has been said 'a question is inadmissible if its purpose is to elicit an opinion on the actual issue before the court'.[10] The principle is reasonably clear and intelligible. Judges and juries have their functions and experts have theirs. The expert who crosses the line dividing these functions ceases to assist, and usurps. The same can occasionally happen in the case of an ordinary witness when an impression he has formed at the time comes close to the issue which the court or jury have to decide. There are, however, real problems about how the line is to be drawn. All opinion evidence is, in some sense, an opinion on the actual issue before the court. It is necessarily directed to the resolution of such issues. If that were not so it would be irrelevant and inadmissible. While court or jury are to be furnished with criteria on which to make their independent judgment it is clear that that judgment is to be applied to conclusions which experts have themselves reached. The court will inevitably want to know how the expert has applied the criteria to the facts in order to reach his conclusion. There is, therefore, much ground which both the expert and court or jury must traverse together. The problem of whether a particular question or piece of evidence transgresses unacceptably on the province of judge or jury does not admit of an easy answer.

The decisions are conflicting. A witness may not be asked for his opinion on whether books are obscene where that is in issue,[11] but in a case involving the validity of a contract of insurance it is competent to ask an expert witness whether certain facts would have influenced a prudent underwriter,[12] which is the very test by which the question of materiality and so of validity has to be determined. On an allegation of professional negligence a somewhat artificial distinction has been made between an opinion on want of skill (inadmissible) and an opinion on improper conduct (admissible).[13] Where, on a charge of murder, the defence is that the victim's wound was self-inflicted it is permissible to seek the opinion of a medical witness as to whether or not the wound could have been inflicted by someone other than the deceased.[14] In *R v Holmes*[15] a medical witness was asked whether the accused knew the nature of his act and that it was wrong although these were the precise issues which the jury had to determine under the McNaghten Rules

10 Walker and Walker *The Law of Evidence in Scotland* para 411(b), p 431.
11 *Galletly v Laird* 1953 JC 16 at 27; *Ingram v Macari* 1983 SLT 61.
12 *Dawsons Ltd v Bonnin* 1921 SC 511 at 517, 519 and 521, 1922 SC (HL) 156 at 160, 166 and 172.
13 *Rich v Pierpoint* (1862) 3 F and F 35.
14 *R v Mason* (1911) 7 Crim App R 67.
15 [1953] 2 All ER 324.

which governed the defence of insanity. On a charge of driving while under the influence of drink a non-expert may, as has been seen, give evidence of his impression that the accused had taken drink but not that he was incapable of driving.[16] In the Republic of Ireland, however, a non-expert witness may be asked for his impression on both questions and that is justified on the view that his impression has an evidentiary value beyond what can be derived from the narration of observed facts.[17] There is no doubt that an expert would be allowed to answer both questions, as is commonly the case where a person's physical or mental capacity is the issue before the court. The true determining factor, it is submitted, is whether or not the witness's opinion can be of assistance to the tribunal of fact.

Often when evidence encroaches on the ultimate issue which court or jury has to determine it will be of a composite character, some of the elements of which may be outwith the range of the expert's skill or the lay-witness's impression. 'Care' Dickson says 'must be taken not to encroach on the province of the jury, by laying before them an opinion founded partly on inferences which do not involve the peculiar skill or knowledge which the witness is supposed to possess'.[18] Even where that objection does not arise, any value which attaches to the witness's opinion or impression on the ultimate issue may be outweighed by its effect in distracting the trier of fact from his duty of independent judgment. That was no doubt what Lord President Boyle had in mind when he spoke of the risk of 'substituting the witnesses for the jury—influencing the latter by the weight of the opinions of these men of skill',[19] but an opinion which encroaches on the ultimate issue does not necessarily substitute the witness for the jury. There may be a risk of the jury's being over influenced, but they remain free to accept or reject the expert opinion and make their own judgment. In *Morrison v Maclean's Trustees* Lord Justice-Clerk Inglis directed the jury that the question of the testator's capacity to test was a question for them and not for the medical witness's to whom it had been put.[20] There may, as has been suggested, have been an implication that an objection to the questions would have been sustained[1] but the direction is equally consistent with a reminder expressed perhaps in strong terms of the jury's duty of independent judgment, a reminder particularly apposite because the foundation in fact for the medical opinion had largely been under-

16 *R v Davis* [1962] 3 All ER 97, [1962] 1 WLR 1111.
17 *A-G v Kenny* (1964) 94 ILTR 185. Cf *Sherrard v Jacob* [1965] NI 151 in which *R v Davis* was followed, Lord Macdermott CJ dissenting.
18 Para 399.
19 *Campbell v Tyson* (1841) 4 D 342 at 343.
20 (1862) 24 D 625 at 631.
1 Walker and Walker *Law of Evidence in Scotland* para 411, p 431.

mined. Where the opinion of an expert, or the impression of a lay-witness, affords assistance on the issue which cannot otherwise be obtained, the evidence will, it is thought, be admitted. On difficult issues 'any jury and justices need all the help they can get'.[2]

Opinion where legal standard applied

It is sometimes said that opinion evidence is inadmissible if it embraces the application of a legal standard. Some of the cases on which evidence has been excluded as encroaching on the issue before the court or jury may be explained on that view.

> 'When a standard, or a measure, or a capacity has been fixed by law, no witness whether expert or non-expert, nor however qualified, is permitted to express an opinion as to whether the person or the conduct, in question, measures up to that standard; on that question the court must instruct the jury as to the law, and the jury draw its own conclusion from the evidence.'[3]

There is no doubt that a witness may not give an opinion on a question of law other than foreign law. That is exclusively the province of the court. If such evidence were allowed it could not properly be of assistance to the jury. It may be for this reason that where liability for fault is at issue questions such as 'who do you think was to blame for the accident?' are regarded as inadmissible even if all the factors bearing on fault are within the knowledge and competence of the expert, or if an eye witness's immediate impression on seeing the event is likely to have included an impression on fault which may be the natural and only comprehensive way in which he can give his evidence. Although the exercise of reasonable care may be a question of fact the concept of fault involves questions of law. There may, however, be borderline cases where a legal standard is dependent on, and practically identical with, a scientific standard as where insanity arises in relation to criminal responsibility. Questions of capacity to test further illustrate the difficulty. The law prescribes what is required for capacity to test but whether or not those requirements are met is largely a matter of scientific assessment. If the witness's evidence has to stop short of the

2 *DPP v AB & C Chewing Gum Ltd* [1968] 1 QB 159, [1967] 2 All ER 504 (opinion of a psychiatrist admitted on whether cards sold with packets of bubble gum were likely to deprave and corrupt children). But such evidence is not competent in the ordinary case where the question is the likelihood of the corruption of adults (*Ingram v Macari* 1983 SLT 61).

3 *Grismore v Consolidated Products Co* 5 NW 2d 646 at 663 (1942). See *Cross* pp 445 and 446.

eventual issue, there is a risk that it may be misconstrued.[4] Diminished responsibility has been the subject of legal definition but, in England, Lord Parker CJ has said that 'although technically the final question "do you think he was suffering from diminished responsibility?" is strictly inadmissible, it is allowed time and time again without any objection'.[5]

Specialised knowledge and province of the expert

Two further rules regarding opinion evidence are given in some textbooks, 1 that only an expert may give evidence on matters requiring special skill and knowledge, and 2 that opinion evidence may not be given on matter which do not require the application of specialised knowledge for their resolution.[6] Both rules are implicit in what has been said about the nature and function of opinion evidence. The first rule is illustrated by *R v Loake*[7] in which the evidence of a non-expert was rejected on a question of insanity. Questions of insanity may not, however, always be beyond the competence of a lay-witness and there is old English authority for the admission of evidence of the impression as to the sanity of a person said to be insane formed by witnesses well acquainted with him.[8] Such evidence is said to be merely a 'compendious mode of ascertaining the result of the actual observation of the witness, from acts done, as to the habits and demeanour' of the person concerned. The second rule is illustrated by cases in which medical evidence has been excluded, where its sole purpose was to show a person's likely state of mind or behaviour and no question of insanity or mental abnormality or deficiency was in issue.[9] In a case[10] which has been described as special on its facts,[11] medical evidence was, however, admitted to show which of two apparently normal persons was the less likely to have behaved in a particular way.

4 Lord Justice-Clerk Inglis' direction to the jury in *Morrison v Maclean's Trustees* (1862) 24 D 625 at 631 is often construed as excluding evidence on the actual question of capacity to test but as indicated above it may have meant merely that although the evidence was admissible the jury had a duty of independent judgment.

5 *DPP v AB and C Chewing Gum Ltd* [1968] 1 QB 159 at 164 and [1967] 2 All ER 504 at 506.

6 *Cross* pp 436–40.

7 (1911) 7 Cr App R 71.

8 *Wright v Doed Tatham* (1838) 4 Bing NC 489 per Parke B at 543–4.

9 *R v Chard* [1971] 56 Cr App R 268.

10 *Lowery v R* [1974] AC 85, [1973] 3 All ER 662.

11 *R v Turner* [1975] QB 834.

CHAPTER 5

Inadmissibility of evidence; secondary evidence; extrinsic evidence qualifying terms of document

SECONDARY EVIDENCE

Secondary evidence suggests by its nature the existence of an original from which it is derived and for which it is a substitute. A copy of a document or object is a typical example. Hearsay evidence is secondary but is subject to distinct rules which have been considered.[1] The general rule is that secondary evidence is inadmissible in the unexplained absence of the primary evidence from which it is derived. This chapter is concerned with the application of that rule to (a) previous judicial determinations regarding the facts in issue, (b) documents and (c) real evidence; and also with the similar rule which excludes extrinsic evidence where a document is constitutive, or is the authentic record, of the rights of parties.

Decrees of courts, etc

The interlocutors and decrees of courts, verdicts of juries, convictions and other records of judicial acts, and extracts of them, are competent and normally conclusive evidence of what is stated therein: eg an extract conviction if ex facie regular is proof of the conviction of the person named therein although it will, of course, be necessary to identify that person with the person to whom it is claimed that the conviction applies and for that oral[2] or fingerprint[3] evidence will

1 Ch 3 above.
2 A reference to a person by name is not sufficient for identification (*Wilson v Brown* 1947 JC 81 at 96; *Bruce v HM Advocate* 1936 JC 93 at 95) and so correspondence of name is not sufficient to identify an accused with the person named in the extract conviction (*Herron v Nelson* 1976 SLT Sh Ct 42). The application of a previous conviction to an accused person may be proved by a prison official although he was not present at the trial to which the conviction relates (Criminal Procedure (Scotland) Act 1975 ss 162 and 357(2)).
3 Criminal Procedure (Scotland) Act 1975 ss 164 and 358.

usually be needed. By virtue of its being a record the extract is, on a literal view, secondary evidence[4] even of the fact of conviction but is treated as primary evidence. Although it proves that the person named was convicted, it does not, however, prove for the purpose of other proceedings that he committed the crime. Similarly, an extract decree in civil proceedings proves that the court decerned, in the terms set forth in the extract, between the parties named therein but, except in so far as it is res judicata between those parties, it does not, for the purpose of any other proceedings, prove the truth of the matters which were in dispute.[5] On those matters the extract decree is hearsay and secondary. The points at issue must be decided on the facts proved in the instant case and not by proof of the conclusions to which others have come. However, by the Law Reform (Miscellaneous Provisions (Scotland) Act 1968, s 10 the fact of a criminal conviction is competent evidence for the purpose of proving in civil proceedings, where it is relevant to do so, that the convicted person committed the offence of which he was convicted and the records of criminal courts are admissible evidence for that purpose.[6]

What is true of interlocutors or decrees is, of course, equally true of notes of evidence. Thus, in *Mackenzie v Mackenzie*,[7] where in a divorce

4 Ch 1 above.

5 In a question with third parties the decree is *res inter alios acta*. In *Stuart v Mags of Edinburgh* 1697 Mor 12536 it was held that a decree was not proof of any matter extraneous to the record, ie any matter on which it was not res judicata. It has been pointed out (Walker and Walker *Law of Evidence in Scotland* para 205, p 226) that that case does not decide that the decree had no evidential value but it is difficult to see on what principle any evidential value could be based. See *Mackenzie v Mackenzie* below.

6 The effect of the conviction is to create a presumption rebuttable on a balance of probabilities: 'Proof of conviction under this section gives rise to the statutory presumption (that the defendant committed the offence) which like any other presumption will give way to evidence establishing the contrary on the balance of probability, without itself affording any evidential weight to be taken into account in determining whether that onus has been discharged' (*Stoppel v Royal Insurance Co* [1971] 1 QB 50 per Buckley LJ); cf *King v Patterson* 1971 SLT (Notes) 40; *Public Prosecutor v Yuvaraj* [1970] AC 913). The view that the conviction itself does not afford any evidential weight conflicts with the view expressed by Davies LJ in *Taylor v Taylor* [1970] 1 WLR 1143 at 1152 that the verdict of a jury was entitled to very great weight in questions of this kind but the giving of such weight to the verdict is inconsistent with the rebuttal of the presumption on a balance of probability. See also *Wright v Wright* (1971) 115 SJ 173. As the conviction is no more than an adminicle of evidence (an evidential fact) for the purpose of proving the commission of the offence, it is thought that any presumptive force it carries can be rebutted on uncorroborated evidence. See generally *Caldwell v Wright* 1970 SLT 111. In an action of defamation conviction of a criminal offence is conclusive evidence under s 12 of the Act of commission of the offence by the person named in the conviction. Both under s 12 and under s 10 problems may arise of whether and to what extent the criminal acts to which the conviction relates correspond with the facts in issue in the civil case (*Caldwell v Wright* 1970 SLT 111; *R v Gosney* [1971] 2 QB 674; *Levene v Roxhan* [1970] 1 WLR 1322).

7 1930 SLT 439.

action it was proposed to introduce the evidence of two witnesses in Australia taken on commission in a previous action of separation, Lord Mackay said that he could not conceive

> 'of any case in which one judge who is bound to act on evidence is entitled to receive either the findings of a previous judge as sufficient or to accept the notes of evidence taken before that judge and without seeing the witness pronounce for himself on the sufficiency of these notes'.

That rule admits of an exception, already seen when considering the hearsay rule, that evidence taken in a previous case may be used in subsequent proceedings where the witness who gave evidence in the previous case is dead.[8]

Lost or destroyed documents

A document affords its own evidence of its terms; the primary evidence of the terms of the document is the document itself. Secondary evidence is admissible only where the document has been lost or destroyed or is for other sufficient reason unavailable for production. In that event the admissibility of secondary evidence depends on whether or not the document is fundamental to the claim.

Where the lost or destroyed document is essential to the constitution of a claim (eg a probative or holograph writ in contracts relating to heritage) or is in fact the foundation of a claim (eg in an action on a contract where the contract had been reduced to writing although writing was not essential for its constitution), secondary evidence is not admissible, but the party founding on the lost or destroyed document must set it up by an action of proving the tenor.[9] That rule suffers an exception where the party against whom the claim is made has destroyed the document or it has been lost or destroyed in his hands. In these circumstances, the party who has destroyed or lost the document is barred from objecting to the other party leading parole evidence to take its place.[10]

Where a document is merely incidental to a claim or constitutes a defence, secondary evidence of its terms is admissible if the loss or

8 *Geils v Geils* (1855) 17 D 397; *Coutts v Wear* (1914) 2 SLT 86; *Hogg v Frew* 1951 SLT 397. See ch 3 above.

9 *Shaw v Shaw's Trustees* (1876) 3 R 813; *Gilchrist v Morrison* (1891) 18 R 599; *Walker v Nisbet* 1915 SC 639; *Elliot v Galpern* 1927 SC 29.

10 *Drummond v Clunas Tiles and Mosaics Ltd* 1909 SC 1049; *Dickson* para 236.

destruction of the document is explained,[11] or it is in the custody of a person beyond the jurisdiction of the court who refuses to give it up or it is 'not reasonably practicable and convenient to produce the primary evidence'.[12]

Copies

It is a common practice in both civil and criminal cases for parties to agree to admit copies as equivalent to principals. In the absence of such agreement the general rule on the inadmissibility of secondary evidence applies to copies.[13] Extracts of judicial decrees, as already noticed, of deeds recorded in registers of deeds and of other entries in public registers such as the Register of Births Deaths and Marriages are, however, admissible in evidence, prove themselves as true extracts and have the same evidentiary status as principals.[14] A similar privilege attaches to certified copies under the Merchant Shipping Acts[15] and other statutes and to sworn copies under the Bankers Books Evidence Act 1879.[16]

Secondary evidence where real evidence available

Proof by secondary means of characteristics of objects which might have been the subject of real evidence is governed by principles similar to those applicable to secondary evidence of documents. The object itself should be produced and in its unexplained absence secondary evidence is not admissible.[17] Because, however, of bulk, cumbersomeness, im-

11 *Dickson* says (para 241) that it must depend on the circumstances of each case whether the party has expended such an amount of care and diligence in searching for the document as will entitle him to prove its contents by secondary evidence. He does not require to exhaust every possible chance of recovering it but must show that he has in bona fide used every means which prudence would suggest as likely to attain that object. Failure by the opposite party to produce a document in his possession when called upon to do so satisfies the test (*Elliot v Galpern* above; *Young v Thomson* 1909 SC 529; *Mitchell v Berwick* (1845) 7 D 382). See generally *Ritchie v Ritchie* (1857) 19 D 507; *A v B* (1858) 20 D 407 at 415; *Clark v Clark's Trustees* (1860) 23 D 74; *Dowgray v Gilmour* 1907 SC 715.

12 *MacLeod v Woodmuir Miners' Welfare Society Social Club* 1961 JC 5. It is thought, however, that this ground for admission of secondary evidence is more readily applicable to real than to documentary evidence.

13 *Dickson* para 227.

14 Ch 3 above.

15 Ch 3 above.

16 S 3.

17 A practice seems at one time to have been sanctioned of admitting secondary evidence where real evidence could have been produced (Hume II 393, *Dickson* paras 1817–22) but a requirement that real evidence should be produced where practicable is in accordance with principle and underlies the exception allowed in *MacLeod v Woodmuir Miners' Welfare Society Social Club* 1961 JC 5. *McGowan v Belling & Co* 1983 SLT 77.

movability, the sheer difficulty or inconvenience of preserving an object in its original state, its disappearance, difficulty of recovery or other practical considerations, it is more often than in the case of documents possible to justify the admission of secondary evidence on the ground that production of the principal is not reasonably practicable and convenient.[18] It is competent for court or jury to view a locus. In that event, the features of the locus are real evidence. Viewing of the locus is, however, uncommon and maps plans, diagrams, photographs and verbal description, all strictly secondary unless they refer to a past state which has been lost, are constantly admitted.

Films, tape and video recordings

Although it has been said that there is no difference in principle between a tape recording and a photograph,[19] that is, it is submitted, true only where the photograph records its subject in a transient state. If the subject of the photograph can without loss of relevant evidential characteristics be produced as real evidence, the photograph is secondary. Because it is a record of sounds, the subject matter of tape recordings is, however, transient and such recordings are, therefore, primary and real evidence.[20] Similar considerations generally apply to films and video-recordings as records of events. A transcript of a tape or a recording made from a tape is, however, secondary evidence. They are, it is thought, inadmissible in the absence of the principal unless that absence is explained on sufficient grounds.[1] There is, however, no rule which excludes secondary evidence where the primary evidence has been adduced and the secondary evidence can assist in its interpretation or evaluation. Accordingly, transcripts and re-recordings may be admissible, subject to proof of accuracy and reliability, in supplement of the primary recording.

EXTRINSIC EVIDENCE QUALIFYING TERMS OF DOCUMENT

General principle

Where an agreement, right or obligation has been reduced to writing it

18 *Punton* (1841) 2 Swi 572; *Maciver v Mackenzie* 1942 JC 51; *MacLeod v Woodmuir Miners' Welfare Society Social Club* above; *Hughes v Skeen* 1980 SLT (Notes) 13.
19 *R v Maqsud Ali* [1966] 1 QB 688.
20 *Hopes and Lavery v HM Advocate* 1960 JC 104 per Lord Justice-General Clyde at 110.
1 They may, however, be admissible in civil cases under the Law Reform (Miscellaneous Provisions((Scotland) Act 1966 s 7(3A) as coming within the definition of document in s 7 of that Act.

is incompetent to contradict, modify or explain its terms by parole evidence or by other extrinsic evidence in the form of prior communings, albeit written, which the final writing had been intended to supersede. The reason for excluding extrinsic evidence is that where parties have embodied their agreement in writing they must be taken to have intended the document to be the authentic record of their transaction and therefore the best possible proof of its terms. To allow parole or other extrinsic evidence to qualify or contradict the writing would be to allow superior evidence to be displaced by inferior.

The principle applies not only to formal deeds but also to missives, letters and other documents which embody terms of contract between parties or obligations undertaken or rights intended to be conferred, provided they are clearly designed for recording and proving the final intention of the parties or grantors.

> 'Where parties agree to embody and do actually embody their contract in a formal written deed, then in determining what the contract really was and really meant, the court must look to the formal deed and to that deed alone. This is only carrying out the will of the party. The only meaning of adjusting a formal contract is that the formal contract shall supersede all loose and preliminary negotiations and there shall be no room for misunderstanding such as may often arise and does constantly arise in the course of long and, it may be, desultory conversations or of correspondence and negotiations in the course of which parties are often widely at issue as to what they will insist on and what they will concede. The very purpose of a written contract is to put an end to the disputes which invariably arise if the matter were left upon verbal negotiations or upon mixed communings partly consisting of letters and partly of conversations.'[2]

The exclusion of evidence of prior communings goes, however, beyond desultory conversations or loose and preliminary negotiations. Even where there has been a written contract evidence of that contract will not be admissible if it has been implemented by a formal conveyance or disposition and that conveyance has been accepted by the disponee. The earlier written contract and all the preceding negotiations are superseded by the formal conveyance or disposition and the rights of parties must be determined solely by the latter. In this connection it is immaterial that the prior contract is referred to in the conveyance unless it is expressly incorporated.[3]

2 *Inglis v Buttery & Co* (1878) 5 R (HL) 87 per Lord Gifford (in the Court of Session) at 102.

3 Gloag *Contract* (2nd edn) p 367.

> 'According to the law of Scotland the execution of a formal conveyance, even where it expressly bears to be in implement of a previous contract, supersedes that contract in toto and the conveyance henceforth becomes the sole measure of the rights and liabilities of the parties.'[4]

Matters outwith the principle

General

As the rule excluding extrinsic evidence depends on the view that the document is the best possible record, the rule does not apply to matters which do not and could not be expected to fall within the scope of the document. The validity of a document may depend on facts which are extrinsic to it as may the question of whether or not a document has become operative. Where there are two or more documents it may not always be clear on intrinsic evidence whether one is to supersede the other or whether they are to be read together. In all those situations extrinsic evidence is admissible.

Validity

Any evidence (otherwise competent) is admissible to show that a writing is not the valid document which it purports to be. Thus, improper execution, fraud, essential error, illegality, incapacity, forgery, impetration by force and fear can all be proved by parole evidence.[5] So too, it is competent to prove by parole evidence that a document does not truly have the character which it purports to bear. Thus, extrinsic evidence may be used to show that an acknowledgment of marriage was a device to give a woman the rights of a widow.[6] In *Young's Trustees v Henderson*,[7] extrinsic evidence was admitted on the question of whether a holograph and subscribed document described in a covering letter as 'rough draft' was or was not a will and after proof it was held that the extrinsic evidence was sufficient to deprive the document of its prima facie character as a will.

Whether document operative

Akin to questions of validity are question of whether a document has

4 *Lee v Alexander* (1883) 10 R (HL) 91 per Lord Watson at 96; cf *Gibb v Cunningham* 1925 SLT 608; *Norval v Addey* 1939 SC 724; *Young v McKellar* 1909 SC 1340.

5 *Steuart's Trustees v Hart* (1875) 3R 192 at 201; *Stewart v Kennedy* (1890) 17R (HL) 25; *Bell Bros (HP) Ltd v Aitken* 1939 SC 577 at 585; Gloag *Contract* (2nd edn) p 365.

6 *Imrie v Imrie* (1891) 19 R 185; cf *Anderson v Forth Marine Insurance Co* (1845) 7D 268; *Fleming v Corbet* (1859) 21D 1034 at 1044; *Smith v Kerr* (1869) 7M 863; *Henry v Miller* (1884) 11R 713 at 716; *Maloy v Macadam* (1885) 12R 431.

7 1925 SC 729.

become operative and also of whether it has ceased to be operative. Where delivery is necessary to bring rights into operation the fact of delivery may be proved by extrinsic evidence. So too, where there is an ex facie valid will extant at the death of a testator and therefore prima facie operative, then parole evidence is admissible to show that prior to the testator's death the will had been sent to his solicitor for the purpose of being destroyed. A similar point is illustrated by *Ferguson v Russel's Trustees*[8] where the testator had made wills in 1878 and 1885 the latter containing a clause of revocation. The testator later destroyed the 1885 will. Proof was allowed that the testator believed that the earlier (1878) will had been destroyed and that he understood he was intestate—such proof being admitted for the purpose of showing that the 1878 will which was still extant on the testator's death did not then become operative. In *Hannay's Trustees v Keith*[9] the position was rather different. The testator had left a formal will with a clause of revocation of previous testamentary writings. On his death there was extant, in addition to the formal will, a holograph will dated a month earlier than the formal will. There was no indication that the holograph will was to operate along with the formal will. In those circumstances it was held incompetent to lead parole evidence that the holograph will was to have effect in spite of the clause of revocation in the later will. To have led such evidence would have been to contradict the formal will. Although extrinsic evidence designed to show whether or not a document has become operative may be led when the document is silent on the matter in issue, it may not be led where it would involve a contradiction of the document. Although, however, a document appears to be ex facie complete and operative a collateral oral agreement may nonetheless be proved to the effect that the operation of the document was conditional upon the happening of an event which has not occurred, ie that it was subject to a suspensive condition. So where damages for breach of contract were sought in *Abraham v Miller*[10] the defender was allowed to prove an extrinsic agreement that the contract should not be binding and effective until it was ratified by the defender's directors—apparently on the view that the defender was not seeking to alter or contradict the terms of the contract but only to show that it had never taken effect.

Relationship between documents

The use of extrinsic evidence to show the relationship between documents is illustrated by *Claddagh Steamship Co v Steven*[11] where the question

8 1919 SC 80.
9 1913 SC 482.
10 1933 SC 171.
11 1919 SC (HL) 132.

was whether two documents each dealing with the sale of a ship formed a single transaction. It was averred that they were merely executorial to give effect to a single agreement dealing with the sale of both ships and that this agreement had not been superseded. It was held that extrinsic evidence was admissible for that purpose and that one of the ships having been requisitioned by the government the purchasers were entitled to refuse to accept a bill of sale of the other ship in spite of there being a separate written contract relating to it.

EXCEPTIONS TO PRINCIPLE

Subject to the above comments it is convenient to consider the rule excluding extrinsic evidence under four headings: evidence 1 to contradict, 2 to supplement, 3 to explain, and 4 to vary the document.

1 Contradiction

The rule that extrinsic evidence may not be admitted to contradict a document admits of few exceptions. There are, however, two situations in which such evidence is admissible. First, it is admissible where both parties are agreed that the document does not accurately represent the agreement they reached. Thus, where creditor and debtor were at odds as to the amount advanced but agreed that it was not the amount stated in the bond, extrinsic evidence was allowed as to what the actual amount was.[12] Second, extrinsic evidence may be admitted to correct clerical errors.[13] No one is allowed to take advantage of a clause of obligation which he admits to be due to a mere clerical error and where an error is not admitted but is obvious from inspection of the document it can be rectified. The cases, however, go a good deal further than that and admit extrinsic evidence not only for the purpose of showing what the true position was where there is a clerical error, either admitted or apparent on the face of the document, but also for the purpose of showing that a clerical error has occured where it is neither admitted nor ex facie apparent.[14]

2 Evidence in supplement of document

Parole evidence may be admitted to supplement a document on matters on which it is silent in the following circumstances:

12 *Hotson v Paul* (1831) 9S 685.
13 Gloag *Contract* (2nd edn) p 435.
14 *Waddell v Waddell* (1863) 1M 635; *Glasgow Feuing & Building Co v Watson's Trustees* (1887) 14R 610; *Krupp v Menzies* 1907 SC 903; *Reid's Trustees v Bucher* 1929 SC 615; *Anderson v Lambie* 1954 SC (HL) 43.

i where there is a collateral agreement separate from the deed, not inconsistent with it and which might naturally be omitted from it, ie on a matter not truly within the scope of the document, extrinsic evidence is admissible.[15] Thus in *Jamieson v Welch* where[16] a house was sold by missive 'with fittings and fixtures. and the disposition did not mention fittings and fixtures, it was held that the purchaser was entitled to lead evidence of the missives on the ground that the fittings and fixtures being corporeal moveables would naturally be transferred by delivery and not in a title to land. The evidence of the missives was supplementary to, and not inconsistent with, the disposition and dealt with matter which might naturally be omitted from it;

ii when a writing is silent on a matter necessarily involved in its interpretation, parole evidence is competent to supply what is omitted in order to make the writing intelligible and effective. Thus, in *Renison v Bryce*[17] extrinsic evidence was admitted to show what had been agreed as the share capital of a company where the document recording the agreement between the parties would not readily have been intelligible without such evidence. There is, here, an overlap between evidence in supplement and evidence to explain a document;

iii extrinsic evidence is admissible to show whether the grantee (not the grantor, at any rate, where the grantor is seeking to escape liability)[18] is an individual or is acting in a representative capacity when the deed is silent on the point and the question arises between the grantee and the grantor in circumstances to which the Blank Bonds and Trust Act 1696 does not apply.[19] Extrinsic evidence may also be admitted to show whether grantors are individuals or representatives in a question between the grantors inter se and, in such a question, to

15 The principle is explained by Dickson 'In such questions' he says 'the nature and object of the writing must be considered so that on the one hand obligations or conditions may not be added to a deed designed for recording all the agreement which the parties made on a particular subject—while, on the other hand, a writing intended to embrace only certain branches or stipulations of an agreement ought not to be stretched to matters beyond its purview; for if it were extrinsic evidence would be excluded on matters which the parties purposely left to be expiscated by that means' (para 1933).

16 (1900) 3F 176.

17 (1898) 25R 421.

18 *Drysdale v Johnstone* (1839) 1D 409; *Anderson v Smith* (1830) 8S 403; *Dickson* para 1018.

19 *Forrester v Robson's Trustees* (1875) 2 R 755. This case is criticised by Gloag *Contract* (2nd edn) p 388 on the ground that it is in contravention of the Blank Bonds and Trusts Act 1696 (see below ch 13) and involves a false distinction between trust and mandate and that the subsequent case of *Laird v Laird & Rutherford* (1884) 12 R 294, in which *Forrester v Robson's Trustees* was distinguished but not doubted on its facts, was based on a false view of what constituted a deed of trust.

show the nature of this relationship if not expressed.[20] The same rule applies to questions between grantees inter se;[1]

iv extrinsic evidence may be admissible to prove that a custom of trade or other customary usage applies to an agreement and was intended by the parties to form part of it.[2] The custom must not, however, be inconsistent with the terms of the agreement—otherwise it is contradictory not supplementary. If, therefore, a contract contains a direct provision expressed in non-ambiguous language it is not permissible to show that by custom of trade certain conditions are annexed to the contract if they are inconsistent with the expressed provision;[3] and

v by the Bills of Exchange Act 1882[4] any fact relating to a Bill of Exchange, cheque or promissory note which is relevant to any question of liability thereon, may be proved by parole evidence. That does not allow the terms of the Bill to be contradicted by parole evidence, but allows the whole facts of the transaction to be established for the purpose of ascertaining the true relations to each other of the persons whose names appear on the Bill and their liability and obligations to each other in respect of it.[5] It does not follow that parole proof of payment or other performance, discharge or variation is competent,[6] and where a bill has been granted

20 *Union Canal Co v Johnston* (1834) 12S 304, (1835) 1 S & M 117; *Drysdale v Johnstone* (1839) 1D 409· *Hamilton & Co v Freeth* (1889) 16R 1022; *Crosbie v Brown* (1900) 3F 83; *Thow's Trustee v Young* 1910 SC 588.

1 *Kilpatrick v Kilpatrick* (1841) 4D 109; *North British Insurance Co v Tunnock & Fraser* (1864) 3M 1; *Moore v Dempster* (1879) 6R 930.

2 The principle is set out by *Dickson* (para 1090) citing *Kirchner v Venus* (1859) 12 Moore PC 361 per Lord Kingsdown: 'When evidence of usage of a particular place is admitted to add to or in any manner to affect the construction of a written contract, it is admitted only on the ground that the parties who made the contract are both cognisant of the usage, and must be presumed to have made their agreement with reference to it.'

3 *Tancred Arrol v Steel Co of Scotland* (1890) 17R (HL) 31. Dickson says (para 1092) that proof of custom is excluded if it is tendered in proof of a matter which the written contract by fair implication embraces. That is, however, so only where the words of the contract are such that it can be implied that custom is excluded. Thus, although parole evidence of the parties' intention in contradiction of the established legal incidents of a contract is generally inadmissible (Gloag *Contract* p 369) a custom of which both parties were aware may be proved in contradiction of such an incident (Gloag *Contract* (2nd ed) p 379). The Sale of Goods Act 1979 (s 55) embodies this principle 'Where a right, duty, or liability would arise under a contract of sale of goods by implication of law, it may be negatived or varied . . . by such usage as binds both parties to the contract'. For cases where there is an implication that custom is excluded see *Gye v Hallam*, (1832) 10S 512; *Alexander v Gillon* (1847) 9D 524; *Stewart v Maclaine* (1898) 36 SLR 233, affd (1900) 37 SLR 623; *Buchanan v Riddell* (1900) 2F 544.

4 S 100.

5 For examples see Gloag *Contract* (2nd edn) p 384.

6 *Nicol's Trustees v Sutherland* 1951 SC (HL) 21. See also *National Bank of Australaisa v Turnbull & Co* (1891) 18R 629 at 634 and 638; *Gibson's Trustees v Galloway* (1896) 23R 414 at 416; *Robertson v Thomson* (1900) 3F 5.

in implement of a written contract, evidence cannot be led in relation to the bill which would have the effect of contradicting the contract.[7]

3 Explanatory evidence

General

The general rule is that the meaning of parties to a deed must be gathered from the words of the deed itself to the exclusion of parole and other extrinsic proof of intention. The duty of the court is not to discover the abstract or secret intention of the parties as distinct from what they have expressed, but to construe and give effect to the words in which they have set forth their final intentions. Extrinsic evidence of intention is generally, therefore, inadmissible whatever form it takes (eg spoken declarations by parties, draft documents, etc)[8] There is therefore no doubt that the principle excluding extrinsic evidence applies to evidence adduced for the purpose of explaining a document but there are some exceptions which are, in the main, to be justified on the view that if the exception were not allowed the document would be unintelligible and incapable of being put into effect.

Patent and latent ambiguities: rules of construction

The fact that the terms of a document are ambiguous does not of itself let in extrinsic evidence as to the meaning of the ambiguous words. In this connection a distinction has often been made between patent and latent ambiguities. Where the ambiguity is patent (ie appears on the face of the document) the resolution of the ambiguity must usually be found from an examination of the terms of the document itself and in particular from such clues as the document as a whole affords to the meaning intended to be attached to the ambiguous words. Where, on the other hand, the ambiguity is latent (ie the words used do not appear on the face of the document to be ambiguous but an ambiguity becomes apparent when the document comes to be applied) recourse may be had to extrinsic evidence in order to resolve the ambiguity. In *Logan v Wright*[9] Lord Brougham said:

> 'The rule [ie the distinction between patent and latent ambiguities and the rule which admits extrinsic evidence for resolving the

7 *Stagg & Robson v Stirling* 1908 SC 675 especially per Lord Kinnear at 680; *McAllister v McGallagley* 1911 SC 112.
8 See *Devlin's Trustees v Breen* 1945 SC (HL) 27.
9 *Logan v Wright* (1831) 5 W & S 242 at 247.

> latter only] is as old as Lord Bacon when he held the Great Seal and that rule holds in all Courts here and in Scotland.'

In *Ritchie v Whish*[10] Lord Brougham's proposition that the rule applies in Scotland appears to have been accepted but it does not seem to have been consistently applied in Scotland[11] and it is doubtful if it still applies in England. It is probably better to discard a rigid distinction of this kind and to approach the matter rather from the standpoint of the basic rules of construction applied to documents.

The meaning normally to be given to words is their ordinary meaning. By that is meant the meaning which persons of ordinary intelligence would give to them.[12] There are, however, some exceptions to the general rule. If the law attaches a particular meaning to the words used they will receive that meaning where the legal prescription is absolute (as may be the case with a statutory prescription); where there is no such absolute prescription, there will be a presumption that the words have been used in the sense which the law attaches to them.[13] If, moreover, it is evident on the face of a document that words have been used in a particular sense, they will be construed in that sense even if it deviates far from the ordinary meaning. If, applying these rules of construction, the words can be given an intelligible meaning, they will be given that meaning unless it appears that, when the document comes to be applied, there is ambiguity. Where the words used cannot be given an intelligible meaning by these rules recourse must be had to the document as a whole to see if it affords any clues as to the meaning which the words should bear and if, after such enquiry, the words remain unintelligible, then extrinsic evidence becomes admissible to explain them. So too, where an ambiguity appears on the application of the document, extrinsic evidence is admissible.

Special meaning

Although the rules noted above have been applied in most cases, extrinsic evidence is admitted rather more freely to explain the terms of a document than to supplement or to contradict it and this freedom has led to some relaxation of the rules. These relaxations are not altogether easy to classify but it may be said that where words, although not absolutely

10 (1880) 8R 101.

11 *Trustees of the Free Church of Scotland v Maitland* (1887) 14R 333; *Anderson v McCracken Bros* (1900) 2F 780; *Von Mehren & Co v Edinburgh Roperie & Sailcloth Ltd* (1901) 4F 232; *Brownlee v Robb* 1907 SC 1302; *Robertson's Trustee v Riddell* 1911 SC 14 are all cases in which the ambiguity was patent but yet extrinsic evidence was admitted.

12 Bell's *Commentaries* (7th edn) I 456; *Dickson* para 1052.

13 Bell's *Principles* para 1694; *Dickson* para 1053.

unintelligible, would lead to an extravagant result if given their apparent meaning, extrinsic evidence may be admitted to show that they were used in a special or restricted sense. Thus, in *Van Mohren v Edinburgh Ropery Co*[14] extrinsic evidence was admitted to show that 'all your requirements in rope' did not mean, as it might appear to mean, everything that the purchaser might require but was restricted to what was required for trade with Iceland, that trade having been what was in the parties' contemplation. An easier case for the admission of extrinsic evidence is *Blacklock v McArthur and Kirk*,[15] where such evidence was admitted to explain 'usual requirements', words which readily invite extrinsic evidence for their elucidation. While dicta such as:

> 'every Court of Justice has a right to have all the information which was in the possession of the parties contracting, to place itself in the situation of the parties for the purpose of putting a construction upon the instrument to which they have become parties'[16]

may be too widely expressed, courts have, in general, been prepared to look at the circumstances surrounding a transaction to see whether a special meaning was intended, at any rate where that special meaning was one attributable to a technical or scientific usage or to common usage among persons carrying on the trade in question. Thus, extrinsic evidence has been admitted to show that a technical meaning was to be attached to 'cutting shop';[17] 'Scotch iron of best quality';[18] 'fair market price';[19] warranted 'no St Lawrence';[20] and, 'statuary'.[1]

Ambiguity on application to facts

Examples of extrinsic evidence being admissible to resolve ambiguities which appear when a deed comes to be applied are numerous. Thus, in *Cathcart's Trustees v Bruce*,[2] where there was a bequest to the children of 'General Alexander Fairlie Bruce'—a bequest apparently quite unambiguous on the face of the deed—and it appeared when the deed came to be applied that there was a General Alexander *James* Bruce and a *Mr* Alexander Fairlie Bruce, extrinsic evidence was admitted to establish whom it had been the testator's intention to benefit. A

14 Above.
15 1919 SC 57.
16 *Forlong v Taylor's Trustees* (1938) 3 S & M 177 at 210.
17 *Watson v Kidston & Co* (1839) 1D 1254.
18 *Fleming & Co v Airdrie Iron Co* (1882) 9R 473.
19 *Charrington v Wooder* [1914] AC 71.
20 *Birrell v Dryer* (1884) 11 R (HL) 41.
1 *Sutton & Co v Ciceri & Co* (1890) 17R (HL) 40.
2 1923 SLT 722.

somewhat similar case was *McFarlane v Watt*[3] where extrinsic evidence was admitted to show what was meant by 'Lands of Craigs' where the seller held Northcraigs and Southcraigs. In that case the principle on which the evidence was admitted was explained as being that 'the document cannot take effect without parole proof to show what is meant'. So too, in *McDonald v Newall*[4] evidence was admitted to show the extent of what was meant by 'the property known as the Royal Hotel' and in particular to show that the subjects pointed out to the purchaser, before the sale, did not include a neighbouring tap-room and stable. A more extreme case is *Naismith's Trustees v NSPCC*[5] where there was a legacy to 'the National SPCC' a description which exactly fitted an English society bearing that name. The English society's claim prevailed against the Scottish society with a somewhat similar description but evidence as to the testator's intention was admitted and it was observed that even where a description in a will exactly fits one person it is still open to another, whom the description partially fits, to establish that he is the person intended. There is, however, a strong presumption in favour of the party accurately and exactly described.[6]

Direct statements of intention

Where extrinsic evidence is admissible, evidence of direct statements of intention by parties or grantors are generally inadmissible because to admit such evidence would open the way for parties too easily to alter deeds and would go against the objective test that a document must be construed according to the meaning of the words used rather than what the parties intended to mean.[7] The only exception to that is perhaps in cases of equivocation of which some of the cases cited above are examples, ie where words used are clearly intended to apply to one person or thing but prove to be capable of being applied to two or more and it is impossible to say from the writing which was intended. In such cases it seems that evidence of direct statements of intention may be admissible.[8]

3 (1828) 6S 556.
4 (1898) 1F 68.
5 1914 SC 76.
6 See also *Fortunato's J F v Fortunato* 1981 SLT 277 in which parole evidence held incompetent to qualify the description of the subjects of bequest.
7 *Devlin's Trustees v Breen* 1945 SC (HL) 27.
8 *Dickson* para 1079. The introduction of direct evidence of intention in such cases was justified on the view that 'the evidence of declarations of the testator has not the effect of varying the instrument in any way whatever; it only enables the court to reject one of the subjects, or objects, to which the description in the will' applies; and to determine which of the two the divisor understood to be signified in the description in the will'; *Doe d Gord v Needs* (1836) 2 N & W 129 per Parke B.

Secret intention; blanks

When extrinsic evidence is admitted it is admitted only for explaining the words actually used and for ascertaining the meaning which parties intended to give to these words. It is never admissible for the purpose of showing that parties secretly intended something different from what they expressed. Accordingly, parole evidence will not be admitted to supply what a writer had meant to say but did not say. Therefore, a total blank in documents cannot be supplied by parole evidence unless the blank is such that the surrounding words are rendered quite unintelligible and it is clear that the words which it is proposed to supply, and no others, are the words which the parties or grantor intended. Thus, in *Sharpe v Sharpe*[9] the court refused to supply words although it pointed out that if one set of words and no others had been available the situation would have been different.[10]

4 Variation

Where a right requires writing for its constitution, it cannot be varied unless by subsequent writing in the appropriate form. Thus, rights conferred by deeds relating to heritage cannot normally be varied unless by probative or holograph writ and a will cannot be varied unless by the subsequent writ of the testator in appropriate testamentary form. Even, however, where writing, although not essential for constitution, has been used to record rights or obligations, the rights and obligations so recorded cannot normally be varied unless by a subsequent writ of the parties. It is necessary to distinguish between the two cases because the qualifications to the general rule differ somewhat according to whether writing was essential for constitution or not.

> 'It may be laid down with more confidence than is usually possible in making general statements that where the relationship of parties is regulated by formal written contract, the averment that the contractual provisions have been altered by a subsequent verbal agreement cannot be proved by parole evidence. Where one party takes his stand on the written contract and the other, either in order to insist on the obligation due to him or in answer to a claim for breach of contract, avers that the terms of the contract were altered, his case is irrelevant if he merely avers a verbal agreement and does not add averments of actings following upon it or offer to prove it by the writ or oath of his opponent.'[11]

9 (1835) 1 S & M 594.
10 See also *Re Follett decd* [1954] 3 All ER 478; and *Re Cory decd* [1955] 2 All ER 630.
11 Gloag *Contract* (2nd edn) p 391.

The rule is illustrated by authority both in relation to contracts requiring writing for their constitution and to those which do not. Thus, in *Turnbull v Oliver*[12] a tenant under a written lease was not allowed to prove by parole an agreement to reduce the rent and in *Stevenson v Manson*[13] an investor was held not entitled to prove a verbal alteration to written instructions given to his stockbrokers.

Where writing essential

Where writing is essential to constitution, variation may not be shown by reference to the oath of the other party or to his informal writ where that writ would not be sufficient to constitute the right or obligation.[14] The reason is that if writing is required for constitution then it is required in the same form for a variation which is, in effect, the constitution of a new right or obligation of the same kind.[15] The fact that a party might swear to there having been a verbal agreement or that his informal writ might show that there was a verbal agreement or an agreement reduced to writing defective in form is irrelevant. However, just as contracts relating to heritage may be entered into by verbal agreement (provable only by writ or oath) followed by *rei interventus*, so a written contract relating to heritage may be varied by a verbal agreement (proved by write or oath) followed by *rei interventus*.[16] Put shortly, the only ways in which rights or obligations requiring writing for their constitution can be varied are ways by which the rights or obligations could themselves be constituted.

Where writing not essential

Where writing is not essential to the constitution of the right or obligation, there are exceptions to the rule that a right or obligation recorded in a document cannot be varied other than by a subsequent document of the parties. The first of these exceptions is that it may be so

12 (1891) 19R 134.
13 (1840) 2 D 1204.
14 *Perdikou v Pattison* 1958 SLT 153.
15 *Carron Co v Henderson's Trustees* (1896) 23R 1042 per Lord Kyllachy at 1048–9 and Lord McLaren at 1054.
16 *Walker v Flint* (1863) 1M 417; *Paterson v Earl of Fife* (1865) 3 M 423; *Phillip v Gordon Cumming's Executors* (1869) 7M 859; *Gibson v Adams* (1875) 3R 144; *Sutherland's Trustee v Millar's Trustee* (1888) 16R 10. Dicta in *Wark v Bargaddie Coal Co* (1859) 3 Macq 467 per Lord Chelmsford LC at 477–9 to the effect that the oral agreement as well as the *rei interventus* could be proved by parole evidence are unnecessary for the decision and inconsistent with principle and with the subsequent authority mentioned above.

varied by reference to the writ or oath of the party having an interest to contradict the variation.[17] Proof of *rei interventus* is not necessary and the writ of the contradictor is sufficient if it provides clear evidence of a verbal variation even although it would not in itself amount to such a variation. Second, a written contract which did not require writing for its constitution may be varied by the subsequent actings of the parties if these actings are such as to be explicable only on the view that the contract had been varied. Variation is implied from the actings. Accordingly, a written contract can be varied in this way although there has been no express agreement to vary or where, although it is alleged that there was an express agreement, that agreement cannot be proved by the writ or oath of the contradictor. It is, however, essential that the actings should be explicable only on the view that the contract has been varied. As Lord Kyllachy said in *Carron Co v Henderson's Trustees*[18] a contract may be 'altered *rebus et factis* for the past and for the future by acts of the parties *necessarily* and *unequivocally* importing an agreement to alter'.

17 *Stevenson v Manson* (1840) 2 D 1204.
18 (1896) 23 R 1042.

CHAPTER 6

Inadmissibility of evidence; exercise of privilege

GENERAL

Privilege is the right to refuse to give or produce evidence which, apart from the exercise of the privilege, would be admissible. It is of the nature of privilege that the exercise of that right is at the choice of the person in whom it is vested and so the privilege may be waived by him. If that is done, no other person can object to the admission of the evidence. For like reasons a party cannot complain of the wrongful rejection of a privilege vested in a witness other than himself and so cannot make such rejection a ground of appeal.[1] On the other hand, he can complain if a witness's claim to privilege is wrongfully upheld for he may thereby have been prejudiced by the exclusion of evidence which ought to have been admitted.[2] It is sometime said on the basis of English authority that as a further corollary matters which are the subject of privilege may be proved by the evidence of a third party or by secondary evidence.[3] That is a question which, where the privilege is statutory, must depend on the interpretation of the statute,[4] but in the case of common law privileges designed to protect a particular class of communication, or a particular relationship, it is thought that the court should not countenance the circumvention of that protection.

1 *R V Kinglake* (1870 22 LT 335; cf *Kirkwood v Kirkwood* (1875) 3 R 235 per Lord President Inglis at 236.

2 *Doe d'Egremont v Date* (1842) 3 QB 609. Cross *on Evidence* (6th edn) p 379, says that the distinction between the wrongful upholding and the wrongful rejection of privilege does not seem to have been taken in other cases but it is submitted that the distinction is fundamental and sound in principle.

3 *Lloyd v Mostyn* (1842) 10 M and W 478 per Parke B at 481–2; *Calcraft v Guest* [1898] 1 QB 759; *R v Tompkins* (1977) 67 Crim App R 181 (cf and contrast *R v Uljee* [1982] 1 NZLR 561). But if a document is brought into court by a party and improperly obtained from him by his opponent, the opponent cannot then tender secondary evidence based on the improperly obtained document (*ITC Film Distributors v Video Exchange Ltd* [1982] Ch 431, [1982] 2 All ER 241).

4 See 'Privilege for communications between husband and wife' p 103 below.

PRIVILEGE AGAINST SELF-INCRIMINATION

'No man is bound to incriminate himself.'[5] That has been said to be 'a sacred and inviolable principle'. Accordingly, a witness has a privilege to refuse to answer questions if the answer would incriminate him. The privilege is excluded by some statutes[6] for matters within their scope and it has been held that the obligation on a bankrupt to answer 'all lawful questions' embraces questions that may incriminate him.[7] Otherwise the privilege is of general application and covers not only answers directly incriminatory but also those from which an inference of guilt may be drawn, or which contain facts forming links in a chain of circumstantial evidence implicating the witness in crime, or leading to the obtaining of evidence on which a charge might be founded against him.[8] It is for the court to decide whether the privilege applies. Dickson says that for this purpose the court will generally be satisfied with the witness's statement that the question has an incriminatory tendency without requiring him to explain how the question bears upon the charge, for that would often, in effect, deprive him of his privilege.[9] Dickson, however, relied on English text-writers and authority and it is now settled in England that the witness's statement is not enough and that the court must judge from the circumstances and the nature of the evidence whether there is a reasonable ground to apprehend danger, having regard to the ordinary course of law.[10] There is a practical problem that the witness may not be able to satisfy the court of the incriminating tendency of the question without, at the same time, incriminating himself. 'The privilege must ... be violated in order to ascertain whether it exists. The secret must be told in order to see whether it ought to be kept.'[11] The only solution seems to be that the court must make the best judgment it can in the circumstances without pressing the witness too far. While the witness's claim to the privilege is not in itself enough, it may be that where it is colourable and appears to be bona fide it should be accepted.[12]

5 *Livingstone v Murrays* (1830) 9 S 161 per Lord Gilles at 162.
6 Eg Explosive Substances Act 1883 s 6(2), Representation of the People Act 1949 s 123(7)(b).
7 *Sawers v Dalgarnie* (1858) 21 D 153 per Lord Benholme at 157. See now Bankruptcy (Scotland) Act 1985 s 47(3).
8 *Livingstone v Murrays* above; *Dickson* para 1789.
9 *Dickson* ibid.
10 *R v Boyes* (1861) 1 B & S 311; *Re Reynolds, ex p Reynolds* (1882) 20 Ch D 294; *Triplex Safety Glass Co v Lancegaye Safety Glass (1934) Ltd* [1939] 2 KB 395, [1939] 2 All ER 613; *Rio Tinto Zinc Co v Westinghouse Electric Corpn* [1978] AC 547, [1978] 1 All ER 434.
11 *R v Cox and Railton* (1884) 14 QBD 153 per Stephen J at 175.
12 Sheriff I D MacPhail's solution that the asking of the question should be forbidden (*Research Paper* para 18–05) has statutory precedents in the Evidence Amendment (Scotland) Act 1874 s 2 and the Criminal Procedure (Scotland) Act 1975 ss 141(F) and 346(F) but is not practicable in all cases. Sometimes neither the questioner nor the court may be aware of the incriminating tendency of the question until the witness objects to answering.

When privilege inapplicable

The privilege does not apply in relation to a crime of which the witness has already been convicted, or to which he has pleaded guilty, or in respect of which he enjoys an immunity from prosecution by virtue of having given evidence for the Crown,[13] and it may be that if he has already made an extra-judicial confession of guilt his invocation of the privilege would be regarded as not in good faith.[14] It is thought too that the witness can have no privilege where he has been tried and acquitted of the crime in question for he has then tholed his assise and cannot be molested further; and in England it has been held that the granting of a pardon under the Great Seal has that effect.[15] The witness's right is limited to declining to answer and he cannot resist being put on oath or being asked the questions to which his privilege applies.[16] If he declines to answer, his doing so and his manner on the occasion are circumstances to be considered in weighing his evidence because 'an innocent man is far more likely to answer with an indignant denial than to avail himself of his privilege'.[17]

Invocation of privilege: effect of denial

The privilege is that of the witness alone.[18] If a question appears to have an incriminating tendency it is the duty of the judge to warn the witness

13 *Macmillan v Murray* 1920 JC 13; cf *McGinley v MacLeod* 1963 SLT 2. See ch 9 below.
14 *Brebner v Perry* [1961] SASR 177.
15 *R v Boyes* (1861) 1 B&S 311.
16 *Don v Don* (1848) 10 D 1046.
17 *Dickson* para 1790. Sheriff I D MacPhail, however, comments that 'it may be assumed that under the common law at present, it is not permissible to draw any adverse inference from the fact that the witness declines to answer the question since otherwise the privilege would be destroyed' and the law of England is that no adverse inference should be drawn from the fact that a privilege is invoked (*Wentworth v Lloyd* (1864) 10 HL Cas 589 at 590–2 per Lord Chelmsford. Cf *Adams v Lloyd* (1858) 3 H & M 351 at 363 per Pollock CB: 'a man may be placed under such circumstances with respect to the commission of a crime, that if he disclose them he may be fixed upon by his hearers as a guilty person, so that the rule is not always a shield of the guilty, it is sometimes the protector of the innocent'. The American Model Code by contrast provides (Rule 233): 'if a privilege to refuse to disclose, or a privilege to prevent another from disclosing, matter is claimed and allowed, the judge and counsel may comment thereon, and the trier of fact may draw all reasonable inferences therefrom'. That provision has not, however, been adopted in the Uniform Rules. The drawing of adverse inferences does not destroy the privilege because the privilege is designed to protect the witness against exposing himself to subsequent criminal proceedings and no inference drawn in the instant case affects that. The question is probably one of circumstances but in most cases it will be impossible to know whether an adverse inference should be drawn.
18 *Kirkwood v Kirkwood* (1875) 3R 235.

that he need not answer it.[19] A party may draw the judge's attention to the need for a warning and somewhat anomalously it appears to be competent to do so by way of objection,[20] but beyond that a party has no interest in the matter. If the privilege is wrongly denied, the evidence is competent for all purposes and it is thought that is so even if the witness is a party because the purpose of the privilege is to protect him from subsequent criminal proceedings and not *qua litigant* in the cause. It is undecided whether the failure of a witness, unwarned and ignorant of his rights, to claim privilege leaves it open for his evidence to be used against him if he is subsequently prosecuted,[1] but where the privilege is claimed and wrongly refused the evidence given is treated as an involuntary statement against interest and so inadmissible in criminal proceedings against the witness.[2]

Incrimination under foreign law

It is undecided whether the privilege extends to answers which might tend to incriminate the witness under foreign law, including English law. In England the privilege is in civil cases confined, by statue, to 'criminal offences under the law of any part of the United Kingdom and penalties provided for by such law',[3] but, before that was enacted it had been held in one case that privilege in respect of incrimination under foreign law could not be allowed because the judge must be able to determine the question as a matter of law[4] and, in another case, that it could be allowed where the foreign law was admitted on the pleadings.[5] There is an obvious problem of verification but where, as may sometimes be the case, the risk of incrimination is obvious, it seems wrong in principle to deny a witness protection against proceedings abroad and, perhaps, extradition in connection with them when, in similar circumstance, he would be protected against proceedings in Scotland.

Liability to penalty

There is no privilege against answering questions where the answer may expose the witness to the risk of civil proceedings against him[6] but in

19 Ibid. *Dickson* para 1790.
20 *Don v Don* (1848) 10 D 1046; *Kennedy v HM Advocate* (1896) 23 R (J) 28; *Dickie v HM Advocate* (1897) 24 R (J) 82.
1 See *Graham v HM Advocate* 1969 SLT 116; cf *R v Sloggett* (1856) Dears CC 656.
2 *R v Garbett* (1847) 1 Dem 236.
3 Civil Evidence Act 1968 s 14(1)(a).
4 *King of the Two Sicilies v Willcox* (1851) 1 Sim NS 301; cf *Re Atherton* [1912] 2 KB 251 at 255. Foreign law is a question of fact and so not a matter of law in the sense indicated (see ch 11 below).
5 *United States of America v McRae* (1868) LR 3 Ch App 79.
6 *Dickson* para 1787.

England the privilege is extended to cases where, by answering, the witness would expose himself to the risk of incurring a penalty civilly recoverable.[7] As penalties have a *quasi-criminal* character the extension may be logical but there is no Scottish authority which requires it and the origins of the rule in England seem to rest on technical features of English law. The matter has received enhanced importance because of the penalties for which the EEC treaty and regulations provide.[8]

Incrimination of spouse

The privilege is against self-incrimination and not against giving evidence which might incriminate anyone else. In England, however, a parallel privilege has now been created in civil cases in respect of questions tending to incriminate a spouse.[9] There appears to have been no such privilege in England at common law[10] but there is no authority in Scotland and the matter may still be open for decision. The view has been expressed that to compel a witness to incriminate his spouse is more repellant than to compel the witness to incriminate himself,[11] and a privilege could be defended on grounds of respect for the matrimonial relationship and the unity of husband and wife. If there is such a privilege, it must be the privilege of the witness because the objection lies in the applying of compulsion to him. It cannot extend to incrimination of a spouse on the offence charged where an accused person gives evidence nor can it apply to incrimination of the accused on that offence where his spouse is a witness whether for prosecution or defence, because to allow it in such cases would be contrary to the clear policy of the law.[12]

Incrimination of company where director a witness

In *Rio Tinto Zinc Corpn v Westinghouse Electric Corpn*[13] the question was raised, but not decided, of the extent to which a director might be able to claim privilege in respect of information incriminatory of his com-

7 (6th edn) p 381.
8 See *Rio Tinto Zinc Corpn v Westinghouse Electric Corpn* [1978] AC 547, [1978] 1 All ER 434.
9 Civil Evidence Act 1968 s 14(1)(b).
10 *Cross* (6th edn) p 384.
11 Report of the Law Reform Committee (England and Wales) which resulted in the Civil Evidence Act 1968 s 14(1)(b), above. See MacPhail *Research Paper* para 18–12.
12 For a spouse of an accused person to have a privilege as a witness to refuse to answer questions incriminating the accused of the offence charged would either, if she were a prosecution witness, defeat the object in her being called, or if she were a defence witness, impose an impossible restraint on her cross-examination. If an accused person who testified were to be able to claim a privilege against incriminating his spouse on the offence charged, that too would greatly hamper cross-examination.
13 [1978] AC 547, [1978] 1 All ER 434.

pany. That raises, in turn, questions of the underlying rationale of the rule. The primary reason, embodied in the maxim *nemo debet prodere se ipsum* is, it is submitted, that there is an essential wrongness in compelling an individual to incriminate himself (or, perhaps, his spouse). Other reasons, such as encouraging potential witnesses to give testimony and maintaining the burden of investigation and proof on the prosecuting authorities (insofar as that is not just a restatement of the primary reason) are, it is submitted, subsidiary and relatively weak. If that is correct, there can be no real objection to compelling a director to give evidence incriminatory of the company of which he is an officer. The company is not a witness and has no privilege. The director is not identified in personality, actual or legal, with his company, and, looking to him as a witness, there is nothing more objectionable in compelling him to give evidence incriminatory of the company than of any other person or organisation in which he might have a financial interest or a duty to serve. Where, moreover, would the privilege end? If it extends to directors, should it not also extend to others to whom responsibility for management of the company's affairs is entrusted and, perhaps, to all employees? Different considerations may possibly apply to the recovery of documents or real evidence.

Imputation of adultery

At common law a witness had a privilege not to answer questions if his answer would tend to show that he had committed adultery.[14] That is, it is submitted, no more than a branch of the privilege against self-incrimination and, as a common law rule, does not survive the disappearance in practice of adultery as a crime. The Evidence (Further Amendment) (Scotland) Act 1874,[15] however, enacts that no witness in any proceeding, whether a party to the suit or not, shall be liable to be asked or bound to answer any question tending to show that he or she has been guilty of adultery unless the witness has already given evidence, in the same proceeding, in disproof of his or her alleged adultery. These provisions form part of an enactment which made parties, and the spouses of parties, competent witnesses in any proceeding instituted in consequence of adultery. The words 'in any proceeding' are capable of, and would ordinarily bear, a wide application[16] but it is submitted that, in context, an interpretation that they refer only to proceedings instituted in consequence of adultery may be justified. This statutory privilege was, within 12 years of its being created, the subject of

14 *Stephens* (1839) 2 Swin 348; *Muir v Muir* (1873) 11 M 529; *Kirkwood v Kirkwood* (1875) 3R 235.
15 S 2.
16 Cf the Guardianship of Infants Act 1925 s 1 as interpreted in *J v C* [1970] AC 668.

trenchant criticism and those criticisms have even more force now.[17] A restrictive interpretation would be in line with the purposes the Act was designed to serve. In contrast with the common law privilege against self-incriminatioin the statutory privilege strikes at questions as well as answers. Accordingly, no evidentiary use can be made of the witness's refusal to answer,[18] and his refusal should not be recorded.[19] The privilege is the privilege of the witness alone and if he elects to give evidence, that evidence is competent.

PRIVILEGE FOR COMMUNICATIONS BETWEEN LEGAL ADVISER AND CLIENT

Communications between a legal adviser and his client are privileged. The rule is ancient. Stair says that advocates 'are not obliged to depone as to any secret committed to them'[20] and in *Leslie v Grant*[1] it was held that the secrets of the cause extended to everything in the case of which the lawyers were informed. The modern privilege is not, however, confined to communications relating to pending, or contemplated, litigation but extends to all communications properly falling within the scope of the relationship.[2] The reason is that the taking of legal advice can never be dissociated from the possibility of eventual litigation and that it is essential for the administration of justice that persons should be able to consult their legal advisers freely without the subject matter of their discussions being under risk of disclosure. It is essential, if the communication is to be protected, that it must be associated with giving or receiving legal advice. 'The mere fact that the person speaking is a solicitor and the person to whom he speaks is his client affords no protection.'[3] Beyond that, what constitutes a communication for the purposes of obtaining legal advice has not been precisely determined but it is doubtful if business firms can obtain protection for their business records merely by the device of depositing them, as it is believed sometimes happens, in solicitors' premises. The matter protected must

17 See Sheriff ID MacPhail *Research Paper* para 18–18 quoting from Lord Trayner 'The Advances of a Generation' (1886) 2 Sc L Rev 57, 89 at 91–2.
18 *Hunt v Hunt* (1893) 1 SLT 157.
19 *Cook v Cook* (1876) 4 R 78.
20 Stair IV 43, 9(8).
1 5 Brown's supp 874.
2 *McCowan v Wright* (1852) 15 D 229 at 237; cf *Greenough v Gaskell* (1833) 1 My & K 98 per Lord Brougham at 103: 'if the privilege was confined to communications connected with suits begun, or intended or expected or apprehended no one could safely adopt such precautions as might eventually render any proceeding successful or all proceedings superfluous'.
3 *Minter v Priest* [1930] AC 558 per Lord Buckmaster at 568.

have formed part of the substance of the actual seeking or giving of legal advice and not have an independent origin.[4] And it is communications alone which are protected, not facts observed.[5] A solicitor must refuse to say whether his client confessed to a crime but must answer if asked whether he came to him wearing blood-stained clothing.

Character of relationship

It is necessary if the privilege is to attach that a relationship of legal adviser and client should have been formed or at least have been contemplated and that the communication should have been made in the course of, or be referable to, that relationship. A legal adviser, for this purpose, comprehends law agent, solicitor and counsel, and communications to them and persons, such as their clerks, who are privy to the relationship, are protected.[6] Where an intermediary is employed, it is thought that the communication remains protected unless there is an independent disclosure to the intermediary because the intermediary is, if but to a limited extent and purpose, the agent or instrument of the party or the adviser.[7] There is, however, no protection where legal advice is sought from persons such as factors or bankers, or accountants who are not professional legal advisers.[8] In *Gavin v Montgomerie*[9] Lord President Hope appeared to allow for an exception to that when he said of the confidentiality between a person indicted for crime and someone who had acted as his agent:

> 'It is not necessary that he be a law agent. It is sufficient that he acts in that capacity. The correspondence clearly related to the impending criminal proceedings; and a person in this position may employ anyone, even a country gentleman, to take evidence or to do other confidential acts and that confidence will be protected.'

That apparent exception is, however, better understood as an instance of the protection afforded to communications made for the purposes of litigation. It is uncertain whether a contemplated relationship of legal adviser and client is sufficient to enable the privilege to attach. In *HM Advocate v Davie*[10] evidence was admitted, under reservation of consideration of its competency by the High Court, of communications between

4 *R v Peterborough Justices, ex p Hicks* [1977] 1WLR 1371; *R v King* [1983] 1 All ER 929.
5 *Bursill v Tanner* (1883) 13 QBD 691 (identity of client); *Brown v Foster* (1857) 1 H & N 736; *Re Cathcart, ex p Campbell* (1870) 5 Ch App 703; *Dwyer v Collins* (1852) 7 Exch 639.
6 *Dickson* para 1665.
7 *Stuart v Millar* (1836) 14 S 837.
8 *Dickson* ibid.
9 (1830) 9 S 213.
10 (1881) 4 Coup 450.

the accused and the solicitor whom he had consulted but who had declined to act for him. Lord Mure seems to have thought the evidence admissible but the point was not decided. There can be no doubt that anything passing after the relationship has been declined is not protected but in relation to communications made while the relationship is still in contemplation, the better view may be that taken in England that the privilege attaches to communications fairly referable to a contemplated relationship.[11] The privilege subsists although the relationship has terminated by the time the question of disclosure arises.[12]

Effect of death of client

In relation to proprietorial matters in which executors have an interest the privilege passes on the death of the client to his executors. It has been suggested that after the death of the client the privilege cannot be waived because death has removed the only person entitled to waive it. But that can be true only of matters (such as, in most cases, a confession of crime) in which executors have no interest. Where the executors have no interest the alternative and better view seems to be that the privilege cannot be invoked because the interest to invoke it rested solely with the deceased and has lapsed on his death. That that is the correct view is supported by *Mackenzie v Mackenzie's Trustees*[13], a declarator of marriage in which protection against disclosure was denied to communications which had passed between a deceased person, to whom the pursuer was alleged to have been married, and his solicitors. That case would also support the view that executors have an interest to assert the privilege only in a question with strangers to the succession (eg creditors of the deceased) who make a claim against the estate, and not in a question with persons who make a claim to participate in the succession.

When privilege not applicable

The privilege does not apply:

1 where the fact that the communication took place forms part of the subject matter of the enquiry or is closely associated with it. This seems to be the ratio of *Kid v Bunyan*[14] where the question at issue was whether the defender had agreed to the terms of settlement of a previous action between the pursuer and the defender. It was held that it was competent to recover letters by the defender to his law agent instructing the latter as to the terms on which the defender was

11 *Minter v Priest* [1930] AC 558. *Cross* pp 389–90.
12 *Dickson* para 1664.
13 *Mackenzie v Mackenzie's Trustees* 1916 1 SLT 271, (1916) 53 SLR 219.
14 (1842) 5 D 193; cf *Anderson v Lord Elgin's Trustees* (1859) 21 D 654.

prepared to settle on the view that those letters were part of the *res gestae*;

2 where the communication is made in the furtherance of any criminal purpose.[15] A client who seeks advice for the purpose of commiting crime cannot expect what he has said to be privileged. That is so whether or not the legal adviser was aware of the criminal purpose. Such communications are, however to be distinguished from (a) communications made after the commission of the crime for the purpose of obtaining advice on the defence to a criminal charge, and (b) communications made for the purpose of obtaining advice on whether or not a proposed course of action would be lawful. In both those cases the communication is privileged, whereas when it is made in furtherance of a criminal purpose, it is not;

3 where the existence of the relationship is in dispute;[16] and

4 in examinations in bankruptcy. The interpretation given to the obligation to answer 'all lawful questions' relating to the bankrupt's estate as excluding any privilege of the bankrupt would appear to apply to communications between legal adviser and client.[17]

Where confidentiality breached; where disclosure necessary to vindicate innocence of third party

There is no Scottish authority on whether the privilege may be invoked when a communication between legal adviser and client is overheard, intercepted or otherwise falls into the hands of a third party, but if the justification of the privilege is, as is commonly asserted, that confidentiality of the relationship is essential to the administration of justice, it would seem that the argument that the law should protect privilege against circumvention as well as direct attack has particular force in this context.[18] There is also no Scottish authority on whether the privilege may be set aside for the purpose of vindicating the innocence of a third party. In *R v Barton*,[19] Caulfield J said:

> 'I cannot conceive that our law would permit a solicitor or other person to screen from a jury information which, if disclosed to the jury, would perhaps enable a man either to establish his innocence or to resist an allegation made by the Crown.'

15 *McCowan v Wright* (1852) 15 D 229; *Morrison v Somerville* (1860) 23 D 232; *Millar v Small* (1856) 19 D 142; *Dickson* para 1678.

16 *Fraser v Malloch* (1895) 3 SLT 211.

17 See p 89 above.

18 See p 88 above. For criticism of the existing English position see Haydon 'Legal Professional Privilege and Third Parties' (1974) 37 MLR 601.

19 [1972] 2 All ER 1192, [1973] 1 WLR 115.

The doctrine so put is attractive but would seem to require some limitation if the purposes the privilege is designed to serve are not to be subverted.

PRIVILEGE FOR COMMUNICATIONS FOR PURPOSE OF LITIGATION

Communications made for the purpose of litigation, even if not between adviser and client, are privileged. Thus, communications made between parties on the same side in an action for the purpose of instructing their common or separate grounds of action or defence, and communications made for similar purposes between parties or their legal advisers and third parties are privileged. 'The general rule is that no party can recover from another material which the other party has made in preparing his case.'[20] A distinction must be made between privileged communications under this head and communications (not privileged) between parties on the same side, or, between parties to the action and third parties which, although relevant to the action, were not made for the purpose of any ground of action or defence. Communications made prior to the raising of the action (*ante litem motam*) will generally fall into the latter category and not be the subject of privilege, whereas communications made *post litem motam* will generally be privileged. Not all communications made after the raising of proceedings and therefore in the strict sense *post litem motam* will, however, be privileged. An admission or confession or other statement made by a party not for the purpose of preparing his case but casually, or for some collateral purpose, will not be privileged. On the other hand, communications made before proceedings commence but with proceedings in view are privileged. Privilege attaches not 'merely after the summons has been raised, but after it is apparent that there is going to be a litigous contention'.[1] It is enough that litigation is 'threatened or mooted'[2] or that 'the parties are at arm's length or are obviously going to be at arm's length'[3] and so privilege may attach to communications made 'after an accident, and even before any

20 Sheriff ID MacPhail *Research Paper* para 18–24 citing *Anderson v St Andrews' Ambualnce Association* 1942 SC 555 per Lord President Normand at 557 and *Robertson v Lanarkshire Steel Co Ltd* 1955 SLT (Notes) 73.
1 *Admiralty v Aberdeen Steam Trawling & Fishing Co* 1909 SC 335 at 340.
2 *Whitehill v Glasgow Corpn* 1915 SC 1015.
3 *Young v National Coal Board* 1957 SC 99 at 105.

claim has been made'. It is convenient and usual to apply the label *ante litem motam* to the communications which are not privileged and *post litem motam* to those which are privileged but the terminology is not strictly accurate; the test is one of purpose rather than of time. Was the communication made for the purpose of enabling the party to prepare his case?

Reason for privilege; employees' reports following accident

The reason for this privilege rests in the nature of adversary litigation.

> 'It is not only settled in practice, but it is a proper consequence of principle that a litigant, in the course of making preparation for the presentment of his ex parte case is not subject to finding himself having inadvertently made preparation for presentment of the case against him.'[4]

The examples of application of the principle, both where the privilege has been upheld and where it has been denied, are too numerous to be cited. Mention may, however, be made of an apparent exception in relation to the recovery of documents which is the field in which most of the examples occur. A report made by an employee present at the time of an accident and made to his employer at or about that time is recoverable.[5] The rule to that effect is well settled, although it is sometimes criticised as anomalous.[6] It is submitted however, that despite the criticisms the rule can be defended in principle. No doubt many accidents, particularly at work, give rise to claims against employers and to litigation, but quite a number do not. The mere fact that there may be a possibility of litigation is not enough to bring privilege into operation. The purpose of such a report may fairly be supposed to be to inform the employer on whether there are circumstances in which 'it is apparent that there is going to be a litigious contention'. Although the employer may subsequently make use of it in preparation of his defence, its purpose is essentially anterior to that. There is also a practical advantage in that:

> 'if such a report is made as part of routine duty, and is a record of the reporter's immediate reaction before he has had the time, opportunity, or temptation to indulge in too much reflection, it may well contain an unvarnished account of what happened and

4 *Anderson v St Andrews' Ambulance Association* 1942 SC 555 per Lord Moncrieff at 559.

5 *Finlay v Glasgow Corpn* 1915 SC 615; *MacPhee v Glasgow Corpn* 1915 SC 990; *Whitehill v Glasgow Corpn* above; *Brennan v David Lawson Ltd* 1947 SLT (Notes) 47; *Russell v Alexander & Sons Ltd* 1960 SLT (N) 92.

6 Eg *Anderson v St Andrews' Ambulance Association* 1942 SC 555 per Lord Moncrieff at 559.

consequently be of value in the subsequent proceedings as a touchstone of truth.'[7]

PRIVILEGE FOR NEGOTIATIONS FOR SETTLEMENT

Communications, whether by way of admission or otherwise and whether written or oral which have been made by a party to a civil action, or by a solicitor or others acting on his behalf and which have been made for the purpose of obtaining a settlement of the action, or, probably in the case of proceedings between husband and wife for the purpose of effecting reconciliation, are privileged. 'It has' as Dickson says,

> 'repeatedly been held incompetent to prove against a party an admission which he has made in an attempt to compromise the case, for such transactions are commonly arranged upon mutual concessions; and the preliminary negotiations are carried on under the implied condition that they will not be evidence in the event of the attempt being unsuccessful.'[8]

Essentially the same reason is given by Lush J in *La Roche v Armstrong*:

> 'To rule otherwise would in many cases make negotiations for the settlement of litigation almost impossible. Unless parties to such negotiation can feel safe in making an offer and stating the facts on which it is based the door to negotiations may be closed. It is for the benefit of litigants and others that statements should be freely made in order to settle litigation.'[9]

It appears that in England, special significance attaches to the use of the words 'without prejudice'[10] but in Scotland these words have no special significance other than perhaps to make the intention of the writer of the communication clear.

Where privilege not applicable

The privilege applies not only to negotiations after an action has been commenced but to negotiations carried out for the settlement of the dispute before that dispute has become the subject matter of legal proceeding. It does not, however, prevent disclosure of the negotiations

7 *Young v National Coal Board* 1957 SC 99 per Lord Justice-Clerk Thomson at 105.
8 Para 305; *Fyfe v Miller* (1835) 13 S 809; *Williamson v Taylor* (1845) 7 D 842; *Fraser v Wilson* (1842) 4 D 1171; *Morrison v Somerville* (1860) 23 D 232.
9 (1922) 1 KB 489.
10 *Cross* p 408, *Dickson* para 306.

after the merits of the dispute have been disposed of, eg on a question of expenses.[11] It is a consequence of the rationale of the privilege that it applies only to proceedings between the parties concerning the subject matter of the negotiations. It cannot, therefore, be invoked in proceedings between strangers to the negotiations, or between one of the parties and a stranger, or probably where the negotiations are incidentally relevant in a litigation between the parties about some other matter. Nor does the privilege extend to anything said, albeit in the course of negotiations, which is not referable to the subject matter of negotiation[12] or is tendered in evidence for a purpose other than showing that settlement was contemplated. Thus, evidence is admissible of a casual admission not made for the purpose of negotiation, or of an illegal threat.[13] The privilege may be invoked by either party.

Conciliation of matrimonial disputes

There is a corpus of English authority affirming privilege for communications made in the course of conciliation of matrimonial disputes. Thus, in *Pool v Pool*[14] the privilege was held to apply to discussions in counsel's chambers between the parties and with a view to reconciliation and in *Henley v Henley*[15] it was held to apply to a statement made to a clergyman where he was acting as a conciliator even if, as in *Henley*, he made the approach to the parties. The privilege applies, although only one party has made the approach to the conciliator who then communicates with the other party and to direct negotiations between the spouses.[16] It is the privilege of the parties and not of the conciliator and if invoked by either party operates to prevent disclosure by the other, or by the conciliator, or by a third party in whose presence the discussions for conciliation took place.[17] It is still an open question whether this aspect of privilege is part of the law of Scotland. If it is no more than an aspect of the privilege for negotiations for settlement it must follow that it is part of the law of Scotland as of England. Sheriff ID MacPhail has, however, pointed out that negotiations for settlement of a matrimonial

11 See *Cutts v Head* [1984] 1 All ER 597, [1984] 2 WLR 349.
12 *Assessor for Dundee v Elder* 1963 SLT (Notes) 35; *Burns v Burns* 1964 SLT (Sh Ct) 21; *Ware v Edinburgh DC* 1976 SLT (Lands Trib) 21.
13 *Waldridge v Kennison* (1794) 1 Esp 143; *Kurtz and Co v Spence & Sons* (1887) 58 LT 438.
14 [1951] P 470, [1951] 2 All ER 563.
15 [1955] P 202, [1955] 1 All ER 590.
16 *Mole v Mole* [1951] P 21, [1950] 2 All ER 328; cf *Pais v Pais* [1971] P 119 [1970] 3 All ER 491.
17 *Theodoropoulas v Theorodoropoulas* [1964] P 311, [1963] 2 All ER 772; *McTaggart v McTaggart* [1949] P 94, [1948] 2 All ER 754.

dispute are to be distinguished in that they are part of the history of the marriage and so have a relevance to the issues before the court which does not arise in other kinds of dispute.[18] On the other hand, the reason behind the rule, the promotion of reconciliation, is no less strong in Scotland than in England. A spouse who gives evidence of what took place at a conciliation interview impliedly waives the privilege.[19] It is submitted that the privilege does not apply to negotiations concerning the custody of access to, or aliment for, a child because these concern a third party (the child) whose interests are primary and supersede those of the parties and to whose welfare the court is bound to give first and paramount consideration.[20]

PRIVILEGE FOR COMMUNICATIONS BETWEEN HUSBAND AND WIFE

In both civil and criminal cases privilege attaches to communications made during the subsistence of the marriage between husband and wife. This privilege is entirely a creature of statute and, indeed, the question was unlikely to arise before the innovations on the competency as witnesses of the spouses of parties to civil proceedings and accused persons in criminal proceedings effected by the Evidence (Scotland) Act 1853[1] and the Criminal Evidence Act 1898[2] respectively. Both those Acts made special provision for the protection of communications between husband and wife. Questions of the effect of the privilege thereby conferred turn on the interpretation of those Acts.

Distinction between criminal and civil cases

So far as criminal proceedings are concerned, the applicable provisions are now to be found in the Criminal Procedure (Scotland) Act 1975 although the words of the relevant sections[3] merely echo the words of the Criminal Evidence Act 1898 s 1. In civil proceedings it is still necessary to have recourse to the Evidence (Scotland) Act 1853. There is a material difference between the wording for criminal cases and that applicable to civil cases. The Evidence (Scotland) Act 1853 provides

18 *Research Paper* para 18–31.
19 *McTaggart v McTaggart* above.
20 Guardianship of Infants Act 1925 s 1.
1 S 3.
2 S 1.
3 Ss 141(b) and 346(d).

that no husband (wife) shall be competent or compellable to give against his wife (husband) evidence of any matter communicated by her to him during marriage. The words 'competent or compellable' are critical. The consequence of these words is that either spouse may invoke the privilege and, indeed, on a strict interpretation it might appear that it was *pars judicas* to take the objection although the statute has not been so construed. In the statutory provisions for criminal cases there is, on the other hand, no mention of the incompetency of disclosure of communications between husband and wife. There is merely a prohibition against compelling a spouse to disclose any such communication. As a result, in criminal cases it is only the spouse who is giving evidence who can invoke the privilege and if the witness spouse chooses to waive the privilege, the other spouse cannot object.

When privilege not applicable

It seems clearly to follow from the statutory provisions in both civil and criminal cases that third parties may be examined as to matters communicated between a husband and wife in their presence and that where written communication between a husband and wife fall into the hands of third parties, these communications may be produced and used in evidence. As the statutes provide a rule only where a husband gives evidence against his wife or vice versa, there would appear to be no privilege in proceedings to which the spouses are not parties.

Despite the generality of the wording of s 3 of the 1853 Act, the privilege does not apply:

1 where the spouses waive the objection;
2 where the conduct of the spouses and their actings towards one another is the subject matter of the enquiry as in divorce; and[4]
3 where a spouse is examined in the bankruptcy of the other spouse.[5]

When privilege ends

Dickson says that confidences between husband and wife are 'perpetually inviolable and that their confidentiality remains, although the marriage has been dissolved by death or divorce'.[6] If that means, as it appears to, that the privilege subsists after dissolution of the marriage, it is impossible to reconcile with the wording of the Acts which relate to the giving of evidence by spouses of a subsisting marriage. It seems to be

4 *Gallacher v Gallacher* 1934 SC 339; *MacKay v MacKay* 1946 SC 78.
5 *Sawers v Dalgarnie* (1858) 21 D 153. See now Bankruptcy (Scotland) Act 1985 s 47(3).
6 Para 1660.

clear that death or divorce bring the protection which the statutes afford to an end. By parity of reasoning it is not ended by judicial separation.

Evidence of marital intercourse

The law of Scotland knows nothing[7] of the former rule of English law that evidence of spouses as to whether or not they had had marital intercourse did or did not take place between them during any period.[9] (Miscellaneous Provisions) Act 1949, however, provides that a husband or wife shall not be compellable to give evidence of whether marital intercourse did nor did not take place between them during any period.[9] The privilege thus conferred on the witness spouse may be invoked 'in any proceedings'.

BANKERS' PRIVILEGE

By the Bankers' Books Evidence Act 1879[10] a banker or officer of a bank is not compellable in any proceedings to which the bank is not a party to prove matter which can be proved by a copy of an entry in the books, unless by order of a judge made for special cause. Bankers and officers of banks may, therefore, be said to have a privilege in relation to matters falling within that statutory provision. It seems, however, that an officer of a bank is compellable to speak to the accuracy of the copy which may be produced and the privilege is designed to protect banks against the disruption which might be caused to them by call for the recovery of their books rather than to protect them against disclosure of any class of information, or to put bankers or officers of banks in any special category as witnesses.

OTHER CONFIDENTIAL RELATIONSHIPS

There are many relationships within which information passing between the parties to the relationship is regarded as confidential and in which disclosure by the recipient of the information may be a civil wrong. Accountants, bankers and medical practitioners are notable examples of the recipients of such confidential information. While the law respects the confidentiality of these relationships to the extent that disclosure, without the consent of the person to whom the duty of confidentiality is

7 *Burman v Burman* 1930 SC 262; *Brown v Brown* 1972 SC 123.
8 *Russell v Russell* [1944] AC 587.
9 S 7.
10 S 6.

owed, will in most circumstances be a civil wrong, there is no privilege against disclosure where the confidential information or communication is relevant evidence in legal proceedings. It may be said that, with the exception of those privileges already noticed in this chapter which can be brought under the heading of confidentiality, the law does not recognise confidentiality as a ground of privilege. Pleas against disclosure on that ground have been frequently refused.[11] A medical practitioner can be compelled to speak to his observations of his patient's condition and, although there seems to be no reported Scottish decision in point,[12] it is settled practice that he may also be compelled to speak to communications passing between him and his patient. A journalist may not claim privilege in respect of the source of his information.[13] It is, however, proper for the holder of confidential information to decline to give evidence about matters of confidence or to disclose them in proceedings for recovery unless ordered to do so by the court. The court may, in its discretion excuse a witness from answering a question which, although relevant, appears to the court to be unnecessary or not to be useful.[14]

PENITENTIAL COMMUNICATIONS TO CLERGYMAN

The only case in which the possibility of privilege for confidential communications seems still to be an open question is that of communications with a clergyman. Dickson[15] regarded the law as not yet settled when he wrote, and the matter has not been much clarified since then.

Hume said[16] that in a criminal case, no call would probably ever be made on a clergyman to disclose any confession of guilt made by a prisoner preparing for his trial, but that it would be otherwise where the confession formed part of the history of the crime. Alison,[17] who seems not to have understood Hume quite accurately, would have extended the privilege to confessions made to a clergyman at any time in order to unburden conscience and obtain spiritual consolation. Macdonald[18] thought that, unless in very special circumstances, the court would not

11 *McDonald v McDonalds* (1881) 8 R 357; *Elder v English and Scottish Law Life Assurance Co* (1881) 19 SLR 195; *Kinloch v Irvine* (1884) 21 SLR 685; *Foster Alcock & Co v Grangemouth Dockyard Co* (1886) 23 SLR 713.

12 *AB V CD* (1851) 14 D 177 at 180.

13 *HM Advocate v Airs* 1975 SLT 177.

14 Ibid at 180.

15 Para 1684.

16 Hume II 350. Hume appears, however, to have taken the view that strictly there was no privilege (ibid).

17 II 471.

18 Pp 314–15.

think it proper to allow the disclosure of a communing of a strictly religious character and that it would probably be held to be privileged. Of the cases, *Anderson and Marshall*[19] is not properly one of disclosure of a confidential communication to a clergyman as two other persons (Ballies of the Burgh) were present when the confession, which the clergyman was allowed to disclose to the court, was made. A similar comment can be made about *Janet Hope or Walker*[20] in which a confession by the prisoner to her jailor, with whom she had had frequent conversations on religious matters, was held to be inadmissible, but it is not clear that the decision was on the basis of the jailor's possible character as spiritual adviser. Lord Justice-Clerk Hope reserved his opinion on 'how far, where a party voluntary unbosoms himself to a clergyman, that disclosure is to be protected'. That question was argued but not decided in *David Ross*[1] in which evidence was admitted from a prison chaplain that he had asked the accused if he had bought poison, but the chaplain was not allowed to give evidence of the answer to the question. In that case, the evidence could, it seems, have been excluded as an involuntary statement made to a person in authority. In *McLaughlin v Douglas and Kidston*[2] the decision proceeded on the assumption that a confession by a penitent to a priest might be confidential, although, in the circumstances of the case, the priest was held to be compellable to answer the actual question put to him. Lord Moncrieff's dictum in *HM Advocate v Parker*[3] that the plea of confidentiality attached only to statements made to a spouse or to a solicitor does not advance the matter greatly as the question of communications with a clergyman was not before him. The trend of the authorities, although inconclusive, is perhaps on balance towards affirming the privilege.

If there is a privilege, the communication must be of a pentential, or other similar, character which would be regarded as confidential within the relationship; it is not enough that the statement is made to a clergyman. Best CJ said in *Broad v Pitt*[4] 'I, for one, will never compel a clergyman to disclose communications made to him by a prisoner; but if he chooses to disclose them I shall receive them in evidence' but, despite that, any privilege is almost certainly that of the person who communicated with the clergyman and not of the clergyman himself. Problems of

19 (1728) Hume II 335. Hume questions the propriety of allowing the disclosure in that case (ibid).
20 (1845) 2 Broun 465.
1 (1859) 3 Irv IRV 434.
2 (1863) 4 Irv 273.
3 1944 JC 49 at 52.
4 (1828) 3 C & P 518.

definition remain. It may be possible to define a 'clergyman' for this purpose as the holder of an office in a religious organisation who in virtue of his office receives penitential communications but there is, perhaps, some arbitrariness in stopping short of spiritual confidants such as the jailor in *Janet Hope or Walker*.

PUBLIC INTEREST IMMUNITY

Evidence is excluded where disclosure would be against the public interest. This topic was formerly discussed under the heading of Crown Privilege, but that is now regarded as an inept description for two reasons:

1 although it is typically information in the hands of government departments and other agencies of the Crown that is protected, the protection extends to information possessed by local authorities and other public bodies unconnected with the Crown where disclosure would damnify the public interest. Persons other than the Crown may, therefore, seek to have evidence excluded on this ground and that is so even if it is a matter of national importance, in which they have no direct interest, that is at stake; and

2 there is properly no question of privilege vested in the Crown or anyone else. It is *pars judicis* to see that the public interest is protected.[5] The Crown, or other body or person with a relevant public responsibility may, where not a party, intervene in order to have the rule invoked but the matter may also be raised by a party with no such responsibility. Because there is no privilege, there can also be no waiver in the strict sense. 'Public interest immunity is not a privilege which may be waived by the Crown or by any party.'[6]

In most circumstances, however, it will be difficult to assert a public interest in non-disclosure where the public body possessed of the information is content that it should be disclosed and if there should be voluntary extrajudicial disclosure it will then become even more difficult to maintain that its use in evidence is against the public interest. Cases can, however, occur in which a public body which is the repository of information to which public interest immunity attaches itself wishes to make use of that information in legal proceedings. If the question were one of privilege, there could be no

5 *Duncan v Cammell Laird & Co Ltd* [1942] AC 624 per Lord Simon at 641.
6 *Air Canada v Secretary of State for Trade (No 2)* [1983] 2 AC 394 per Lord Fraser at 436, [1983] 1 All ER 910 at 917.

bar to its doing so but, under the rule of public interest immunity, it may be restrained. Such a case occurred in *Hehir v Commissioner of Police of the Metropolis*[7] where the plaintiff, in an action for alleged false imprisonment and malicious prosecution on the part of the police, successfully objected to his being cross-examined on a statement he had made for the purposes of a police enquiry. The whole subject matter of the enquiry was immune from disclosure because of the public interest in encouraging candour and the Commissioner of Police had no authority to set that immunity aside. It has, however, been suggested that where a public interest immunity exists for the benefit of a third party (whose goodwill it is in the public interest to maintain) that party may waive the immunity. That again can be said not to be a true case of waiver because, where the beneficiary is content that there should be disclosure, there is no longer a public interest in secrecy.[8] Thus, there is a general public interest that sources of police information should remain confidential but, if a particular informer is content that his identity should be revealed, there is no longer a public interest in non-disclosure so far as he is concerned.

Ministerial certificate

Where, as is the common case, objection to disclosure is taken on behalf of the Crown, a certificate will be granted by a minister, or, in some cases, by a Permanent Under-Secretary, stating the grounds on which immunity is claimed. A ministerial certificate should not be lightly granted.

In *Robinson v State of South Australia*[9] Lord Blanesburgh said:

> 'The privilege is a narrow one most sparingly to be exercised. The foundation is that the information cannot be disclosed without injury to the public interest and not that that documents are confidential or official which alone is no reason for the non-production. The fact that the production might in the particular litigation prejudice the Crown's own case or assist that of the other side is no such "plain overriding principle of the public interest" as to justify any claim for privilege. In truth the fact that the documents if produced might have any such effect upon the fortunes of the litigation is of itself a compelling reason for their production, one only to be overcome by the gravest considerations of state policy or security.'

7 [1982] 2 All ER 335, [1982] 1 WLR 715.
8 [1982] 2 All ER 335 at 341, [1982] 1 WLR 715 at 723.
9 [1931] AC 704.

Nor is it a good ground for a ministerial certificate if:

> 'the consequences of disclosure might involve the department or the government in parliamentary discussion, or in public criticism, or might necessitate the attendance as witnesses or otherwise of officials who have pressing duties elsewhere. It is not enough that the minister of the department does not want to have the documents produced. The minister, in deciding whether it is his duty to object, should bear these considerations in mind, for he ought not to take the responsibility of withholding production except in cases where the public interest would otherwise be damnified, eg where disclosure would be injurious to national defence or good diplomatic relations, or where the practice of keeping a class of document secret is necessary for the proper functioning of the public service.'[10]

Ministerial certificate not conclusive

Although stringent tests for the granting of a certificate were laid down by the courts, it was at one time the law of England that the Minister was the sole judge of whether those tests were satisfied. A ministerial certificate was automatically effective. Dicta in *Duncan v Cammell Laird* had been to the effect that the same rule applied in Scotland, but in *Glasgow Corpn v Central Land Board*[11] it was held that the court had an inherent power to overrule the ministerial objection where the interests of justice, as balanced against the other aspects of the public interest, so required. The law of England has now been brought into line with the law of Scotland by *Conway v Rimmer*[12] in which the House of Lords reversed its own previous decision in *Duncan v Cammell Laird.* Where, however, a ministerial certificate is granted, it is only for weighty reasons that it will be overridden.

Distinction between 'class' and 'contents' cases

In *Rogers v Secretary of State for the Home Department*[13] Lord Salmon said:

> 'There are also classes of documents and information which for years have been recognised by the law as entitled in the public interest to be immune from disclosure. In such cases the affidavit

10 *Duncan v Cammell Laird & Co Ltd* [1942] AC 624.
11 1956 SC (HL) 1.
12 [1968] AC 910.
13 [1973] AC 388 at 412, [1972] 2 All ER 1057 at 1071; cf *Conway v Rimmer* [1968] AC 910 at 952, [1968] 1 All ER 874 at 888 per Lord Reid.

> or certificate of a minister is hardly necessary. I refer to such documents as Cabinet Minutes, minutes of discussions between Heads of Government Departments and despatches from ambassadors abroad.'

A distinction has, accordingly, been made between cases where a document belongs to a protected class and cases where protection is sought because of the particular information contained in a document. The distinction is not, however, one of principle and even Cabinet papers are not automatically immune.[14] In both cases, a balance may have to be struck between the merits of disclosure in the interests of justice and the merits of maintaining secrecy from the other standpoints of public interest at stake and, in both cases, the court, if in doubt, may inspect the documents privately.[15] No doubt new classes of protected documents may be developed but the primary question in most 'class' cases is whether the class for which protection is claimed falls into, or is analagous to a recognised category. There may, however, be further questions of whether the documents do properly come within the class and of whether proper consideration has been given to the necessity for protection against disclosure in the particular case. On those issues, except perhaps the last, the ministerial certificate can add little to what the court can ascertain for itself, if necessary, by inspection of the documents. In cases, however, in which protection is claimed on the ground of the particular contents of the document, the ministerial certificate is central to the estimation of the hazard to the public interest involved.

Oral evidence; interrelation with rules on recovery

Questions of public interest immunity most often arise in relation to recovery of documents but the immunity also applies to the giving of oral evidence and to the use of documents in evidence.[16] Where a minister certifies that the disclosure of a document is contrary to the public interest, he may make a similar certification in respect of the giving of oral evidence about the matters to which the document relates. In questions of recovery of documents, the general rules on recovery operate along with, and may sometimes obscure, the rules on public interest immunity. Thus, although the latter were much debated in the

14 *Air Canada v Secretary of State for Trade (No 2)* [1983] 2 AC 394 at 432, [1983] 1 All ER 910 at 915 per Lord Fraser.

15 Ibid. Cf *Burmah Oil Co Ltd v Bank of England* (1980) AC 1090 per Lord Edmund Davies at 1129.

16 See *Hehir v Commissioner of Police for the Metropolis* [1982] 2 All ER 335, [1982] 1 WLR 715.

Air Canada v Secretary of State for Trade (No 2)[17] it is thought that the question on which the decision ultimately turned, that the plaintiff could not show that the documents would support his own case was an English procedural rule on discovery rather than a rule of public interest immunity.

Governmental interests protected

Matters of vital national importance are clear cases for upholding public interest immunity. Older cases in which the decision was against disclosure of information concerning military campaigns,[18] or the design of submarines in time of war would,[19] no doubt, still be followed although the absolute character which they attached to the ministerial certificate is no longer the law. Generally, that will be true of all those affairs of state in which the need for secrecy is well recognised and a ministerial certificate that such an interest is jeopardised is unlikely to be overridden. But in Australia it has been held that the fact that documents are held by the intelligence services of the state is not in itself a source of automatic immunity.[20] In areas where there is no such central national interest and immunity is claimed on some less obvious ground which is said to be essential for the functioning of the public service, the development of the law since *Glasgow Corpn v Central Land Board* and, more especially since *Conway v Rimmer* has been such that many of the older cases must now be regarded as less authoritative. To that, the observations of Lord Keith of Kinkel in *Burmah Oil Co Ltd v Bank of England* are apt:[1]

> 'There can be descerned in modern times a trend towards more open governmental methods than were prevalent in the past. No doubt it is for parliament and not for courts of law to say how far that trend should go. The courts are, however, concerned with the consideration that it is in the public interest that justice should be done and should be publicly recognised as having been done. The law may demand, no doubt only in a very limited number of cases, that the inner workings of government should be exposed to public gaze.'

In that case, Lord Denning MR had said:

> 'Now I can understand that privilege in regard to high questions of state policy, such as those dealing with foreign affairs or the

17 [1983] AC 394, [1983] 1 All ER 910.
18 *Asiatic Petroleum Co Ltd v Anglo-Persian Oil Co Ltd* [1916] 1KB 822.
19 *Duncan v Cammell Laird & Co Ltd* [1942] AC 624.
20 *Alister v R* (1983) 50 ALR 41.
1 [1980] AC 1090 at 1134.

> defence or security of the realm. But I do not think it should be extended to commercial transactions undertaken by the government or Bank of England.'[2]

The House of Lords, however, considered that the formulation of policy on such matters as 'part of the inner working of the government machine'[3] was an appropriate ground for the claim of public interest immunity although it seems that the claim would not have prevailed had the documents, in fact, been necessary for the just disposal of the cause.

Norwich Pharmacal Co v Customs & Excise Commissioners[4] and *Alfred Crompton Amusement Machines Ltd v Customs & Excise Commissioners*[5] both concerned information which came into the possession of the Commissioners in connection with the performance of their statutory duties. In the former case disclosure was ordered, and, in the latter case refused. The main point of distinction seems to have been that in the *Norwich Pharmacal* case the third parties, about whom the information was sought, were wrongdoers and so the House of Lords held that disclosure of their names could not be adverse to the proper administration of the Customs service nor to the legitimate interests of the person concerned for which confidentiality might have been claimed in the public interest. Those features were not present in the *Alfred Crompton Amusement Machines Ltd* case which concerned confidential communications with third parties against whom no wrong was alleged. The cases are illustrative of the principle enunciated in *Burmah Oil Co Ltd v The Bank of England*[6] that the burden of making out a claim for immunity may be very heavy (although the ministerial certificate may go a long way to discharging it) but that once the balancing stage has been reached the scales must tip decisively in favour of disclosure before it will be ordered.

Criminal investigations; police reports and information

The investigations at the instance of the Crown with a view to criminal prosecution are generally immune but the court will order production of Crown precognitions where withholding them would manifestly cause injustice and there is no special reason of state requiring them to be protected.[7] There appears to be no automatic, or even prima facie protection of the names of persons who have given information to the Crown but the Lord Advocate will not be required to divulge them if he

2 [1979] 1 WLR 473 at 486.
3 [1980] AC 1090 at 1144 per Lord Scarman.
4 [1974] AC 133, [1973] 2 All ER 943, [1973] 3 WLR 164.
5 [1974] AC 405, [1973] 2 All ER 1169.
6 [1980] AC 1090 at 1125 and 1127, [1979] 3 All ER at 717 and 719.
7 *Dickson* paras 1654 and 1655 and cases cited there.

states that it would be prejudicial to the public service to do so.[8] The protection is less strict than that accorded in England where, in civil proceedings 'sources of police information are a judicially recognised class of evidence excluded on the grounds of public policy'.[9] The Scottish authorities are, however, old and not easily reconciled with more recent authorities on the irrecoverability of police reports. In *Carmichael v SCWS Ltd*[10] Lord Wark said that as a deceased police officer who had made a report could have been cited as a witness had he been alive, production of his report could not affect the public interest more than his giving oral evidence would have done, but that view was disapproved in *Rogers v Orr*[11] and in *McKie v Western SMT Co*[12] Lord President Cooper said:

> 'It seems to me to be indispensible to the efficient working of the system of detection and prosecution of crime in Scotland that the officers making such reports or communications should know when they are making them that they are protected by absolute immunity from the risk of subsequent disclosure. The only method of securing absolute candour and freedom in the making of such reports—and without these qualities their value is largely destroyed—is an absolute guarantee against publication.'

As a matter of practice, the police will generally supply an abstract from the report of an incident giving names of witnesses and other particulars and will themselves generally consent to the precognosced.

Although police reports will usually be immune from disclosure they, as well as other information in the hands of the police for which protection may be sought, are subject to the general rules on public interest immunity. Thus, in *Rogers v Secretary of State for the Home Department*[13] disclosure was refused of documents relating to a letter written by a police officer to the Gaming Board which the plaintiff claimed to be defamatory of him, not on the ground that the letter was a police document but because its production might jeopardise the working of the public service. Similarly, in *Neilson v Laugharne*[14] where disclosure was sought of statements made for the purpose of a police

8 *Dickson* paras 1652 and 1653, Hume II 135, Burnett 313; Alison II 94. *Henderson v Robertson* (1853) 15 D 292.

9 *Rogers v Secretary of State for the Home Department* [1973] AC 388 at 407, [1972] 2 All ER 1057 at 1067 per Lord Simon of Glaisdale; cf *D v NSPCC* [1978] AC 171 per Lord Simon of Glaisdale at 241; *Marks v Beyfus* [1890] 25 QBD 494.

10 1934 SLT 158.

11 1939 SC 492.

12 1952 SC 206 at 215.

13 [1978] AC 388, [1972] 2 All ER 1507.

14 [1981] QB 736, [1981] 1 All ER 829.

disciplinary enquiry, the Court of Appeal held that in every case the test was whether disclosure would inhibit the performance of the statutory function in question. The principle is reconcilable with *Conway v Rimmer*[15] although the result is in some contrast. The plaintiff in that case had been dismissed from the police force after having been unsuccessfully prosecuted for theft. He sued on the ground of malicious prosecution and disclosure was, on his application, ordered both of probationary reports on him and of a report to the Director of Public Prosecutions about the circumstances of the alleged thefts. The probation reports were regarded as routine documents and secrecy for the report to the Director of Public Prosecution was not essential after the prosecution had been completed. Any public interest in their non-disclosure could not prevail against their critical importance for the doing of justice in the case.

Extension beyond agencies of central government

'The categories of public interest are not closed and must alter from time to time whether by restriction or extension as social conditions and social legislation develop.[16]

The perception embodied in the above principle may be taken as the basis of the modern development of public interest immunity beyond interests protected by agencies of the Crown. A claim made by a local authority or other public body in respect of a matter which, although in its hands, involves questions of national public interest against disclosure, may be supported by a ministerial certificate and fall to be treated in the same way as other cases of national interest. In other cases, however, the burden of showing a case of immunity will not easily be discharged. That the interests of the local authority or other body are affected is not in itself sufficient.[17] There must be a recognised public interest of general importance at stake. And even where there is such an interest, it will be more readily outweighed than in the case of vital interests of state by the importance of disclosure in the interests of justice.[18] A claim has, however, been upheld in relation to information given to a local authority to enable it to discharge its statutory duties in relation to the care of children[19] and, in *D v NSPCC*[20] disclosure was refused where the plaintiff sought information as to the identity of an

15 [1968] AC 910, [1968] 1 All ER 874.
16 *D v NSPCC* [1978] AC 171 at 230, [1977] 1 All ER 589 at 605.
17 [1978] AC 171 at 245, [1977] 1 All 589 at 618 per Lord Edmund Davies commenting on *Blackpool Corpn v Locker* [1948] 1 QB 349, [1948] 1 All ER 85.
18 See *Campbell v Tameside Metropolitan BC* [1982] QB 1065, [1982] 2 All ER 791.
19 *Re D (Infants)* [1970] 1 All ER 1088, [1970] 1 WLR 599.
20 [1978] AC 171, [1977] 1 All ER 589.

informant who had given the Society unfounded information about the alleged ill-treatment by the plaintiff of her daughter. The Society had a statutory power, although not a duty, to bring care proceedings in respect of children and the immunity was upheld largely by analogy with the immunity of police informers. At the same time, the view that public interest immunity was confined to the organs of central government was explicitly rejected. Those cases all show the maintenance of confidentiality as an aspect of the public interest in some circumstances, but the mere fact that a public body is possessed of confidential information does not confer an immunity. Thus in *Science Research Council v Nasse*[1] a case of alleged discrimination in relation to employment, a claim for public interest immunity was rejected in respect of confidential reports upon successful applicants for the post in respect of which discrimination was alleged. Even if the employer was a public body, the interest in question was of a private, and not a public, nature.

Applicability to criminal cases

In principle, public interest immunity applies to criminal cases as well as to civil. It has, however, been said that 'if medical documents, or indeed other documents, are relevant to the defence in criminal proceedings, Crown privilege should not be claimed'[2] and that is applicable even to prosecutions for minor offences. But that is an admonition as to practice, not a rule of law. Crown privilege has been sustained where a vital national interest was at stake.[3] It is submitted, however, that in such cases, the non-availability, through no fault of his own, of evidence which might have assisted the accused's defence is a matter to be taken into account on a consideration of whether there is reasonable doubt as to his guilt. Where no such vital national interest is at stake, the balance will nearly always fall in favour of disclosure. So, in England, the protection afforded against disclosure of the identity of police informers does not obtain where the information is required to establish innocence in a criminal trial,[4] and, in Scotland, a conviction has been quashed where the trial court had upheld an objection by a police officer to disclosing the name of his informant.[5]

1 [1980] AC 1028, [1979] 3 All ER 673, [1979] 3 WLR 762.
2 *Conway v Rimmer* [1968] AC 910 at 942, [1968] 1 All ER 874 at 881 per Lord Reid quoting the Lord Chancellor at 197 HL Official Report (5th series) col 745.
3 *R v Hardy* (1794) 24 State Tr 199; *R v Watson* (1817) 32 State Tr (1); *R v Cubbett* (1831) 2 State Tr NS 789 and *R v O'Connor* (1846) 4 St Tr NS 935.
4 *Rogers v Secretary of State for the Home Department* [1973] AC 388 at 407, [1972] 2 All ER 1057 at 1067 per Lord Simon of Glaisdale.
5 *Thomson v Neilson* (1900) 3 F (J) 3.

CHAPTER 7

Inadmissibility of evidence: evidence irregularly obtained; statements made on precognition

EVIDENCE IRREGULARLY OBTAINED

Documents which are required for use in evidence in civil cases are recovered by commission and diligence. Where an object, other than a document, is required for use in evidence the court may grant an order for its exhibition or, if it cannot be brought to court, for its inspection.[1] In criminal cases, the Crown recovers documents and objects by means of a warrant to search which may be included in the warrant to arrest, or a special search warrant specifying the things to be seized and the places to be searched. The accused recovers by petition to the court for an order to recover and, in the case of recovery of documents, that order will be for commission and diligence similar to that granted in civil cases.[2] Documents and real evidence are regularly recovered if they are obtained under any of those procedures or if they otherwise come legitimately into the possession of the party who wishes to produce them as where he is the owner or has obtained them for purposes of production with the owner's consent. It may, however, happen that the party who wishes to produce a document or object has obtained it clandestinely from the owner, or has obtained it by violent means or in purported reliance on a diligence or warrant but in excess of the powers granted. In those cases, recovery is said to be irregular and questions arise of whether the document or object can be produced and used in evidence.

Civil cases

The law on the effect of irregular recovery in civil cases is unsettled. In *Rattray v Rattray*[3] a letter which the pursuer had stolen from the Post

1 See *MacTaggart v MacKillop* 1938 SLT 594.
2 *Downie v HM Advocate* 1952 JC 37; *Hasson v HM Advocate* 1971 SLT 199.
3 (1897) 25 R 315.

Office was admitted at the proof before the Lord Ordinary without objection. In the Inner House, however, the question of its admissibility was raised. The case is not an authority on the admissibility of illegally obtained evidence because, although opinions were expressed, a decision on the point was not necessary for the decision on the merits, and the admissibility of the document could, in any event, be defended on the ground that objection had not been taken timeously. Two of the four Inner House judges were, however, of the opinion that the letter was admissible on inter alia the general ground, as put by Lord Trayner, that 'the policy of the law in later years (and I think a good policy) has been to admit almost all evidence which will throw light on disputed facts and enable justice to be done'.[4] The opposite argument was put by Lord Young, 'I think that the court is bound to take notice of the statute law enacting that the pursuer's conduct was a crime . . . and to reject as evidence anything obtained by a violation of the law and still held by the person who did that act'.[5]

In a number of subsequent cases, evidence which may have been irregularly obtained was admitted without objection[6] and in *MacColl v MacColl*[7] Lord Moncrieff felt constrained reluctantly and, it is felt, unnecessarily, to follow the opinions in *Rattray* in favour of admissibility. In *Duke of Argyll v Duchess of Argyll* Lord Wheatley had, at an interlocutory stage,[8] felt similarly constrained, but when at the proof he held that stolen diaries were admissible in evidence, he did so after considering the authorities in criminal cases which, as is discussed later, reject the view that irregularity or illegality of recovery is irrelevant to admissibility. 'There is' Lord Wheatley said, applying the law as stated by Lord Justice General Cooper in *Lawrie v Muir*:

> 'no absolute rule, it being a question of the particular circumstances of each case determining whether a particular piece of evidence should be admitted or not. Among the circumstances which may have to be taken into account are the nature of the evidence concerned, the purpose for which it is used in evidence, the manner in which it is obtained, whether its introduction is fair to the party from whom it has been illegally obtained and whether its admission will in fairness throw light on disputed facts and enable justice to be done.'[9]

4 Ibid at 318–19.
5 Ibid at 320.
6 *MacNeill v MacNeill* 1929 SLT 251; *Turner v Turner* 1930 SLT 393; *Watson v Watson* 1934 SC 374.
7 1946 SLT 312, 1946 SN 80.
8 1962 SC 140.
9 1963 SLT (Notes) 42.

Indeed, as Lord Wheatley recognised, it may be appropriate to take a narrower view of admissibility in civil than in criminal cases. In criminal cases, the view can be maintained that the public interest in the conviction of those guilty of crime should not be prejudiced merely because of excess on the part of a public officer and that the courts should be slow to reject evidence indicative of guilt on the grounds of such excess unless the reliability of the evidence is tainted by the means by which it was recovered or there are other compelling reasons for its rejection. In civil cases, on the other hand, there would seem to be little objection to a general rule that a party should not gain an advantage by his own wrong. In actions concerning status, of which all the cases mentioned are examples, a broader approach, approximating to the rule in criminal cases and therefore still falling short of unqualified admissibility, may be justified.

Criminal cases

The general principle

Subject to a discretion to exclude, at one time very restricted[10] but enlarged by the Police and Criminal Evidence Act 1984,[11] the rule of English law in criminal as well as in civil cases, is that the court is not concerned with how relevant evidence has been obtained and that it is, therefore, admissible despite any irregularity in its recovery.[12] The only exceptions appear to be evidence which cannot be produced without reference to an inadmissible confession and evidence obtained in contempt of court.[13] At least, since 1949, Scots law has followed a different course.[14]

The starting point was *HM Advocate v McGuigan*[15] in 1936. Lord Justice-Clerk Aitchison held that the police had been entitled to act without delay and without a warrant when they searched the tent of the accused shortly after his arrest, in connection with charges of murder, rape and theft. There was, therefore, no irregularity. The Lord Justice-Clerk went on, however, to say that, if there had been an irregularity, it would not have followed that the evidence would have been inadmissible.

10 *R v Sang* [1980] AC 402, [1979] 1 All ER 122.
11 S 78.
12 *Kuruma Son of Kaniu v R* [1955] AC 197, [1955] 1 All ER 236.
13 *Cross on Evidence* (6th edn) p 432.
14 See J W R Gray 'The Admissibility of Evidence Illegally Obtained in Scotland', 1966 Jur Rev 1 to which the author acknowledges his indebtedness.
15 1936 JC 16, 1936 SLT 161.

> 'An irregularity in the obtaining of evidence does not *necessarily* make that evidence inadmissible ... Rules as to saerch and warrant must, no doubt be strictly observed and never lightly departed from; but, on the other hand, they must always be reasonably interpreted in the light of the circumstances of the particular case.'[16]

Those words were taken up by Lord Justice General Cooper in the later Full Bench case of *Lawrie v Muir*[17] in which he referred to the need to take into consideration two conflicting interests:

> '(a) the interest of the citizen to be protected from illegal or irregular invasions of his liberties by the authorities, and (b) the interest of the state to secure that evidence bearing upon the commission of crime and necessary to enable justice to be done shall not be withheld from courts of law on any mere informal or technical ground.'[18]

There is, therefore, a balance to be struck between the interest of the citizen and interest of the state and the use of the words 'does not *necessarily* make that evidence inadmissible' in *McGuigan* had shown there was no absolute rule.

> 'Irregularities require to be excused, and infringements of the formalities of the law in relation to these matters are not likely to be condoned. Whether any given irregularity ought to be excused depends upon the nature of the irregularity and the circumstances under which it was committed. In particular, the case may bring into play the discretionary principle of fairness to the accused which has been developed so fully in our law in relation to the admission in evidence of confessions or admissions by a person suspected or charged with crimes. That principle would obviously require consideration in any case in which the departure from the strict procedure had been adopted deliberately with a view to securing the admission of evidence obtained by an unfair trick. ... On the other hand to take an extreme example figured in argument, it would usually be wrong to exclude some highly incriminating production in a murder trial merely because it was found by a police officer in the course of a search authorised for a different purpose or before a proper warrant had been obtained.'[19]

16 Ibid at 18 italics supplied.
17 1950 JC 19, 1950 SLT 37.
18 Ibid at 26.
19 Ibid at 27.

The result is that there is an inclusionary discretion to be exercised on a consideration of whether the irregularity can be excused and of fairness to the accused. Prima facie evidence irregularly obtained is inadmissible but it may be admitted if the irregularity can be excused and its admission would not prejudice a fair trial for the accused.

Reconciliation of interests

The basis of reconciliation of conflicting interests adopted in *Lawrie v Muir* has been influential beyond Scotland and has been widely approved, but it has left uncertainties as an examination of *Lawrie v Muir* and subsequent cases shows. In *Lawrie v Muir* evidence was held to be inadmissible which had been obtained as a result of a search by inspectors of a company whose function it was to secure the return of milk bottles to their rightful owners. The search had been carried out in good faith under warrants issued by the Scottish Milk Marketing Board for the inspection of premises of distributors with whom the Board had contracts. The accused had no contract with the Board but had allowed the inspectors to examine her premises when they produced their warrants to her. The search was, therefore, irregular in that it proceeded on a bona fide but false representation of authority. The facts bear some resemblance to those in *Fairley v Fishmongers of London*[20] where evidence obtained as the result of a search by an inspector employed by private prosecutors was held to be admissible. The inspector had no warrant but was accompanied by an official of the Ministry of Food who held a warrant entitling him to enter premises in connection with the enforcement of food regulations but had no concern with the legislation dealing with the possession of unclean salmon with which the inspector of the private prosecutors was concerned and under which the prosecution was brought. The distinction between the two cases is not easy to draw. Reference is made in *Fairley* to the absence of any deliberate departure from strict procedure in order to obtain evidence by an unfair trick but in *Lawrie* too, there had been neither a deliberate departure nor an unfair trick. Possible points of distinction are that in *Fairley* a warrant could probably have been obtained had it been sought and that the offence was more serious than in *Lawrie*. But it is a dangerous principle to say that irregularities can be condoned where compliance would have been easy, or that the more serious the crime, the less weight need be given to the irregularity. In *McGovern v HM Advocate*[1] there was a technical assault when finger-scrapings were obtained from an accused person who was under suspicion of breaking into an office and blowing

20 1951 JC 14, 1951 SLT 54.
1 1950 JC 33, 1950 SLT 133.

open a safe with explosives but who had not, at the time the scrapings were taken, been formally apprehended or charged. It was held that the irregularity could not be excused and that the evidence was inadmissible. But the scrapings could lawfully have been taken only a short time later and could have been taken at the time if the requisite procedures had been followed. The distinction between that case and *Fairley*, in which it was said that the inspector could have obtained a warrant if he had applied for one, is slight.

In *HM Advocate v Turnbull*,[2] the premises of the accused, who was an accountant, were searched under a warrant relating to charges of making fraudulent income tax returns. A large number of documents, which were not examined at the time, were recovered and passed to the Inland Revenue Authorities for examination. As a result, further charges were brought arising from documents which had been recovered and unrelated to the original charges. At the trial objection was taken to the admission of these documents and the objection was sustained. There was, it was said, no urgency and it was not a case of documents having been incidentally recovered in the course of a lawful search, but a mass of material which was not plainly incriminating had been abstracted and deliberately retained for examination.

> 'The examination of private papers in the hope of finding incriminating material was interference with the rights of the citizen. Therefore to hold that evidence so obtained was admissible would . . . tend to nullify the protection afforded to a citizen by the requirement of a magistrate's warrant, and would offer a positive inducement to the authorities to proceed by irregular methods.'[3]

A comparison may be made with *HM Advocate v Hepper*.[4] The accused had consented to the search of his house in connection with a matter other than that with which he was eventually charged. At his trial, objection was taken to evidence about the finding of an attaché case which was relevant to the trial but unconnected with the purpose for which the search had taken place. The primary ground of decision was that there was no irregularity as urgency justified the course taken and the article had been found incidentally in the course of a lawful search. Even if it was not plainly incriminating, it was, it was said, of a very suspicious character. In these circumstances the evidence was admissible even if, contrary to the primary ground of decision, it was irregularly obtained.

2 1951 JC 96, 1951 SLT 409.
3 Ibid at 103.
4 1958 JC 39, 1958 SLT 160.

Guidelines

It is probably inevitable that there should be fine distinctions in any attempt to reconcile interests which are not commensurable or easy to compare. The uncertainty of debatable cases on the borderline may be regretted but that uncertainty does not undermine the utility or the justice of a rule which requires irregularity to be excused and due consideration given to fairness to the accused before evidence irregularly obtained is admitted. Some guidelines emerge:

(a) Urgency goes primarily to justification[5] but where it is insufficient to justify, it may be an element in excuse.[6]

(b) That the irregularity was due to mistake or oversight rather than deliberate intent is favourable to, although not conclusive of, excuse.[7]

(c) A deliberate irregularity, even if it consists in no more than the retention and examination of papers which fall outwith a warrant will usually be fatal to excuse.[8]

(d) Incriminating evidence, or evidence of a very suspicious character, is admissible where it is found incidentally to a lawful search, although extraneous to the purposes of the search, either because (i) its recovery is justifiable where urgency so requires, or (ii) its recovery without further procedure is excusable.[9]

(e) That the defect which gave rise to the irregularity was readily curable, is relevant to excuse but is not always sufficient.[10]

(f) The seriousness of the offence is relevant to excuse but its role in that connection may be ambiguous and has to be seen in the light of the other circumstances.[11]

EVIDENCE RESULTING FROM INADMISSIBLE CONFESSION

Inadmissible confessions are a species of evidence irregularly obtained. They are, however, subject to special rules which have been discussed earlier.[12] A problem remains of the admissibility of evidence discovered as a result of an inadmissible confession. That evidence may take the form of documentary or real evidence, or of facts observed.

5 *McGuigan v HM Advocate* 1936 JC 16, 1936 SLT 161.
6 Dicta in *Lawrie v Muir* 1950 JC 19, 1950 SLT 37. Cf *HM Advocate v Hepper* above.
7 *Fairley v Fishmongers of London* 1951 JC 14, 1951 SLT 54, but cf *Lawrie v Muir* above.
8 *HM Advocate v Turnbull* 1951 JC 96, 1951 SLT 409.
9 *HM Advocate v Hepper* 1958 JC 39, 1958 SLT 160.
10 *Fairley v Fishmongers of London* above, but cf *McGovern v HM Advocate* 1950 JC 33, 1950 SLT 133.
11 *Lawrie v Muir* 1950 JC 19, 1950 SLT 37, *Fairley v Fishmongers of London* 1951 JC 14, 1951 SLT 54.
12 Ch 3 above.

In *Chalmers v HM Advocate*[13] a youth, in response to police questioning took the police to a field and pointed out a location at which a purse was found. The finding of the purse was incriminatory of the youth only if considered in the context of the youth's actings. Those actings were held to be assertive conduct against the youth's interest (ie the equivalent of a confession) and to be involuntary and inadmissible. The decision is authority for the view that the obtaining of evidence as a consequence of a confession, or its equivalent in conduct, does not, even if the evidence is confirmatory of the confession, render an otherwise inadmissible confession admissible. Nor can the consequent evidence be admitted along with evidence that it was obtained as a result of what the accused had said without specifying the content of the statement for that is to invite the jury to speculate as to what the accused has said. *Chalmers* does not, however, decide whether evidence obtained as a result of an inadmissible confession is admissible if it has relevance independently of the confession because the finding of the purse in *Chalmers* had no such relevance. It is submitted that where there is independent relevance in the consequent evidence, that evidence is admissible.

If a person on whom suspicion has centred is interrogated by the police otherwise than for such limited purposes as the clarification of statements he has already made, the evidence so obtained will be inadmissible, but the inadmissibility of the evidence does not make the interrogation as such improper. Indeed, as pointed out by the Thomson committee[14] it may be the duty of the police to pursue questioning of that kind, eg for the purpose of discovering the whereabouts of a missing child or stolen property. The answers to the questions will be inadmissible but it does not follow that the evidence to which those answers lead should also be inadmissible. The problem is, it is submitted, to be resolved in the same way as the admissibility of evidence irregularly obtained. The interrogation of a suspect solely for the purpose of obtaining answers which will lead to evidence incriminatory of him may be unjustifiable. The use at the suspect's trial of evidence so obtained offends just as much as the direct use of his answers against the maxim *nemo debet prodere se ipsum*. But if the questioning is justifiable, as may be the case where it has some other object, the fact that incidentally leads are obtained to evidence incriminatory of the accused, does not render that evidence inadmissible. Or there may be circumstances in which the questioning although strictly irregular can be excused. Again, evidence to which that questionning leads but which has relevance independently of the questionning or the answers to it may be admissible. That view

13 1954 JC 66.

coincides, it is thought, with the conclusion of the Thomson committee[14] that evidence recovered as a result of inadmissible confessions might be admitted provided (a) the prosecution does not disclose in evidence the source of the information and (b) the information was not obtained by methods which the court decides are unfair in the circumstances.

STATEMENTS MADE ON PRECOGNITION

Admissibility of precognition

In *McNeillie v HM Advocate*,[15] Lord Justice General Clyde expressed disapproval of the cross-examination of a witness about statements he had made 'under the confidential circumstances of precognition' and the generally accepted modern practice is that statements made on precognition are not admissible in evidence.[16] Before considering this question further it is necessary to distinguish two senses in which the word precognition may be used: (a) the act of ascertaining from a potential witness what his evidence is likely to be; and (b) the document in which the precognoscer's account of what the potential witness is likely to say is recorded.[17] Lord Justice-Clerk Thomson was using the word in the latter sense when he said:

> 'one reason why reference to precognition is frowned on, is that in a precognition you cannot be sure that you are getting what the potential witness has to say in a pure and undefiled form. It is filtered through the mind of another, whose job it is to put what he thinks the witness means into a form suitable for use in judicial proceedings. This process tends to colour the results. Precognoscers as a rule appear to be gifted with a measure of optimism which no amount of disillusionment can damp.'[18]

The general inadmissibility of a witness's precognition in that sense requires little argument. It is usually not an account of what the witness has actually said but is the precognoscer's reconstruction or interpretation. Moreover it is not the original evidence of what the witness said to the precognoscer but is, in the technical if not in the etymological

14 Department Committee on Criminal Procedure in Scotland (2nd Report) 1975 Cmnd 6218, para 7.27.
15 1929 JC 51.
16 Sheriff I D Macphail *Research Paper* para 19–47. Walker and Walker *The Law of Evidence in Scotland* p 368, para 343(b). See however *Livingston v Strachan Crerar & Jones* 1923 SC 794 per Lord Murray and Lord Justice-Clerk Alness and *MacTaggart v HM Advocate* 1934 JC 33.
17 Walker and Walker ibid.
18 *Kerr v HM Advocate* 1958 JC 14 at 19.

sense, hearsay; the original evidence is the precognoscer's testimony of what was said to him. It is also a partial account both in the sense that it was compiled from the standpoint of one party and, usually, in the sense that it is incomplete, although those are considerations which go to weight rather than admissibility. Further consideration requires, however, to be given to the general inadmissibility of evidence of statements made on precognition in the sense of accounts in the form of original evidence of what a potential witness actually said to the precognoscer in the course of being questioned about what his testimony was likely to be. The precognoscer may, of course, not be able to remember what was actually said but that is no reason for rejecting his testimony where he does recollect, and he may be able to refresh his memory by notes made at the time or even, perhaps, by reference to the precognition if it is in fact a contemporary and accurate record.

Admissibility of statements proved to have been made

The admissibility of statements made on precognition can arise in three contexts: 1 as exceptions to the rule against hearsay; 2 as prior consistent statements adduced for the purpose of supporting a witness's credibility where that is competent; and 3 as prior inconsistent statements for the purpose of attacking a witness's credibility.[19] The second of those categories has not been judicially considered in relation to precognitions but must be governed by similar considerations to those applying to the third. The exceptions to the rule against hearsay in which questions of the admissibility of statements made on precognition are likely to arise are those which admit statements against interest made by a party and statements made by persons who are deceased by the time of trial or proof. Despite what is said about the general inadmissibility of statements made on precognition there is authority for the admission of such statements when they are against the interest of a party to a civil action and have been made in the course of precognition in other proceedings.[20] There is, however, also authority that such statements are not admissible in criminal proceedings;[1] a distinction which is hard to justify on any ground of principle. The inadmissibility of statements made on precognition by persons subsequently deceased is but an instance of the inadmissibility, subject to certain qualifications, of statements by deceased persons where they were made for the purposes of litigation and that rule, although it carries echoes of ancient notions on the incompetency of witnesses, is well established.[2] The preponderance of older

19 Ch 3 above.
20 *Fraser v Wilson* (1842) 4 D 1171 at 1173; *Morrison v Sommerville* (1860) 23 D 232 at 238.
1 *Cook v McNeill* (1906) 8 F (J) 57.
2 Ch 3 above.

authority supports the admission of statements made on precognition for the purpose of attacking the credibility of a witness by proving his prior inconsistent statements.[3] Their admissibility for that purpose is also supported by the unqualified terms of the relevant provisions of the Evidence (Scotland) Act 1852[4] and the Criminal Procedure (Scotland) Act 1975,[5] but is contrary to modern practice.

Precognition and privilege

The modern practice of the absolute or virtually absolute exclusion of statements made on precognition seems for the reasons just given to rest on a questionable basis. Two arguments for their exclusion, both based on privilege, can, however, be advanced. Statements made on precognition are, it can be said, *post litem motam* communications for the purposes of litigation and as such are privileged. That is correct but it is a reason for objection by one party to questions or evidence by another party about what his (the first party's) witnesses have said on precognition, and for no more. Second, it can be said that the witness has a privilege in respect of what he has said on precognition. That may be what Lord Justice General Clyde had in mind in *McNeillie* when he spoke of 'the confidential circumstances of precognition'. As has been seen, however, confidentiality does not in itself attract privilege[6] and the reasons for an exception in the case of statements made on precognition are obscure. If the rule is one of privilege it is subject to waiver.

Character of precognition

It may sometimes be difficult to determine the distinction between what constitutes a statement made on precognition and other statements. The essence of precognition is, however, that it is concerned with preparation for the institution of proceedings or preparation for proof or trial. Accordingly a statement made to the police before an arrest is made is not a precognition and if otherwise competent is admissible.[7] Similarly,

3 *Inch v Inch* (1856) 18 D 997; *Luke* (1866) 5 Irv 293; *Robertson* (1873) 2 Coup 495; *Whyte v Whyte* (1884) 11 R 710. In some of these cases, however, the objection seems not to have been taken. See contra *O'Donnell & Maguire* (1855) 2 Irv 236; *Emslie v Alexander* (1862) 1 M 209; *Dysart Peerage Case* (1881) LR 6 HL (Sc) 489 per Lord Watson at 509; and *Lauderdale Peerage Case* (1885) LR 10 HL (Sc) 692 per Lord Seldrone LC at 7110.

4 S 3.

5 Ss 147 and 349.

6 Ch 6 above.

7 *Gilmour v Hanson* 1920 SC 598. Cf *HM Advocate v Stark* 1968 SLT (Notes) 10 and *Hall v HM Advocate* 1968 SLT 275.

statements made by fellow employees to an employee carrying out investigations into the occurrence of an accident are not regarded as having been made on precognition.[8]

8 *McNeill v Richard Costain (Civil Engineering) Ltd* (27 November 1970 unreported) cited by Sheriff I D Macphail in *Research Paper* para 12–24.

CHAPTER 8

Inadmissibility of evidence: judicial knowledge; judicial admissions; personal bar

JUDICIAL KNOWLEDGE

Judicial knowledge and judicial admissions operate to limit the scope of proof by evidence in that evidence is unnecessary and, in the latter case, incompetent on the matters to which they relate.

Facts which are common knowledge, either in the sense that every well-informed person knows them or that they are generally accepted by informed persons and can be ascertained by consulting appropriate works of reference, are deemed to be within judicial knowledge. The result is that evidence is unnecessary unless one wishes to attack the commonly accepted view or to meet such an attack.

Scots law

Scots law in all its aspects, including decision of all Scottish courts and of the House of Lords in Scottish appeals is within judicial knowledge. Judicial notice is also taken of decisions of the Judicial Committee of the Privy Council, of the House of Lords in English cases and of English courts where those decisions have reference to a branch of law assimilated to Scots law or to the interpretation of a statute which applies also to Scotland or are of persuasive authority on a point of Scots law. When, however, under the Scottish rules of international private law English law is the lex causae by which the decision of the case is governed it must be proved as foreign law.

Foreign law

Foreign law is not within judicial knowledge and where at issue in a case the relevant foreign law must be proved by evidence or by one of the other means noted later.[1] For that reason, a question of foreign law is said to be a question of fact.

1 Ch 11 below.

Statutes, statutory instruments, law reports, etc

It follows from the fact that matters of law are within judicial knowledge that statutes,[2] statutory instruments,[3] royal proclamations (once published in the Gazette)[4] and reported decisions of the courts do not require to be produced or proved. It is sufficient to refer to any reputable edition of the statutes or statutory instruments, to the official Gazette in the case of royal proclamations and to any reputable report in the case of judicial decisions. In case of dispute as to the terms of an Act of Parliament reference should, however, be made to a copy bearing to be printed by the Queen's Printer[5] in the case of UK Acts and to the Record Edition in the case of Scottish Acts.[6] Judicial knowledge extends only to the general law of Scotland and local or private enactments require to be proved. Byelaws and regulations made by some local or other authority under statutory or common law powers are proved by the production of a copy and a witness to speak to the copy[7] unless in the case of regulations or byelaws made under statute, the statute in question otherwise provides for their proof or provides that they are to have the same effect as an Act of Parliament. On somewhat similar principles, Acts of the General Assembly of the Church of Scotland require to be produced and proved, which is done by producing an extract attested by the Clerk of Assembly.[8] Private Acts of Parliament passed before 1850 require to be produced by the party founding on them and to be proved. Proof is by a copy sworn to be collated with the Parliament Roll in the case of UK Acts[9] and probably by production of the Record Edition in the case of Scottish Acts. Private Acts passed since 1850 are, however, for purposes of judicial notice, deemed to be Public Acts and are judicially to be taken notice of unless they bear a clause expressly taking them out of the ordinary category[10] in which case they require to be produced and proved in the same way as Acts passed before 1850.

Orders in council made since 1948 are statutory instruments.[11] Orders

2 *Macmillan v McConnell* 1917 JC 43 per Lord Justice-Clerk Scott Dickson at 47; *Herkes v Dickie* 1958 JC 51 at 55, 57, and 58.
3 *Sharp v Leith* (1892) 20 R (J) 12 per Lord McLaren at 15–16; *Hutchison v Stevenson* (1902) 4 F (J) 69 per Lord McLaren at 72; *Snell v Unity Finance Co Ltd* [1964] 2 QB 203.
4 Crown Office Act 1877 s 3.
5 Dickson para 1105.
6 Thomson and Innes (eds) *The Act of the Parliaments of Scotland* (1844–75).
7 *Dickson* paras 1316–17.
8 Walker and Walker *The Law of Evidence in Scotland* p 223, para 202.
9 *Dickson* para 1105. Some pre-1850 UK private legislation contains, however, a provision that it is to be judicially noticed as a public Act.
10 Interpretation Act 1978 ss 3 and 22(1), Sch 2 para 2.
11 Statutory Instruments Act 1946 s 1(1).

in council made before 1948, if made pursuant to statute, do not require proof.[12] Other orders in council made before then probably require to be produced and proved (prima facie evidence is a copy of the Gazette purporting to contain the order or a copy bearing to be printed by the Government Printer or under the superintendence of Her Majesty's Stationery Office or certified copy or extract).[13] Acts of Sederunt and of Adjournal are also now statutory instruments[14] and the general rule seems to be that, in any event and of whatever date, they do not require production or proof although there is some doubt about Acts prior to 1893.[15] In the event of doubt as to the terms of an order in council made since 1948 or made pursuant to statute prior thereto reference should be made to a copy bearing to be printed by the Queen's Printer. In case of doubt as to the terms of an Act of Sederunt or Act of Adjournal it seems that reference should be made either to the original Books of Sederunt or Adjournal or to an extract given by the clerk of court or keeper of the records. Acts of the Scottish Privy Council before 1708 are proved by an extract from the Register, certified by the keeper of the records.[16]

The above provisions may be modified by specific statutory provision dealing with particular types of case. Thus, the Criminal Procedure (Scotland) Act 1975 provides that in a summary trial production of a print or copy of any order by a department of state or government or local authority or public body made under powers conferred by statute should be received as evidence of the due making confirmation or existence of such order but without prejudice to any right competent to the accused to challenge such order as being ultra vires of the authority making it or on any other competent ground.[17]

Duty of bringing law to the attention of the court

The fact that matters of law are within judicial knowledge does not mean that the court can be left to arrive at conclusions of law unaided. The maxim of continental jurisprudence *jus novit curia* which is there interpreted as putting on the court an obligation to ascertain the law applicable to a case has, in that interpretation, no counterpart in our system. It is the function of counsel or, where counsel are not employed,

12 *Macmillan v McConnell* 1917 JC 43.
13 Documentary Evidence Act 1868 s 2, Documentary Evidence Act 1882 s 2.
14 Statutory Instruments Act 1946 s 1(2).
15 By the Rules Publication Act 1893 s 4, Acts of Sederunt and Adjournal became statutory rules and were noticed as part of the general law. That seems to have been the practice even before then. See *Walker and Walker* pp 222–3, para 201.
16 Public Records (Scotland) Act 1937 s 9.
17 S 352(2).

of solicitors to refer the court to all the law applicable to the case whether in statute, statutory instruments or other delegated legislation or in decided cases and to give the court every assistance in ascertaining the applicable law. The court's duty is to decide the case on the points of law argued before it and it has no obligation, even within the confines of such points of law, to ascertain for itself the relevant authorities. It is the function of counsel or solicitor to bring the authorities to the notice of the court and their duty as officers of the court extends to seeing that all relevant authorities, at any rate if clearly in point are brought to the attention of the court. In *Glebe Sugar Refining Co Ltd v Greenock Harbour Trustees*,[18] Lord Birkenhead LC said:

> 'This House expects and indeed insists that authorities which bear one way or another upon the matters under debate shall be brought to the attention of their Lordships by those who are aware of the authorities. This observation is quite irrespective of whether or not the particular authority assists the party who is so aware of it.'

The principle is applicable not only to the House of Lords but to any court.

Ordinary meaning of words

The ordinary meaning of English words, terms, phrases and expressions, so far as met with in current literature or standard dictionaries, is presumed to be within judicial knowledge. When, however, a word or phrase is alleged to have a special or technical meaning or is capable of more than one meaning in the question at issue, it may be competent or necessary to prove the applicable meaning by evidence. Judicial knowledge is not deemed to extend to such special or technical meanings. The difficulty is to decide whether a word is a technical term and so requiring to be proved by evidence or is part of the ordinary language and therefore within judicial knowledge. The question is further complicated by the fact that certain technical terms may be of such frequent occurrence, particularly in matters litigated before the courts, that despite the general rule to the contrary they become part of judicial knowledge, at any rate in certain contexts. In *Sutton & Co v Ciceri*[19] proof was allowed as to the meaning of 'statuary' but in *Griffiths' & Co Factor v G's Executor*[20] the meaning of 'effects' was held to be within judicial knowledge. In *Oliver v Hislop*,[1] it was held that a sheriff of a border

18 1921 SC (HL) 72.
19 (1889) 16R 814, (1890) 17R (HL) 40.
20 (1905) 7F 470.
1 1946 JC 20.

county did not require to be instructed by evidence as to the meaning of technical terms in local statutes for the regulation of Tweed Fisheries and that therefore where the libel referred to a 'cleek' as similar to a rakehook in a prosecution under a statute referring to 'rakehooks or similar engines' the resolution of the question so raised was within judicial knowledge.

Facts of science and nature

The ordinary facts of nature or science do not require proof. These include the basic facts of human and animal biology and behaviour including the normal propensities and conduct of men, women and children and animals.

The normal period of gestation is an example of a type of fact of this kind which has given rise to some difficulty, for although the normal period is within judicial knowledge the courts have had difficulty in coming to any conclusion short of the most extreme instances as to minimum and maximum possible periods. In *Marshall v Marshall*[2] the Court refused to hold that 308 days was impossible and in *Gaskill v Gaskill*,[3] it was held, after hearing evidence, that 331 days was possible. Similar difficulties have attended the question of the age for childbearing. In *Rackstraw v Douglas*[4] it was held—somewhat perversely one might think—that judicial knowledge did not entitle the court to hold that a woman of 81 was past childbearing but in *G's Trustees*[5] a majority of seven judges held that there was a presumption that a woman of 53 would have no issue although that presumption might be rebutted by evidence. The decision in *G's Trustees* was reached as explained by the Lord Justice-Clerk: 'as a conclusion based upon common experience and medical opinion of which the Court is sufficiently certiorated by medical-legal works of high authority'.

That dictum both shows the increasing tendency in matters of judicial knowledge attended with some technical complexity to recognise text-books on the relevant branch of science as authority for the statements contained in them. Questions of the period of gestation and of the age for childbearing show an interplay between judicial knowledge and evidence because although the basic facts and extremes are within judicial knowledge, evidence in most cases will be required to resolve the particular issue.

2 1934 SN 80.
3 [1921] P 425.
4 1917 SC 284.
5 1936 SC 837.

Ward v Abraham,[6] is an example of normal human propensities and conduct being within judicial knowledge. In that case which arose out of injury sustained by a girl as a result of a cricket ball being propelled from an adjoining garden, the Lord Justice-Clerk said:

> 'Cricket is in itself a dangerous game only in very special circumstances. It is a game which we all know—and judges must to some extent proceed on common knowledge—boys play wherever they can get a place to play it in.'

In *Hogg v Cupar District Committee*[7] the Court, however, refused to accept as common knowledge that a horse always backed when its nosebag was taken off.

Notorious public facts; matters of common occurrence

Judicial knowledge extends to the construction of buildings, cars, ships and familiar machinery but only insofar as elementary principles are concerned. It also extends to the facts of history and geography insofar as these are generally known and to notorious public and national events, eg the officers of state, the government departments, the existence of peace or war, the failure of important banks, general economic conditions, the facts of the almanac, weights and measures, currency, and general geographic situations. The ordinary customs of business, methods of book-keeping, banking and stockbroking and the ordinary professional or business conduct of any large class of society are also within judicial knowledge as are the ordinary incidents of industrial activity. 'I must say' said Lord Guest in *Devine v Colvilles Ltd*:

> 'that without evidence to the contrary I should have thought it self-evident that an explosion of such violence that it causes fear of immediate danger to the workers does not occur in the ordinary course of things in a steelworks if those who have the management use proper care.'[8]

It is, however, only usages which are of wide application and of common knowledge that fall within judicial knowledge. If the usage or custom is a special one or is of limited application and applies only in some particular trade or branch of the trade it must be proved.

In all questions of judicial knowledge it is necessary that the matters brought within that category should be generally known, or at least

6 1910 SC 299 at 302.
7 (1912) 1 SLT 57.
8 1969 SC (HL) 67 at 100.

within a class of knowledge which is generally ascertainable. A judge is not entitled to rely on his private knowledge.[9]

JUDICIAL ADMISSIONS

Judicial admissions in civil cases must take one of three forms: 1 admissions on record; 2 admissions by minute; or 3 admissions at the Bar.

Admissions on record

An admission on record is, if clear and unqualified, conclusive against the party making it and may therefore be founded upon by the other side as establishing the fact in question and doing away with the necessity of leading evidence to prove it.[10] Care, however, requires to be exercised in judging the effect of an admission.[11] Admissions cannot be taken apart from their qualifications and must be read along with all the explanations and statements that accompany them[12] and in general admissions will be strictly construed against the party founding upon them. The record is to be looked at as a whole and isolated passages are not to be founded on in disregard of the main averments.

Only admissions on the closed record are judicial admissions so as to bind the party making them but admissions made on the open record and withdrawn may, if the party gives evidence, be put to him in cross-examination and, failing satisfactory explanation, will tell heavily against him and have a very damaging effect on his credibility. It remains an element of proof to be considered along with the other facts of the case.

> 'It was competent to retract before closing the record; but the fact of the admission having once been made remained nevertheless an element of proof to be considered by the judge along with the other facts of the case which element would be entitled to more or less weight according to the circumstances in which the admission had originally been made.'[13]

So, too, statements made on record in an inferior court and departed from in a new record in the Court of Session, can be used to show that

9 *Morrison v Monro* (1854) 1 Irv 599, cf *Hattie v Leitch* (1889) 16 R 1128; *McCann v Adair* 1951 JC 127.
10 *Wilson v Clyde Rigging and Boiler Scaling Co* 1959 SC 328.
11 *Spindlow v Glasgow Corpn* 1933 SC 580.
12 *Walker v Garlick* 1940 SLT 208.
13 *Bathgate v Macadam* (1840) 2 D 811.

the party had given a different account elsewhere of the matter in issue.[14]

An averment by a party is not the equivalent of an admission and is, unless proved, of no factual significance.[15] In certain circumstances, however, an averment may amount to an implied admission[16] and an admitted averment binds both parties so that the party making the admission as well as the other party can found on it.

It is incompetent to lead evidence to contradict an admission made on record but such evidence may become competent if it is not objected to at the first available opportunity.[17]

2 Admissions by minute

Minutes of admissions may take the form either of joint minutes for both (or all) parties to the action or of a minute on behalf of one party.

A joint minute by its nature binds all the parties to it and constitutes a contract between them to admit the facts stated therein. Similarly a minute of admission by one party binds that party.

Admissions by minute should be construed along with the admissions and averments on record. Minutes of admission must be used with caution as it is uncertain (as in the case of admissions on record) what the result of an admission may be. 'Once adjusted the minute forms the evidence in the case; it is the proof at large, in synthesis, and its statements of admitted facts must be regarded as final.'[18] Its adjustment has been described as 'one of the most difficult and delicate tasks which fall to the lot of counsel'.

3 Verbal admissions

Verbal admissions are made at the bar by counsel or, where counsel is not employed, by a solicitor. They have the same effect as admissions made on record or by minute but the terms of such admissions are not so readily verifiable. Accordingly, it is generally preferable if such admissions are on matters of importance that they should be recorded in a minute. Where an interlocutor bears to proceed on a verbal admission and that admission is inaccurately recorded, the interlocutor should be immediately challenged.[19]

14 *Stuart v Mitchell* (1833) 11 S 1004.
15 *Lee v National Coal Board* 1955 SC 151 especially per Lord Sorn; *Stewart v Glasgow Corpn* above especially per Lord President Clyde at 39; *Wilson v Clyde Rigging & Boiler Scaling Co* 1959 SC 328.
16 *Dobson v Colvilles* 1958 SLT (N) 30 per Lord Sorn, reported only in the Opinion of Lord Wheatley (Ordinary) in *Wilson v Clyde Rigging & Boiler Scaling Co* above at 330.
17 *Brown's Ex v North British Steel Foundry Ltd* 1967 SLT 421; SLT (N) 112.
18 *London & Edinburgh Shipping Co v The Admiralty* 1920 SC 309 per Lord Dundas at 318.
19 *Lauder v The National Bank* (1918) 1 SLT 43.

Admissions in criminal cases

At common law the only competent forms of judicial admission are the accused's pleas of guilty. Accordingly a conviction which proceeds on any other form of purported judicial admission is null.[20] The common law rule, however, now suffers an exception where the accused is legally represented. In such a case neither the accused nor the prosecutor need lead proof of any fact which is admitted by the other party nor prove any document the terms and application of which are not in dispute and a copy of any document may by agreement be accepted as equivalent to the original.[1] Where facts or documents are admitted in this way the admission must be recorded in a minute lodged with the clerk of court. Admissions that a document is a form of certificate which may afford proof of certain matters under stature does not constitute an admission of these matters if the certificate is not produced.[2]

If a prosecutor does not accept a plea of guilty he cannot thereafter rely on it[3] and in solemn procedure where an accused pleads guilty to part of the indictment before the jury is empanelled and the trial proceeds on the remainder, his plea of guilty is not properly before the jury and reference to it is incompetent.[4]

PERSONAL BAR

Personal bar in its English counterpart of estoppel has been described as a rule of evidence[5] but in most of its applications it seems properly to be a matter of substantive law[6] or the law of remedies. There may, however, be instances in which a party is personally barred by his conduct from objecting to evidence which would otherwise be inadmissible or, perhaps, from leading evidence which would otherwise be admissible. Thus a party in whose possession primary evidence has been lost or destroyed can be said to be personally barred from objecting to his opponent's leading secondary evidence[7] and a party who has failed to object timeously to the admission of evidence for which there is no

20 *Tullis v Millar* (1899) 1 F (J) 75.
1 Criminal Procedure (Scotland) Act 1975 ss 150 and 354.
2 *Evans v Wilson* 1981 SCCR 60.
3 *Strathern v Sloan* 1937 JC 76.
4 *Walsh v HM Advocate* 1961 JC 51. There is no corresponding rule in summary procedure (*McColl v Skeen* 1980 SLT (Notes) 53).
5 *Low v Bouverie* [1891] 3 Ch 82 per Bowen LJ at 105.
6 See *Canadian & Dominion Sugar Co Ltd v Canadian National (West Indies) Steamships Ltd* [1947] AC 46 per Lord Wright at 56; *Mills v Cooper* [1967] 2 QB 459 per Diplock LJ at 468.
7 Ch 5 above.

basis on record can be said to be barred from objecting to its subsequent use.[8] But personal bar cannot cure a radical defect. Failure to object to hearsay does not make it competent evidence.

8 Ch 10, p 165 below.

CHAPTER 9

Competency and compellability of witnesses

GENERAL

The history of the Scottish rules of evidence was, from an early stage, characterised by a marked distrust of oral testimony and, as a consequence, by highly restrictive rules which rendered large classes of persons incompetent as witnesses.[1] These rules came close to excluding practically anyone likely to have any familiarity with the cause and where there was scantity of evidence witnesses in some of the excluded categories came to be received *cum nota* (ie under reservation of credibility). Inevitably the restrictive rules gave way to pressures for a more general relaxation. In the nineteenth century those pressures gained added impetus and they found statutory expression in the Evidence (Scotland) Acts 1840, 1852 and 1853, the Evidence (Further Amendment) (Scotland) Act 1874, and the Criminal Evidence Act 1898. The general principle of the modern law is that all who are capable of giving intelligible evidence are competent as witnesses and that all who are competent are compellable. This chapter is concerned with the few exceptions or qualifications to that general rule.

MENTALLY ILL AND MENTALLY DEFECTIVE

Persons suffering from mental illness or who are mentally defective are not necessarily incompetent as witnesses. The witness must be able to give coherent testimony and to understand the distinction between truth and falsity but it is not essential that he should understand the nature of the oath and instead of being sworn, or making an affirmation, he may

1 Stair IV 43,7. Hume II 339 ff.

be admonished to tell the truth.[2] The witness must also be able to understand the subject matter on which he is to be examined.[3] Delusions or irrationality on a particular matter do not necessarily render the witness's evidence valueless on others.[4] The extent and nature of the mental illness or defect must be considered in relation to the subject matter of the enquiry. It is for the court to determine the competency of the witness and evidence may be led for that purpose.[5] The effect on the witness of his being examined must be taken into account.[6]

DEAF, DUMB AND INARTICULATE

The competency of a person as a witness is not affected by his being deaf or dumb unless communication with him is impossible. The usual and preferable way of taking evidence from persons afflicted in this way is through an interpreter using the recognised sign language for the deaf and dumb. Failing that, however, questions may be put and answered in writing.[7] If that too is impracticable, any form of communication may be adopted which the witness can use and which can be understood and interpreted.[8] Anyone who understands the particular form of communication may act as an interpreter. A witness who, although not deaf and dumb, is inarticulate may be examined in that way.[9]

CHILDREN

There is no age limit below which a child is not competent as a witness. As in the case of the mentally ill and mentally defective it is for the judge to determine whether the child has the necessary capacity to give evidence, having regard to his ability to distinguish truth from falsehood and give a coherent account. The matter can usually be decided by examination of the child by the court but, if need be, other evidence

2 *Black* (1887) 1 White 365.
3 *Buckle v Buckle's Curator* (1907) 15 SLT 98.
4 *Dickson* para 1553.
5 *McKenzie* (1869) 1 Coup 244; *Black* above; *Stott* (1894) 1 Adam 386. It is also competent to examine the witness as a preliminary to his giving testimony (*O'Neil & Gollan* (1858) 3 Irv 93).
6 *Tosh v Ogilvy* (1873) 1 R 254 at 257; *Kilpatrick Parish Council v Row Parish Council* (1911) 2 SLT 32.
7 *Dickson* para 1556 states a preference for written questions and answers but that view is not now followed.
8 See *Rice* (1864) 4 Irv 493; *Montgomerie* (1855) 2 Irv 222.
9 *Howison* (1871) 2 Coup 153.

may be heard.[10] At least in a civil case the court may refuse to accept a child as a witness if it is unsuitable that he should give evidence in view of the nature of the case and his tender years.[11] In any proceedings in relation to any conduct contrary to decency or morality in which a child or young person is called as a witness, the court may direct that everyone be excluded from the court during the taking of his evidence other than officers of the court, parties and their counsel or solicitors, persons otherwise directly concerned in the case, and bona fide press representatives.[12] A child as young as three and a half was admitted in one case where the charge was of assault against her.[13] In some of the older cases the decision on the competency of the child as a witness seems to have turned on whether or not he had made a *de recenti* statement[14] but it is thought that that is a consideration which goes to credibility rather than competency.

Children under the age of 12 are not put on oath but are admonished to tell the truth, as are children over that age if they do not understand the nature of the oath.[15] Children over 14 will be presumed to know the nature of the oath unless the contrary appears.

ACCUSED AS DEFENCE WITNESS

At common law an accused person was not a competent witness at his own trial. The only way in which he could get his own account of events before the jury was if he had emitted a judicial declaration. The Crown was not obliged to read such a delcaration at the trial but it was the practice to do so if the accused so desired or if it served the interests of the prosecutor. By the Criminal Procedure (Scotland) Act 1975,[16] re-enacting provision first introduced by the Criminal Evidence Act 1898, an accused person is now a competent witness for the defence on his own application. By the same Act,[16] as amended by the Criminal Justice (Scotland) Act 1980[17] he may' if he consents, be called as a witness by a co-accused provided he has not already given evidence on his own behalf and been cross-examined by that co-accused. Where the accused

10 *Dickson* paras 1543 and 1548.
11 *Robertson v Robertson* (1888) 15 R 1001.
12 Children and Young Persons (Scotland) Act 1937, s 45.
13 *Millar* (1870) 1 Coup 430.
14 *Thomson* (1857) 2 Irv 747; *Millar* above.
15 *Dickson* para 1549.
16 Ss 141 and 346.
17 S 28.

gives evidence in his own defence it is usual for him to be the first witness called and there is obvious merit in that course. The requirement of the Act that if he is the only witness to facts called by the defence he must be called immediately after the close of the evidence for the prosecution is, however, rather difficult to understand. It appears that if he is the sole witness to facts he must give his evidence before any expert testimony is given but if there is more than one defence witness to the facts there is no restriction on his place in the order of witnesses whether or not there is expert testimony. An accused person who gives evidence may refuse to answer any question regarding a communication between himself and his wife during the subsistence of their marraige but not any question which tends to criminate him as to the crime charged.[17] The circumstances in which he may be cross-examined on whether he has committed or been convicted of, or been charged with, any other offence or is of bad character are considered elsewhere.[18]

JUDICIAL EXAMINATION AND DECLARATION

It is still competent, although rare, for an accused person to emit a declaration. Under procedures introduced by the Criminal Justice (Scotland) Act 1980[19] the prosecutor may now, at the accused's judicial examination, question him with a view to eliciting any denial, explanation, justification or comment which the accused may have as regards (a) matters averred in the charge (provided the particular aim of the line of questions is to determine (i) whether any account which the accused can give ostensibly discloses a category of defence such as alibi, incrimination or consent of the victim and (ii) the nature and particulars of that defence) or (b) the alleged making, by the accused to, or in the hearing of, an officer of police of an extrajudicial confession relevant to the charge (provided the accused has received a written record of the alleged confession), or (c) what is said in any declaration emitted by the accused. The questions should not be designed to challenge the truth of anything said by the accused and there should be no reiteration of a question which the accused has refused to answer and no leading questions. The sheriff must ensure that all questions are fairly put to, and understood by, the accused and must tell an accused who is represented by a solicitor that he may consult that solicitor before answering any question. The accused may decline to answer a question and at his subsequent trial his having so declined may be the subject of

18 Ch 2 above.
19 S 6 enacting amendments to the Criminal Procedure (Scotland) Act 1975 s 20 and inserting a new s 20A.

comment by the prosecutor, the presiding judge, or any co-accused only where, and insofar as, the accused, or any witness called on his behalf, avers something which could have been stated appropriately in answer to that question. The record of the examination, including a record of any declaration emitted, is to be received in evidence without being sworn to by witnesses. The court may, on the application either of an accused or the prosecutor refuse to allow the record or any part of it to be read to the jury or, in a summary trial, to be received in evidence. The principles on which that discretion may be exercised are not defined but would seem to include any irregularity in the record or in the examination or any circumstance which would make the use of the record prejudicial to the accused.

ACCUSED AS WITNESS AGAINST CO-ACCUSED

An accused person can never, as long as charges against him are outstanding, be a competent witness for the prosecution at his own trial. If, however, he pleads guilty[20] or the charges against him are withdrawn,[1] he becomes a competent and compellable witness for the prosecution against any co-accused. If he is not called as a witness by the prosecution he is, in these circumstances, also a competent and compellable witness for a co-accused subject,[2] where the charges against him have been withdrawn, to privilege against self-incrimination.

An accused person is also, subject to the same privilege, a competent

20 Criminal Procedure (Scotland) Act 1975 ss 141(3) and 346(3) as inserted by Criminal Justice (Scotland) Act 1980 s 28. It is necessary for this purpose that he should have 'pleaded guilty to all charges against him which remained before the court (whether or not he has been sentenced)'. The appropriate time for determing the co-accused's competency as a witness is when he is called to give evidence and he is competent if, by that time, the only outstanding charges against him are those to which he has pleaded guilty (*HM Advocate v Ferrie* 1983 SCCR 1). It is not necessary for notice to be given but the court may grant such adjournment as may seem just.

1 If the charges are withdrawn he is, in effect, no longer a co-accused (see below) against any further proceedings for the offences with which he was charged. He cannot, however, in solemn procedure be called as a prosecution witness unless his name is included in a list of witnesses or unless he is called in pursuance of the new provisions on additional evidence (see ch 12 below). It is, however, sufficient for the prosecutor's purpose in this connection that he was included in a list of witnesses for another accused (Criminal Procedure (Scotland) Act 1975 s 82A).

Where the co-accused has pleaded guilty, ss 141(3) and 346(3) of the 1975 Act apply and no notice need be given. If the charge against the co-accused has been withdrawn notice must be given unless his name has been included in a list of witnesses (*Lindie v HM Advocate* 1974 JC 1, 1974 SLT 208) or the right to notice has been waived by the prosecution (*Lowson v HM Advocate* 1943 JC 141).

and compellable witness for his co-accused where their trials have been separated.[3]

SPOUSE OF ACCUSED

At common law a spouse was not a competent witness either for prosecution or defence at the trial of the other spouse. The only exception to that was where the spouse was the victim of the offence. In that event the spouse against whom the offence had been committed was both competent and compellable at the instance of the prosecutor as a witness against the other spouse.[4] The offence need not be one of bodily injury. Cases include forgery[5] and theft[6] as well as assault. The rule that the victim spouse is a competent and compellable witness against the other spouse is unaffected by statute and remains in force.

Under the Criminal Evidence Act 1898 and also a number of other statutes, dealing with particular offences, which that Act effectively superseded, a spouse became a competent witness for the defence of the other spouse on the latter's application.[7] A spouse of one accused was not, however, a competent witness for the defence of a co-accused. In certain offences a spouse was also a competent but never, apart from the common law exception, a compellable witness for the prosecution.[8] These statutory provisions are now obsolete in view of an amendment to the Criminal Procedure (Scotland) Act 1975[9] made by the Criminal Justice (Scotland) Act 1980.[10] The spouse of a person charged with an offence may now be called as a witness by that person or by a co-accused or by the prosecutor. The consent of the person charged is not necessary to the calling of his spouse as a witness by co-accused or prosecutor but the spouse is not compellable at their instance in any case where he or she would not be so compellable at common law. It was undecided under the previous statutory enactments whether a spouse was compellable at the instance of the other spouse. The wording of the 1980 Act, although not explicit, by implication puts compellability beyond a doubt.[11] The witness spouse may not be compelled to disclose any

3 *Bell & Shaw v Houston* (1842) 1 Broun 49; *Morrison v Adair* 1943 JC 25.
4 *Harper v Adair* 1945 JC 21; *Foster v HM Advocate* 1932 JC 75.
5 *Foster v HM Advocate* above.
6 *Harper v Adair* above; see also *Millar* 1847 Ark 355 (false accusation of crime).
7 S 1.
8 *Leach v R* [1912] AC 305.
9 Ss 143 and 348.
10 S 29.
11 *Hunter v HM Advocate* 1984 SLT 434.

communication made between the spouses during marriage and that is so whether he or she is a witness for the prosecution or defence.

COMMENT ON ACCUSED'S FAILURE TO GIVE EVIDENCE

The failure of an accused person to give evidence must not be commented on by the prosecutor.[12] The prohibition is absolute but breach is not necessarily fatal to conviction.[13] The statute by contrast places no restraint on comment by the judge and as a result it might be thought that, within limits of fairness, he might comment freely. It has, however, been held that such comments should be made only with restraint and where there are special circumstances which require[14] it and that 'if it is made with reference to particular evidence which the panel might have explained or contradicted, care should be taken that the evidence is not distorted and that its true bearing on the defence is properly represented to the jury'.[15]

No form has been laid down which judicial comment, if made, should follow but there are, no doubt, a number of cases in which the form commended by Lord Parker CJ in *R v Bathhurst*[16] would be appropriate; that the jury should be told:

> 'The accused is not bound to give evidence, that he can sit back and see if the prosecution have proved their case, and that, while the jury have been deprived of the opportunity of hearing his story tested in cross-examination the one thing they must not do is assume that he is guilty because he has not gone into the witness box.'

A careful comment probably requires reference to the accused's right not to testify and remain silent. Although a strong comment may be appropriate where an explanation from the accused is obviously called for and is not forthcoming,[17] it goes too far even in such a case to say that it is essential for the accused to go into the witness box.[18] The failure of an accused person to put forward an innocent explanation should not, in

12 Criminal Procedure (Scotland) Act 1975 ss 141(b) and 346(b).
13 *Ross v Boyd* (1903) 5 F (J) 64; *McAttee v Hogg* (1903) 5 F (J) 67; *McHugh v HM Advocate* 1978 JC 12.
14 *Scott (A T) v HM Advocate* 1946 JC 90; *Knowles v HM Advocate* 1975 JC 6.
15 *Scott (A T) v HM Advocate* 1946 JC 90 per Lord Justice-General Normand.
16 [1968] 2 QB 99, [1968] 1 All ER 1175. A Scottish court might not, however, follow the view taken in *R v Mutch* [1973] 1 All ER 178 that the form adopted in *R v Bathhurst* should be followed in almost every case.
17 See *Hardy v HM Advocate* 1938 JC 144.
18 *R v Sparrow* [1973] 2 All ER 129, [1973] 1 WLR 488.

general be a matter for comment where the accused rests his defence on a simple denial of the prosecution case.[19]

COMMENT ON FAILURE OF ACCUSED'S SPOUSE TO GIVE EVIDENCE

The Criminal Procedure (Scotland) Act 1975 as amended stipulates: 'The failure of the spouse of an accused to give evidence shall not be commented on by the defence or the prosecutor'.[20] The intention, no doubt, is to preclude comment by one accused on the failure of another accused's spouse to testify in his defence as well as comment by the prosecution. The provision is, however, curiously expressed. Taken in its strict terms, it would prevent an accused from explaining his failure to adduce the evidence of his own spouse but it is probably not to be so read. Comment by the judge is competent and is governed by similar principles to those applicable to the failure of an accused person to testify. Such comment can, however, it is thought, be proper only in relation to a party at whose instance the spouse was a compellable witness. It would, therefore, seem to be wrong for the judge to comment on the prosecution's failure to lead the evidence of the spouse of one of the accused, or on an accused person's failure to lead the evidence of a spouse of a co-accused.

ACCOMPLICES

No incompetency attaches to the evidence of a *socius criminis* (accomplice), but if he is adduced as a witness for the prosecution his evidence is received *cum nota*, ie subject to 'a special scrutiny, over and above the general examination which a jury has to apply to all the material evidence in every case' and the jury must be specifically directed accordingly.[1] It is undecided whether the same reservation applies to the evidence of a *socius* who is a defence witness but it is submitted that it does not. It is true that fairness is bilateral and so applies to the public interest represented by the Crown as well as to the accused, but the reason for the reception *cum nota* of the evidence of Crown witnesses who are accomplices is that 'there is always a temp-

19 *R v Mutch* above.
20 Ss 143(3) and 438(3) as amended by Criminal Justice (Scotland) Act 1980 s 29.
1 *Wallace v HM Advocate* 1952 JC 78 per Lord Justice-General Cooper at 82.

tation to minimise their part in the crime and blacken the accused'.[2] It is difficult to see how that consideration can have any part to play when the *socius* is a defence witness. The need to receive the evidence of a *socius* with caution should not preclude a rational appriasal of its value. An accomplice is not necessarily motivated by malice towards the accused and unless there has been some improper pressure or inducement he has, as a Crown witness, no interest to speak anything other than the truth. 'The penitent thief is not a figment of the imagination, and the *socius criminis* is by no means the only type of witness likely to concoct false evidence.'[3]

A *socius criminis* is a person who has been convicted of, or pleaded guilty to, the offence with which the accused is charged or who gives evidence confessedly as an accomplice.[4] A co-accused, unless he falls into one of these categories, is not an accomplice for this purpose even if there is evidence which points to his participation in the crime.[5] It is undecided whether other witnesses should be treated as *socii* where it appears on the evidence that they have that character. In *Wallace v HM Advocate* Lord Keith said, 'I should . . . hesitate to say that the court has any duty or right to arrogate to itself the task of saying that such a witness, who after all is not on trial, is a *socius* in the offence with which an accused is charged'. It is submitted that that reasoning has cogency.[6] It may be, however, consistently with that, that the jury should be directed that if they come, on the evidence, to the conclusion that a witness was a *socius* they should then treat his evidence with appropriate caution.

Indemnity for accomplice when Crown witness

Where a *socius* who has not been convicted or pleaded guilty is adduced by the Crown as a witness he cannot thereafter be prosecuted for the

2 *Dow v McKnight* 1949 JC 38 per Lord Jamieson at 55. See also *Slowey v HM Advocate* 1965 SLT 309.

3 *Dow v McKnight* 1949 JC 38 per Lord Justice-General Cooper at 57.

4 *Wallace v HM Advocate* 1952 JC 78 per Lord Keith at 83. Lord Keith included a person who 'is charged along with an accused' in the category of *socius* but that was disapproved in *Slowey v HM Advocate* above.

5 *Slowey v HM Advocate* above. It is wrong to give a *cum nota* warning in respect of an accused person because he is entitled to the presumption of innocence (see *Martin v HM Advocate* 1960 SLT 213; *McGuiness v HM Advocate* 1971 SLT (Notes) 7; *McCourt v HM Advocate* 1977 SLT (Notes) 22). Such a direction is wrong if given as a matter of law even in relation to evidence by one accused in which he incriminates another accused but it seems to be permissible to indicate to the jury that it may be open to them on the facts to regard such evidence with reserve (see *McGuiness v HM Advocate*).

6 See *Murdoch v HM Advocate* 1955 SLT (Notes) 57.

crime charged. 'By the very act of calling him as a witness, the prosecutor discharges all title to molest him for the future with relation to the matter libelled.'[7] As a result, he has no privilege against self-incrimination so far as that matter is concerned and is compellable to answer all questions relating to it.[8] He has, however, no indemnity in relation to other offences even if arising out of the same event or related in their circumstances. The libel in support of which he gives evidence is the measure of his indemnity.[9] In relation to these offences he retains, therefore, his privilege against self-incrimination and may refuse to answer questions which might show his implication in them even if these questions also have a bearing on the crime charged.

A private prosecutor cannot bind the Crown and so a *socius* who is adduced by him as a witness obtains no indemnity except against him. On the other hand, it is thought that the protection afforded to a Crown witness is sufficiently ample to cover all proceedings.

JUDGES AS WITNESSES

In *Muckarsie v Wilson*[10] it was said that it was incompetent to call a judge of the Supreme Courts as a witness to judicial proceedings before him, although probably not to other events in court not forming part of the judicial proceedings such as a riot or assault. In earlier cases, however, judges were examined of consent and in the later case of *Monaghan*[11] the court declined to express an opinion on the competency of citing a judge of the Supreme Courts. Judges of inferior courts are competent witnesses to proceedings before them[11] and it is difficult to justify a distinction unless it be that, in the case of judicial proceedings in the Supreme Courts, there should normally be means other than the judge's testimony by which the evidence and other features of the judicial proceedings can be proved, whereas in the inferior courts the judge's notes may be the only record. If, however, that is the ground of distinction the incompetency as witnesses of judges of the Supreme Court would seem not to be absolute.[12] There is no doubt that a judge is a competent witness to anything not forming part of his duty in court.[13]

7 Hume II 366–7.
8 *Macmillan v Murray* 1920 JC 13.
9 *McGinley & Dowds v MacLeod* 1963 JC 11, 1963 SLT 2; *O'Neill v Wilson* 1983 SLT 573.
10 1834 Bell's Notes 99.
11 (1834) 2 Broun 131.
12 Any incompetency there is seems, in any event, not to be radical as in a number of cases judges have consented to appearing as witnesses (*Harper v Robinsons & Forbes* (1821) 2 Mur 383; *Gibson v Stevenson* (1822) 3 Mur 208; *Stewart v Fraser* (1830) 5 Mur 166).
13 *Muckarsie v Wilson* above.

JURORS AND ARBITERS

Jurors may not give evidence of the jury's deliberation with a view to challenge of the verdict.[14] That is, however, a rule of finality of verdicts rather than of competency of witness or of evidence.[15] It is undecided what protection against disclosure, if any, should be accorded for other purposes to the deliberations of a jury but it is conceived that if the content of these deliberations was relevant to a question of criminal or, perhaps, of civil, liability it would be admissible in evidence and the jurors would be competent and compellable witnesses. It is sometimes said that arbiters are competent witnesses in actions for enforcement or reduction of their awards only in relation to certain matters.[16] Again, however, that is not properly a rule of competency of witnesses or evidence but of the grounds on which an arbitral award may be challenged.[17]

PROSECUTORS AS WITNESSES

In *Graham v McLennan*[18] a burgh prosecutor who was also a superintendent of police gave evidence. That was held to be an incompetent procedure and there were dicta to the effect that no matter what the circumstances might be a prosecutor in a criminal case could not give evidence and that the fact that he did so was sufficient ground for quashing a conviction.[19] Lord Ardwall, however, contented himself with the more limited proposition that 'in the circumstances set forth in the stated case the prosecutor was not a competent witness'. In *Ferguson v Webster*[20] it was held that the procurator fiscal of the Police Court was not a competent witness for the defence. These cases rest on the view that a public prosecutor should be present merely in the exercise of his official duties and that it was undesirable that someone who had prepared the case and read the precognitions should be a witness.[1] The objection, therefore, is to the competency of the prosecutor in the sense of the person who has prepared and conducted the case for the

14 *Pirie v Caledonian Railway Co* (1890) 17 R 1157; Hume II 429–30; *Dickson* paras 1642–6.
15 *Pirie v Caledonian Railway Co* (1890) 17 R 1157 per Lord President Inglis at 1161.
16 *Dickson* para 1639.
17 The arbiter's competency as a witness is coextensive with the ground on which his award may be reduced. See *Black v John Williams & Co (Wishaw) Ltd* 1923 SC 510 1924 SC (HL) 22 at 28–9.
18 1911 SC (J) 16.
19 Per Lord Justice-Clerk at 19.
20 (1869) 1 Coup 370.
1 Per Lord Justice-General at 374, per Lord Deas at 374–5.

prosecution. The person in whose name the prosecution is brought is a competent witness if he has not also conducted the case.[2]

In *Mackintosh v Wooster*[3] some doubt was cast on the absolute dicta in *Graham v McLennan* and on the soundness of *Ferguson v Webster*, the qualified statement of Lord Ardwall in *Graham v McLennan* was preferred and it was said that there was no absolute rule.[4] There may, therefore, be circumstances in which even a prosecutor who has conducted the case will be a competent witness. The principle which the court was concerned to establish in *Ferguson v Webster* was the inconsistency between personal knowledge of facts vital to the case and the discharge by a public prosecutor of his duties. 'It would be the duty of anyone so situated to decline from the outset all interference, either official or judicial, in a case in which he knew he had important testimony to give from his own personal knowledge.'[5] It was observed that if that duty were breached, there was no doubt that 'a remedy would be found to prevent the ends of justice from being defeated'.[6]

PRESENCE IN COURT

General

At common law a person who had been present in court during the hearing of evidence could not, thereafter, be tendered as a witness.[7] As an exception to that rule an expert witness might remain in court during the hearing of evidence of fact but not of other expert evidence.[8] Otherwise the bar to competency was absolute. Its absolute character was removed by the Evidence (Scotland) Act 1840[9] which provided that in any trial before any judge of the Court of Session or before any sheriff, it should not be imperative on the court to reject any witness against whom it was objected that he or she had, without the permission of the court and without the consent of the party objecting, been present in court during all or any part of the proceedings. It is implicit in that wording that the court has a power, no doubt only to be exercised for cause, to permit a potential witness to be present in court while evidence is being heard and, thereafter, to receive him as a witness. In any event, however, the court has a discretion under the Act to admit a witness who has been present in court where it appears that his presence was not the

2 *Mackintosh v Wooster* 1919 JC 15.
3 Ibid.
4 Per Lord Dundass at 19 and Lord Guthrie at 20.
5 Per Lord Deas at 375.
6 Ibid. Cf per Lord Justice-General at 374.
7 *Dickson* para 1599.
8 *Dickson* para 1761.
9 S 3.

consequence of culpable negligence or criminal intent and that the witness had not been unduly instructed or influenced by what took place, or that injustice will not be done by his or her examination.[9] The 1840 Act continues to apply to civil cases. In criminal cases the matter is now governed by provisions of the Criminal Procedure (Scotland) Act 1975[10] which are in practically identical terms. It is *pars judicis* to take the point and, if it is taken, it is for the party seeking to adduce the witness to satisfy the court that its discretion may be properly exercised in his favour.[11] It has been suggested that the witness may be examined for that purpose or independent evidence[12] led but an explanation tendered at the Bar may, it is thought, sometimes be sufficient. It must be shown both (a) that there was no culpable negligence or criminal intent, and (b) either that the witness was not unduly instructed or influenced by what took place in his presence or that injustice will not be done by his being examined. The culpable negligence or criminal intent in question is probably that of the party seeking to adduce the witness. Witnesses commonly remain in court after they have given evidence and their presence in court in that connection is not in practice treated as a barrier to their recall.

Parties, advocates, agents, experts

At common law neither parties nor their advocates or agents were competent as witnesses. They were, of course, commonly present in court but the objection to their competency did not rest on that presence but applied in any event. Accordingly, the statutory provisions modifying the common law requirement to reject a witness against whom it is objected that he has been present in court during the proceedings do not apply to them. Nor is there anything in the enactments abolishing the objection on the ground of agency and partial counsel (by which advocates and solicitors were excluded as witnesses) and making it competent to adduce and examine a party to the cause as a witness which would make the presence in court of parties or their advocates or agents any objection to their competency.[13] Accordingly, parties, their advocates and agents, may give evidence although they have themselves been present in court during the hearing of other evidence and even although they have been actively engaged in the conduct of the case.[14]

10 Ss 140 and 343.

11 *Macdonald v Mackenzie* 1947 JC 169. Cf *Ryan v Paterson* (1972) 36 Jo Crim L 111.

12 *Macdonald v Mackenzie* 1947 JC 169 per Lord Mackay at 174.

13 Evidence (Scotland) Act 1852 s 1, Evidence (Scotland) Act 1853 ss 2, 3 and 4, Evidence (Further Amendment) (Scotland) Act 1874 ss 1 and 3, Criminal Evidence Act 1898 s 1 (now Criminal Procedure (Scotland) Act 1975 ss 141 and 346).

14 *Campbell v Cochrane* 1928 JC 25.

In the case of a party it may, however, be the subject of adverse judicial comment if the evidence of other witnesses is led in his presence before he gives evidence when that could have been avoided by his giving evidence at an earlier stage.[15] For that reason it is good practice that a party who is to be a witness should be the first witness on his own behalf. In any event, the fact that he has heard other evidence before giving his own is a matter to be taken into account in weighing his evidence.[16] A party is, however, always entitled to be present[17] and in a criminal case on solemn procedure the presence of the accused normally is essential.[18]

The common law rule that an expert witness might be allowed to be present during the hearing of evidence of fact is unaffected by statute. Permission is usually granted if there is no objection[19] but consent of parties is not essential and in a criminal case it has been allowed in the face of an objection by the Crown.[20]

BANKERS

Under the Bankers' Books Evidence Act 1879[1] a banker, or officer of a bank, is not compellable in any legal proceedings to which the bank is not a party to produce any banker's book the contents of which can be proved under the Act or to appear as a witness to prove the matters, transactions and accounts recorded therein unless by order of a judge made for special cause. The contents of bankers' books can be proved under the Act by a copy which has been examined against the original and the copy can be proved either by affidavit or by the testimony of an

15 *Penman v Binny's Trustees* 1925 SLT 123.
16 *Fraser v Smith* 1937 SN 67.
17 *Penman v Binny's Trustees* above.
18 Criminal Procedure (Scotland) Act 1975 s 145(1) as amended by Criminal Justice (Scotland) Act 1980 s 21. The 1980 Act introduced a proviso that if, during the course of his trial, an accused so misconducted himself that in the view of the court a proper trial could not take place unless he was removed, the court might order him to be removed for so long as his conduct might make necessary. In that event the trial may proceed in his absence but if he is not legally represented the court must appoint counsel or a solicitor to represent his interests during his absence. In summary procedure trial for certain statutory offences may proceed in the absence of the accused (s 338) and a summary complaint may be disposed of on the accused's plea of guilty by letter without the necessity of his appearance. The statutory power to proceed in an accused's absence where he misconducts himself does not, however, apply to summary trials.
19 *Milne* (1863) 4 Irv 301; *Pritchard* (1865) 5 Irv 88; *Laurie* (1889) 2 White 326; but cf *Granger* (1878) 4 Coup 86.
20 *Murray* (1858) 3 Irv 262 but permission may be refused if the accused objects (*Dingwall* (1867) 5 Irv 466 at 471).
1 S 6.

officer of the bank.[2] If the latter expedient is necessary an officer of the bank is compellable for that purpose.

SPOUSE OF PARTIES IN CIVIL CASE

The Evidence (Scotland) Act 1853[3] enacts that it shall be competent to adduce and examine as a witness the husband or wife of any party, but unlike its English counterpart,[4] does not specifically make the spouse compellable. The discrepancy can be variously interpreted. On the one hand, it can be said that it would be remarkable if Parliament intended to enact different rules for England and Scotland; on the other hand, as Parliament thought it necessary to refer to compellability in the English statute the omission of any such reference from the Scottish Act may be significant. It has been held, on an interpretation of the Criminal Evidence Act 1898, that words rendering a spouse competent as a witness carry no implication of compellability[5] but the considerations affecting the interpretation of criminal legislation are rather different from those applicable to civil cases. 'It is one thing for the state to renounce the evidence of unwilling spouses in its own interests but another for it to deprive private litigants of such evidence'.[6] It is thought that the general principle applies that, in the absence of a rule to the contrary, a competent witness is to be taken to be compellable. That interpretation consists with the exceptions from compellability contained in the enacting section from which it may be inferred that, apart from these exceptions, the witnesses to whom the section refers are compellable.

SOLEMN CRIMINAL PROCEDURE: REQUIREMENT OF NOTICE

In criminal cases under solemn procedure the prosecutor may examine only those witnesses whose names have been included in the list annexed to the indictment and, if he obtains leave to do so, any other witnesses whose names and addresses are contained in a written notice given to the accused not less than two clear days before the jury is sworn.[7] Likewise,

2 Ss 4 and 5.
3 S 3.
4 Evidence (Amendment) Act 1853.
5 *Leach v R* [1912] SC 305.
6 Clive *Husband and Wife* (2nd edn) p 372 (see Sheriff ID Macphail *Research Paper* para 4–03).
7 Criminal Procedure (Scotland) Act 1975 ss 79 and 81. Notice is not required of witnesses to the accused's declaration or to prove the application of an extanct conviction (s 79(2)).

the accused must give written notice of the names and designations of any witness he wishes to examine who are not on the Crown list, at least three clear days before the jury is sworn, but if he is unable to give such notice and can satisfy the court, before the jury is sworn, of his inability the court may allow the witnesses to be examined giving such remedy to the prosecutor by adjournment or postponement of the trial or otherwise as shall seem just.[8] The prosecution can waive its right to notice but otherwise these provisions are peremptory.[9] The accused need not, however, give notice of his own intention to give evidence[10] and the prosecutor or the accused may, without giving notice but subject to the power of the court to grant such adjournment or postponement of the trial as may seem just, call as a witness a co-accused who has pleaded guilty to all charges against him which remain before the court.[11] The time for determining whether any charges against the co-accused remain before the court is when he is tendered as a witness.[12] Permission may be granted for the leading of additional evidence or evidence in replication, although the witness has not been included in a list of witnesses or notice given.[13] In circumstances other than those just indicated notice requires to be given of intention to call a co-accused as a witness[14] and notice has also to be given if a spouse of an accused is to be a witness whether for the other spouses's defence or the defence of a co-accused, or for the prosecution. It is competent for the prosecutor to examine any witness included in any notice lodged by the accused and for the accused to examine any witness included in any list or notice lodged by the prosecutor or by a co-accused.

COMPELLABILITY OF WITNESS NOT CITED

It was at common law an objection to the competency of a witness that he had appeared without being cited. That objection was removed by the Evidence (Scotland) Act 1852,[15] but it has been questioned whether

8 Ibid s 82(2).
9 *Lindie v HM Advocate* 1974 SLT 208.
10 *Kennedy v HM Advocate* (1898) 2 Adam 588.
11 Criminal Procedure (Scotland) Act 1975 ss 141(3) and 346(3) as added by Criminal Justice (Scotland) Act 1980 s 28. These provisions apply although the co-accused has pleaded guilty before the trial at an accelerated diet (*Monaghan v HM Advocate* 1984 SLT 262).
12 *Lindie v HM Advocate* above.
13 Criminal Procedure (Scotland) Act 1975 ss 149, 149A, 350 and 350A as substituted by Criminal Justice (Scotland) Act 1980 s 30. See ch 13 below.
14 *Lindie v HM Advocate* 1973 SLT 208.
15 S 1 (now Criminal Procedure (Scotland) Act 1975 ss 138 and 341 for criminal proceedings).

witnesses thus made competent are also compellable.[16] There is, however, little room for doubt that the ordinary rule that compellability follows on competency applies. Citation is designed to secure attendance within the precincts of the court. Any person there present who has knowledge of matters relevant to the subject matter of the enquiry may be compelled to give evidence unless there is ground to the contrary.[17] Accordingly, a witness brought but not examined by one party, may, as long as he remains within the precincts, be compelled to give evidence at the instance of the other party.[18]

THE SOVEREIGN, OTHER HEADS OF STATE AND THEIR FAMILIES

The law of England has been said by the law officers of the Crown to be that the Sovereign is neither competent nor compellable as a witness,[19] but modern textbooks refer only to her non-compellability and seem to assume her competency.[20] Non-compellability as an attribute of sovereignty may be a necessary constitutional principle but the bar to competency is less easy to explain or defend and there is no Scottish authority which supports it. The evidence of other members of the Royal Family is both competent and compellable. Foreign heads of state, members of their families forming part of their household and their private servants have the same immunities and privileges as are conferred on the head of a diplomatic mission, the members of his family forming part of his household and his private servants by the Diplomatic Privileges Act 1964, except that the restrictions by reference to nationality or residence contained in that Act do not apply.[1] A certificate by, or on behalf of, the Secretary of State is conclusive evidence on any question of whether any country is a state for this purpose or as to the person to be regarded as the Head of State.[2]

DIPLOMATS

Under provisions of the Vienna Convention applied as law in this

16 *McDonnell v McShane* 1967 SLT (Sh Ct) 61.
17 Ibid. Cf *Watson v Livingston* (1902) 5 F 171.
18 See *Parker v NB Railway Co* (1900) SLT 18.
19 *R v Mylius* (1911) Times, 2 February. See Sheriff ID Macphail *Research Paper* para 3–04.
20 Eg *Cross on Evidence* (6th edn) p 203.
1 State Immunity Act 1978 s 20.
2 Ibid s 21.

country by the Diplomatic Privileges Act 1964[3] the head of a diplomatic mission or any member of the diplomatic staff of the mission is not obliged to give evidence. The privilege appears to be personal to the individual diplomat and if he elects to give evidence he is a competent witness. The same privilege is extended to members of the diplomat's family forming part of his household, provided they are not citizens of the UK and colonies, and to members of the administrative and technical staff of the mission, together with members of their families forming part of their respective households, provided they are not citizens of the UK and colonies or permanently resident there. If any question arises of whether any person is entitled to such a privilege, a certificate issued by or under the authority of the Secretary of State is conclusive evidence of any fact relating to that question. The privilege may be withdrawn by Order in Council on the ground of lack of reciprocity. Where a diplomat is a national of, or permanently resident in, the UK or colonies he enjoys inviolability in respect of official acts performed in the exercise of his functions but is not otherwise immune from giving evidence.

CONSULAR OFFICERS AND STAFF; INTERNATIONAL ORGANISATIONS

The staff of foreign consulates and the corresponding officers of Commonwealth countries[4] may be called upon to attend as witnesses in the course of judicial or administrative proceedings. No coercive measure or penalty may, however, be applied to a consular officer should he decline to do so, with the result that he is, in effect, non-compellable. That is true, however, only of consular officers holding career appointments. Honorary consular officers and also all members of the administrative, technical or service staff are compellable as witnesses, except that they are not obliged to give evidence concerning matters connected with the exercise of their functions or as expert witnesses with regard to the law of the state they represent. The immunity of consular officers who are citizens of the UK and colonies,

3 Ss 2, 3 and 4, Sch 1, Arts 1, 31(2), 37(1), (2) and 38.
4 Consular Relations Act 1968 s 1, Sch, Arts 1, 41, 45, 59 and 71; Diplomatic and Other Privileges Act 1971 s 4 and Sch (consular and similar officers of the Republic of Ireland and Commonwealth countries).

British subjects, or a British protected person, or who are permanently resident in the UK or colonies, is similarly restricted.

Immunity similar to the above may be extended by order in council to members of international organisations and participants in international conferences.[5]

5 International Organisations Acts 1968 and 1981.

CHAPTER 10

Conduct of proof or trial

At proof or trial evidence is led without any introductory statement except that in a civil jury trial there is an opening speech to the jury before the pursuer's evidence is led and, if the defenders lead evidence, there is a similar speech for the defenders.

ORDER OF PROOF

A decision on who is to lead in the proof does not determine any question of onus but the guiding consideration is that evidence should be led first on behalf of the party on whom the legal burden of proof rests. That usually means in a civil case that evidence is first led on behalf of the pursuer and in a criminal case it is always first led on behalf of the prosecutor.

Evidence is led by each witness being examined on behalf of the party who adduces him then cross-examined by the other party or parties and, finally, examined again by the party who adduced him. The first examination on behalf of the party who adduces the witness is called 'the examination in chief'. The examination for the other party or parties is called 'cross-examination' and the final examination on behalf of the party adducing is called 're-examination'. Each witness is examined in chief, cross-examined and re-examined before the next witness is called and examined. The examination in chief is preceded by the witness taking the oath or affirming. Examination in chief, cross-examination and re-examination should all proceed without interruption apart from such interruption as is necessary for the opposing party to object to questions on lawful grounds and such limited interruption as the judge may think it necessary to make. At the conclusion of re-examination the judge may question the witness further in order to clarify matters which he considers obscure but, in general, judicial questioning should be limited. If at the close of re-examination or of the judge's questions, any party wishes to ask further questions or, if at a later stage it is desired to have a witness recalled that may be done only by leave of the Court and the question should then normally be put to the witness by the judge although parties may propose questions for the judge to put to the witness.

FORM AND NATURE OF QUESTIONS

All questions should relate to matters relevant to the issues in the case and should be designed to elicit only evidence of an admissible kind. In cross-examination, and in some circumstances in examination in chief and re-examination, questions may also be asked which, although not relevant to the issue, are relevant to the credibility of the witness.[1] In examination in chief and in re-examination, leading questions may not be asked. A leading question is a question which is so framed that it suggests to the witness the answer which he is to give (eg to ask a witness in a case of murder 'Did you see the accused plunge the knife into the victim?'). An alternative form which leaves the answer open should be used. The only exceptions to the rule against leading questions in examination in chief or re-examination are where the questions relate to matters of narrative or of an introductory nature or are about matters which are not to any substantial degree in dispute or, perhaps, where the witness is hostile (to be considered later). Leading questions ought to be objected to, but even where objection is not taken, use of leading questions has a serious adverse effect on the value of evidence.[2]

HYPOTHETICAL QUESTIONS

It is sometimes said that hypothetical questions should not be asked. That is, however, too broadly expressed. Hypothetical questions are often essential. To elicit expert testimony it is necessary to put to the witness the hypothesis on which his opinion is asked. A distinction should be made between two senses of the term 'hypothetical question'.[3] First of all, a hypothetical question may be directed to what the consequences would have been, if they had occurred, of actions or events which in fact did not take place. Second, the hypothetical question may ask the witness to assume a certain state of facts which either has been proved or

1 Witnesses may always be cross-examined as to their own credibility and if a witness turns out to be adverse to the party adducing him it will usually be competent to question him on his credibility. Where it is competent to lead evidence of previous consistent statements, or *de recenti* statements, or previous inconsistent statements (chap 3 above) witnesses may, of course, be examined to that effect.

2 *McKenzie v McKenzie* 1943 SC 108, where Lord Justice-Clerk Cooper said of the habitual and presistent use of leading questions in examination in chief on central issues of disputed fact that it will 'not only displace entirely the confidence we ought to put in the deposition of a witness but may make the answer as given a worthless answer'.

3 See Walker and Walker *Law of Evidence in Scotland* p 361, para 339(c).

which it is intended to prove. There can be no objection to a hypothetical question, otherwise leigtimate, of the second type although, of course, it runs the risk of adverse comment if proof is not forthcoming of what it was intended to prove. The first type of hypothetical question raises more difficulty. Purely fanciful questions should be excluded but in most cases they would, in any event, be excluded as irrelevant. Sometimes hypothetical questions of the first kind may be necessary (eg in seeking to assess the materiality of a breach of contract it may be necessary to ask what would have happened if the breach had not taken place). Disapproval of hypothetical questions of this kind was expressed in the Outer House in *AB v CD*[4] but it is thought that that disapproval which is, in any event, difficult to reconcile with *Bairner v Fels*,[5] cannot apply to all such questions. The objection to hypothetical questions is probably due to a confusion. Such questions may often be irrelevant or seek inadmissible opinion evidence. For that reason hypothetical questions, at any rate of the first type, have sometimes been treated as if they were in themselves objectionable. The true tests are, however, probably those of relevancy. If a hypothetical question satisfies these tests there seems to be no reason why it should be excluded. To that the qualification should, however, be made that a hypothetical question ought not to be put to a witness where the hypothesis is a matter within the witness's knowledge until he has had an opportunity of admitting or denying the hypothesis.

SCOPE OF CROSS-EXAMINATION; FOUNDATION FOR DEFENCE

Cross-examination is not limited to matters on which the witness has given evidence in examination in chief but may range beyond those matters so as to elicit facts not already brought out which may be in favour of the case of the cross-examiner or with a view to destroying the credibility of the witness. Cross-examination should, however, at least cover all the matters on which the witness has given evidence in chief with the sole exception of matters which are not in controversy. Failure to cross-examine a witness on a matter on which he has given evidence in chief may bar the cross-examiner from leading evidence on that matter or render evidence he has already led of little value. Failure to cross-examine does not, however, amount to an admission so as to remove the need for corroboration of the evidence in chief.[6]

4 1957 SC 415.
5 1931 SC 674.
6 *Stewart v Glasgow Corpn* 1958 SC 28.

A defender in cross-examining the pursuer's witnesses must lay the foundation for any case he hopes to establish. By that is meant that the defender must put to each of the pursuer's witnesses such part of his own case as may be supposed to be within the knowledge of the witness. The purpose of this rule is to give the witness an opportunity of dealing by denial or explanations with the matter which the defender intends to prove. There may sometimes be doubt about what matters are within the witness's knowledge and there is no obligation to put every part of the defender's case to a witness just in case it may be a matter on which he might comment. Proof should not be

> 'uselessly overburdened by the needless expedient of putting the defender's case to every witness for the pursuer when under cross-examination. On the other hand, the most obvious principles of fair play dictate that, if it is intended later to contradict upon a specific and important issue to which the witness had deponed or to prove some critical fact to which that witness ought to have a chance of tendering an explanation or denial, the point ought normally to be put to the witness in cross-examination. If such cross-examination is omitted, the witness may have to be recalled with the leave of the court, possibly on conditions as to expenses, and in some circumstances the omission may cause fatal damage to the case'.[7]

CROSS-EXAMINATION AND EVIDENCE BEARING ON CREDIBILITY

Cross-examination as to credibility may include questions on the witness's relationship to a party, his interest in the case, his motive for giving evidence, prejudice and, subject to the privilege against self-incrimination, the witness's character. Questions as to character may include cross-examination as to previous convictions inferring dishonesty.[8] As the evidence of prostitutes[9] and of accomplices[10] is suspect, it is, subject to privilege, competent to examine witnesses as to whether they bear that character. Except in cross-examination of the witness

7 *McKenzie v McKenzie* (1943 SC 108 per Lord Justice-Clerk Cooper.

8 Scottish practice confines cross-examination on convictions to convictions relating to dishonesty such as theft, fraud, or perjury as it is only such convictions which are thought to reflect on the witness's credibility. In England, a much wider latitude is allowed although restriction has been recommended (*Cross on Evidence* (6th edn) pp 288–9).

9 *Tennant v Tennant* (1883) 10 R 1187. There may, however, be some doubt as to whether this authority would now be followed.

10 *Dow v McKnight* 1949 JC 38. See ch 9 above.

whose credibility is under attack evidence cannot be led if its only purpose is to reflect on a witness's credibility. Therefore, if a witness denies a conviction for a crime of dishonesty, his commission of the crime cannot be proved whether by production of an extract conviction or otherwise.

PREVIOUS INCONSISTENT STATEMENTS OF WITNESS

The general rule that evidence cannot be led if its only purpose is to reflect on the witness's credibility, suffers an exception in the case of previous inconsistent statements made by the witness. Evidence of such inconsistent statements may be led under a rule introduced by the Evidence (Scotland) Act 1852, s 3 and now embodied for criminal cases in the Criminal Justice (Scotland) Act 1975.[11] Where it is intended to lead such evidence the witness in question must first be cross-examined as to his having made the inconsistent statement. A similar course should be followed where the need emerges to discredit one of one's own witnesses. In such an event an opportunity must be taken in the course of examination of the witness to put to him his previous inconsistent statement and if that is not done evidence of the inconsistent statement will be incompetent. Despite the generality of the words of the statute it is probably not competent to put to a witness a statement made by him on precognition or to lead evidence of such a statement.[12]

In cross-examination there is no objection to leading questions and they may be an important tactical weapon. If, however, the witness's evidence turns out to be favourable to the cross-examiner it may be more effective if given in the witness's own words rather than by assent to a series of leading questions.

SCOPE OF RE-EXAMINATION

The only peculiarity of re-examination is that it must be confined to matters which have been dealt with in cross-examination. Its purpose is to give the party who has adduced the witness an opportunity of clearing up difficulties or ambiguities which may have emerged from cross-examination or to seek to repair the damage which cross-examination may have done. It is not an opportunity for him to put his case to the

11 Ch 3 above.
12 Ch 7 above.

witness all over again, still less for the introduction of new matter. Subject to these qualifications, the rules for re-examination are the same as those for examination in chief.

CONCURRING WITNESSES

In civil cases it is competent, in order to save time, to hold one witness as concurring in chief and cross with the previous witness. This can, of course, only be done with the consent of parties and is, in fact, of rare occurrence. The concurring witness is sworn and parties then state that they are holding him as concurring with a named previous witness. The previous witness may then be taken as corroborated by the concurring witness. This procedure is not open in criminal cases.[13]

RECALL OF WITNESS

So long as the proof is not formally closed a judge may recall a witness who has been examined either *ex proprio motu* or, in his discretion, at the request of one of the parties.[14] This power is sparingly exercised and is limited to cases where it is necessary to clear up some point which has been left in doubt or uncertainty or where a later witness has given evidence on which the witness to be recalled could not have been interrogated while in the witness box. It is a possible course in criminal as well as civil cases.[15]

USE OF DOCUMENTS TO REFRESH THE MEMORY

In general, evidence must be given from a witness's own unaided recollection. An expert witness may, however, refresh his memory by referring to textbooks and any witness may refresh his memory by referring to a note or other record made by himself at the time of the event or transaction in question or so soon thereafter that the matter is

13 *Cafferty v Cheyne* [1939] JC 1.
14 Evidence (Scotland) Act 1852 s 4.
15 *Davidson v McFadyen* 1942 JC 95. The common law power to recall a witness in a criminal case is limited to clearing up ambiguities (*Lindie v HM Advocate* 1974 JC 1 at 6, 1974 SLT 208 at 211. See also Renton and Brown *Criminal Procedure according to the Law of Scotland* (3rd edn) para 18–79). In addition, however, under the Criminal Procedure (Scotland) Act 1975 ss 149, 149A, 350 and 350A, as substituted by the Criminal Justice (Scotland) Act 1980 s 30, the judge may permit the recall of a witness for the purpose of leading additional evidence, or evidence in replication, for which those sections provide (see p 167 below).

still fresh in the witness's memory. It must not be a precognition or other record made by someone other than the witness unless perhaps where notes have been taken down by someone else at the witness's dictation and under his supervision or have otherwise been made under his immediate observation.

Notes used for this purpose need not themselves be admissible evidence and in many cases they will not be so. In principle there seems to be no reason that the note should be lodged as a production. A distinction has, however, sometimes been drawn between the use of notes to refresh or stimulate the memory of the witness and the use of notes as a substitute for his memory. In a practical sense that distinction is very difficult to maintain. There is, however, authority for the view that in the latter event (ie where the notes are a substitute for the witness's memory) they may be used by the witness only if they are proved to have been accurately made and if, in a solemn criminal trial at any rate, they are a production.[16]

When documents are used to refresh a witness's memory the cross-examiner is entitled to see them for the purpose of his cross-examination but he is only entitled to see such parts of the witness's notes as he has used for the purpose of refreshing his memory.[17] Where a witness has made notes but has not used them for that purpose there is no right of access to the notes.[18]

HOSTILE WITNESSES

In English law 'hostile witness' is a technical term to which distinct legal rules attach.[19] The general principle of English law is that a party adducing a witness must be held as putting forward the witness as a person of credit. He may not, in examination in chief or re-examination of the witness, seek to destroy that witness's credit by putting to him previous inconsistent statements—nor may he lead evidence from other witnesses of previous inconsistent statements by the witness in question. An exception is, however, allowed in the case of what is called a 'hostile witness'. Not every unfavourable witness adduced by a party is a hostile

16 See *Macpherson* (1845) 2 Broun 450 and *Gibb* (1871) 2 Coup 35.
17 *Niven v Hart* (1898) 25 R (J) 89.
18 *Hinshelwood v Auld* 1926 JC 4.
19 See *Cross* pp 269 ff. See also *Lowe v Bristol Omnibus Co* 1934 SC 1, in which Lord Justice-Clerk Aitchison referred to the English practice and said 'For myself I should very much deprecate its introduction, especially in this kind of case, where it is notorious that witnesses who are perfectly honest may observe the same thing in different ways and what is more important that the recollections of witnesses of what they did observe may vary from time to time'.

witness. A witness who merely fails to prove what he was expected to prove is not hostile. A hostile witness is a witness who shows that he does not desire to tell the truth at the instance of the party who calls him. If the judge gives leave to treat a witness as hostile he may then be examined as to previous inconsistent statements and these statements may be proved in evidence.

Mention has been made of the position in English law because, although it is clear that the law of Scotland on this matter is entirely different, some confusion has existed.[20] In Scotland too there is, of course, prima facie an assumption that a witness adduced by a party is put forward by that party as a witness of credit and in some Scottish authorities there is a reflection of the view that the party must be held as accepting the testimony of a witness whom he adduces. In general, however, Scots law has acknowledged the right of a party to depart from the evidence of a witness adduced by him and has not laid down any technical rules as to the treatment of witnesses as hostile.[1] Circumstances may compel a party to adduce a witness who has an adverse interest to him or a prejudice against him. Moreover, witnesses may go back on what they are expected to say and give unexpected evidence adverse to the party calling them. In such circumstances, a party is entitled to seek to discredit the witness insofar as his evidence is adverse. The leave of the court is not required. Subject to the court's seeing that the witness has fair play, counsel may examine the witness as he thinks best and, provided the witness has been given a fair opportunity of answering any charge of unreliability or untruthfulness, may invite the course to disbelieve his testimony. This is the rule in both civil and criminal cases.[2]

It is not clear on the Scottish authorities whether the party adducing a witness who turns out to be hostile is then entitled to use techniques of cross-examination such as the use of leading questions.[3]

OBJECTIONS TO EVIDENCE

Objection to evidence should be taken as soon as the objectionable question is asked or, if the objectionability does not lie in the question

20 *Low v Bristol Omnibus Co* above.
1 *Avery v Cantilever Shoe Co* 1942 SC 469 per Lord President Normand.
2 *Frank v HM Advocate* 1938 JC 17 at 22.
3 See *Gall v Gall* (1870) 9 M 177 per Lord President Inglis: 'A party is often obliged from the exigencies of this case to adduce, a witness whom he cannot expect to be favourable to him, and he is, I think, in the circumstances entitled to treat the witness as a hostile witness whom he is examining in chief'.

but in the answer which is given, as soon as the objectionable feature of the answer emerges. Objection may be on any of the grounds of competency or relevancy which have been mentioned, or on the ground that insufficient notice of the line of evidence has been given in the pleadings (that there is 'no record for the evidence'). The objection may be to a particular question or to a particular item of evidence and a question may be objectionable where, although formally apparently correct, it is designed to elicit inadmissible evidence. Objection to the 'line' (ie trend) of evidence should be taken as soon as a question which seeks to introduce an inadmissible line of evidence is asked.

Failure to take objection at the appropriate time will not entitle the court or jury to rely on clearly incompetent or irrelevant evidence but where the objection is on the ground of insufficient notice on record or on some other ground which does not go to the fundamental competency of the evidence, a party may be held to have waived all right to criticise the admission of the evidence by not having taken objection at the appropriate time.[4]

Ruling on objection; reservation

When an objection is taken the judge may rule on it at any time and in a jury trial must do so. In a civil proof, it is open to the judge, and is often convenient, to allow the evidence to be led under reservation of its competence and relevance and if that is done the competency and relevancy of the evidence objected to may be considered after the proof has been concluded. The disadvantages of this procedure are that the proof is burdened by evidence which may have in the end to be discarded and that there is some risk of the judge's mind being influenced by matters which ought to be excluded from his consideration. There is also a practical risk that matter reserved may at the end of the day be overlooked. The advantages of the procedure are that it enables the court to decide the question of admissibility after all the evidence has been led and it may often be easier to make such a decision then, especially on questions of relevancy, than it would have been at an earlier stage. There is also the considerable advantage that if evidence is allowed under reservation it is available for consideration by the appeal court even if the judge of first instance should, after hearing all the evidence, have decided that it was inadmissible.

It is, unfortunately, obscure what the proper course to be followed in summary criminal trials is. In *Clark v Stuart*[5] the Court not only approved the admission of evidence under reservation of its competency and

4 *Brown's Executors v North British Steel Foundry Ltd* 1967 SLT 421.
5 *Clark v Stuart* 1950 JC 8.

relevancy but expressly commended that practice as the proper course to be followed in order to allow the question of law raised by the objection to be examined if necessary by a higher court. Only exceptional circumstances, it was said, would justify the exclusion outright of what might be an important chapter of evidence. Unfortunately for the clarity of the law, a contrary view has since been expressed without considering *Clark v Stuart*.[6]

ADDITIONAL PROOF

Civil cases

After the proof has been closed it is only on the strongest grounds that further evidence may be led.[7] The court will not open up the proof to examine a witness who could have been but was not called or to hear evidence on part of a case of which proof has been neglected. Allowance of additional proof must, therefore, be regarded as highly exceptional. In cases originating in the Court of Session the Lord Ordinary or, if the case is reclaimed, the Inner House, has at common law the power to allow additional evidence to be led provided it could not have been previously obtained by the exercise of reasonable diligence. In the Sheriff Court the Sheriff Principal,[8] but not the Sheriff,[9] may allow additional proof, and if the case is appealed to the Court of Session the Inner House has a statutory power to allow additional proof.[10] The statutory power to be exercised 'if necessary' has been interpreted as meaning if necessary in the interests of justice.[11]

In jury trials it is, of course, once the trial is over, no longer possible to lead evidence before the jury and if further evidence is to be led the only course open is to have a new trial at which all the evidence will probably require to be led again. A new trial on the ground that new evidence has come to light which could not have been previously obtained by the exercise of reasonable diligence (*res noviter veniens ad notitiam*) is competent but the rule is strictly applied and a new trial on these grounds will be granted only in compelling circumstances.[12] New trials cannot be granted in criminal cases.

6 *MacLeod v Woodmuir Minors' Welfare Society Social Club* 1961 JC 5 at 8.
7 McLaren *Court of Session Practice* p 562.
8 Sheriff Courts (Scotland) Act 1907 s 27.
9 The sheriff has no general power to allow additional proof (see Dobie *Sheriff Court Practice* p 225) but he may allow additional proof after amendment or after the late production of documents (ibid).
10 Court of Session Act 1868 s 72.
11 *Gairdner v McArthur* 1915 SC 589. See also *Macfarlane v Raeburn* 1946 SC 67.
12 See Thomson and Middleton *Manual of Court of Session Procedure* pp 318 ff.

Criminal cases

At common law the prosecutor could not lead new evidence after his case had closed and so could not lead evidence in replication of matter introduced by the defence which had taken him by surprise. The Criminal Procedure (Scotland) Act 1975 contains new provisions for the leading of additional evidence, including evidence in replication. The Act provides that the judge may, on a motion of the prosecutor or defence made after the close of that party's evidence and before the commencement of the speeches to the jury, or in a summary trial before the prosecutor proceeds to address the judge on the evidence, permit the applicant to lead additional evidence but only where the judge (a) considers that the additional evidence is prima facie material, and, (b) accepts that at the time the party's evidence was closed either (i) the additional evidence was not available and could not reasonably have been made available, or (ii) the materiality of such additional evidence could not reasonably have been foreseen by the party. The judge's powers extend, on a motion of the prosecutor, to permitting additional evidence for the purpose of contradicting evidence led by the defence which could not reasonably have been anticipated by the prosecutor, or providing proof of a prior inconsistent statement made by a defence witness. Permission may be granted although it involves recall of a witness and although a witness or production concerned is not included in any list lodged by the parties or notice given where that is required. An adjournment or postponement may be allowed before permitting the additional evidence to be led.[13]

EVIDENCE AND CROSS-EXAMINATION WHERE THERE ARE SEVERAL PARTIES

1 Co-defender

Where two or more defenders are separately represented evidence elicited in cross-examination of the pursuer's witnesses by one defender may be used in evidence both for and against the others.[12] It is common for second and subsequent defenders formally to adopt the first defender's cross-examination but it is doubtful if that is strictly necessary as the rule that evividence elicited in cross-examination by one defender is evidence both for and against the other does not seem to rest on adoption.[14] The practice of adopting cross-examination may have

13 Criminal Procedure (Scotland) Act 1975 ss 149, !49A, 350 and 350A as substituted by Criminal Justice (Scotland) 1980 s 30.
14 *Ayr Road Trustees v Adams* (1883) 11 R 326.

arisen from the need (which obtained at least in former practice) for a defender to adopt evidence given in chief on behalf of another defender on which he wished to found. It is sometimes said that one defender is not entitled to cross-examine another defender's witnesses except where one defender is blaming another. The exception takes most of the content out of the rule if it be such. In this respect, as in the others, it is thought that the particular rules which have been developed in former practice can now be safely disregarded and that modern practice sanctions treating all evidence in the case, however elicited, as evidence in the cause and so available for and against all parties.[14]

2 Co-pursuers

Cases where pursuers have conflicting interests are rare and it is sometimes said that where there is no conflict of interest there is no right to cross-examine. It may, however, happen that where pursuers, although their interests do not conflict, are separately represented, a witness for one pursuer may give evidence without touching on some matter on which he could give evidence and on which another pursuer would wish to have his evidence or he may not be questioned as fully on some point as another pursuer would wish. It is difficult to see why there should be any objection in principle in that situation to the other pursuer examining him on the matters which have not been adequately covered. Where there is a conflict of interest it seems that there is a right to cross-examination and that view has been affirmed in salvage cases.[15]

3 Co-accused

As compared with the modern tendency to get away from technical rules in civil cases where there are several parties some technical rules until recently persisted, or appeared to persist, in the criminal trial of more than one accused.

At common law an accused person was not competent as a witness at his own trial. There could therefore be no question of one accused calling another as a witness unless the trials had been separated or the accused whom it was proposed to call as a witness had pleaded guilty during the trial or at an earlier diet or the prosecution had withdrawn the charge against him. Nor at common law could there be any question of one accused cross-examining a co-accused who had given evidence on his own behalf. The Criminal Evidence Act 1898 did not affect the incompetency of one accused calling another as a witness but by making an accused person a competent witness in his own defence it opened the

15 *Boyle v Olsne* 1912 ST 1235.

question of his being subject to cross-examination by a co-accused. It was held that there was a right to cross-examine but only where the witness had given evidence incriminating the co-accused.[16] The restrictions on freedom to cross-examine and on calling another accused as a witness have now been removed by an amendment to the Criminal Procedure (Scotland) Act 1975 which provides:

> 'The accused may—
> (a) with the consent of a co-accused, call that other accused as a witness on the accused's behalf; or
> (b) ask a co-accused any question in cross-examination if that co-accused gives evidence,
> but he may not do both in relation to the same co-accused.'[17]

A co-accused who is examined or cross-examined has no privilege against self-incrimination on the offences with which he is charged. Evidence so elicited is, it appears, available for or against both accused. It is not the evidence of an accomplice and is not to be received *cum nota*.[18]

The law was at one time understood to be that evidence given by a witness for one accused was not evidence against another accused although it might be relied on in his favour.[19] It is, however, now settled that evidence of any witness in the case is evidence in support or rebuttal of any charges in respect of any of the accused.[20] It follows that if a witness for one accused gives evidence against another accused the latter has a right to cross-examine and even if there is no such adverse tendency in the witness's evidence it seems right that a co-accused should be entitled to examine the witness in order to elicit evidence in his favour.

The fact that evidence by one accused is available as evidence for or against the other does not mean that a prosecutor is entitled to cross-examine an accused on questions irrelevant to his own guilt. If an accused person gives evidence incriminating another accused person the prosecutor may take advantage of that evidence but he is not entitled to cross-examine for the purpose of eliciting it.[1] The prosecutor, of course, cross-examines last.

16 *Gemmell & McFadyen v MacNiven* 1928 JC 5.
17 Ss 141 and 346 as amended by Criminal Justice (Scotland) Act 1980 s 28.
18 Ch 9 above.
19 *Young v HM Advocate* 1932 JC 63 per Lord Justice-General Clyde at 73. Cf *Morrison v Adair* 1943 JC 25.
20 *Todd v HM Advocate* 1984 SLT 262.
1 *Young v HM Advocate* 1932 JC 63 per Lord Justice-General Clyde at 74. *Sed quaere* if this is still the law.

OATH AND AFFIRMATION

The testimony of witnesses is given after they have taken the oath or made an affirmation to tell the truth. The usual form of oath is 'I swear by almighty God that I will tell the truth, the whole truth and nothing but the truth' and the prescribed form of affirmation is 'I (witness's full name) do solemnly, sincerely and truly declare and affirm that I will tell the truth, the whole truth and nothing but the truth'.[2] An affirmation has the same force and effect as an oath, with the result that false testimony is perjury.[3] A witness who objects to the usual form of oath on the ground that it is contrary to his religious belief may take the oath in a form appropriate to his belief and such an oath is equally binding. Where, however, it is not reasonably practicable to administer an oath in the manner appropriate to the witness's religious belief, he may be required to affirm.[4] Anyone objecting to taking an oath is entitled to affirm.[5] The testimony of children and of persons who, because of their mental condition, are unable to understand the nature of an oath may be given after being admonished to tell the truth.[6]

2 Oaths Act 1978 s 6.
3 Ibid s 5(4).
4 Ibid s 5(2) and (3).
5 Ibid s 5(1).
6 Ch 9 above.

CHAPTER 11

Requirements of proof; specialities of documentary and real evidence; foreign law

'Public document' is not a term of art but it is used in this chapter as a general heading for records and other official documents recognised by law as being kept for a public or statutory purpose. Acts of Parliament, subordinate Scottish and UK legislation and interlocutors and decrees of courts have already been considered.[1] The treatment of public documents in this chapter is concerned with the use in evidence of the other principal categories of public documents.

PARLIAMENTARY JOURNALS AND THE GAZETTES

The Journals of Parliament are proved by examined copies. They are evidence that the proceedings to which they relate took place but not of the truth of any matter of fact asserted in the course of those proceedings.[2] The evidentiary significance of the official gazettes is similar. They are evidence of the making and terms of proclamations, orders, regulations and other public official acts published in them but they do not constitute evidence of a private right conferred even where that right flows from the Crown.[3] Where notices concerning individuals in their private capacity are published in the Gazette, eg sequestrations, the Gazette is evidence that a notice in those terms was published but is not evidence of any fact narrated.[4] A complete copy of the Gazette which bears to be such will be accepted as authentic on production.[5]

1 Chs 5 and 8 above.
2 *Dickson* para 1110; Bell's Princ para 2210.
3 *Dickson* para 1112.
4 *Dickson* para 1113.
5 *Dickson* para 1112.

PUBLIC REGISTERS AND OFFICIAL RECORDS

Public records such as the Register of Birth, Deaths and Marriages are evidence of facts recorded in them which fall within the purview of the record.[6] Thus these registers are evidence and, by statute, sufficient evidence of the facts of birth, marriage and death respectively,[7] although other evidence will be required to identify the persons named in the record. Proof of the entry in the Register is by an extract or an abbreviated certificate.[8] Registers kept under statute by professional bodies and military registers afford evidence in the same way of the matters they are designed to record. And generally any official record required to be kept by a public officer is evidence of the facts which it was his duty to record but not of other matters.[9] Thus the Books of a Burgh have been admitted to prove the appointment of a Burgh official.[10] The admissibility of these records is independent of the admissibility of documents compiled under a duty to record in terms of the Law Reform (Miscellaneous Provisions) (Scotland) Act 1966.[11]

SHIPS' LOG BOOKS

Under the Merchant Shipping Acts ships' log books and certain other documents pertaining to ships are admissible as evidence of the matter stated therein where these matters are stated in pursuance of the Acts or 'by any officer in pursuance of his duties as such officer'.[12] Entries are proved by a copy or extract if it is proved to be an examined copy or purports to be signed and certified by an officer to whose custody the original document was entrusted.[13] The doubt which at one time existed as to whether entries admissible under the Merchant Shipping Act 1894 could, by themselves, constitute sufficient evidence for proof has now

6 *Dickson* paras 1104 and 1204.
7 Registration of Births, Deaths and Marriages (Scotland) Act 1965 s 41(3). Apart from statutory provision the registers were evidence but not *probatio probata* of the facts contained in them (*Dickson* para 1204). The statutory provision does not apply to pre-1855 Registers. The trustworthiness of entries in the earlier registers is dependent on the regularity with which the particular register was kept (*Dickson* para 1173).
8 S 43(3) above.
9 *Dickson* para 1209.
10 *Hunter v Hill* (1833) 11 S 989. Cf *Williams v Dobbie* (1884) 11 R 982 (lighthouse records as evidence of weather).
11 Ch 3 above.
12 Merchant Shipping Act 1894 s 695.
13 Ibid s 695(2).

been removed by a provision that they shall be sufficient evidence.[14] They are not, however, exhaustive of proof and so, if other evidence is led or if there is reason for doubting their accuracy, they may not be conclusive.

VALUATION ROLL AND ELECTORAL REGISTER

The Valuation Roll is competent and in certain cases conclusive evidence of the rateable valuation of property during the year to which it relates.[15] It is also evidence of tenancy and occupation but is not conclusive of these matters. The Electoral Roll is evidence only of the right to vote and is normally conclusive of that.[16]

MINUTES OF LOCAL AUTHORITY AND COMPANY MEETINGS

The minute books of a local authority are received in evidence without further proof.[17] They are therefore self-authenticating and prove their own terms. It is thought that this has the result that they afford evidence of what took place at the meeting (eg what resolutions and orders, etc were passed), contrary to the general rule that the primary and normally only admissible evidence of what took place at a meeting is the evidence of those who were present at it and that the only evidentiary significance of a minute is as a statement against the interest of those who accepted it. The minutes of general meetings of companies and of meetings of directors are evidence of the proceedings at the meeting if they purport to be signed by the chairman at that or the next succeeding meeting.[18]

OFFICIAL DOCUMENTS IN SUMMARY CRIMINAL CASES

In a summary criminal case any letter, minute or other official document issuing from the office or in the custody of any government department is when produced prima facie evidence of the matters contained in it.[19] A copy bearing to be certified by any person having authority to certify is equivalent to the original. No witness is required to swear to the document nor is proof required of signature or of authority to certify.

14 S 695(1) as amended by Merchant Shipping Act 1970, Sch 3, para 3.
15 Armour *Valuation for Rating* (5th edn) para 2–26.
16 Representation of the People Act 1949 s 39(1).
17 Local Government (Scotland) Act 1973 Sch 7, para 7.
18 Companies Act 1985 s 382(2).
19 Criminal Procedure (Scotland) Act 1975 s 353.

Similar provisions apply to the proof of any order made by a government department or local authority or public body under statutory powers. A print or copy is evidence of the due making, confirmation and existence of the order but without prejudice to the accused's right to challenge it as ultra vires.

PROOF BY CERTIFICATE

There are numerous statutory provisions providing for proof of certain matters by certificate. They present a varied and sometimes confusing range of terms about the evidentiary effect of the certificate. A provision that a certificate is 'conclusive evidence' means that it establishes the fact certified and that it is incompetent to contradict it by other evidence.[20] Where a certificate is said to be 'sufficient evidence' it does not require to be corroborated or supported by other evidence. It may be contradicted by other evidence but in the absence of such evidence or, it is thought, of circumstances giving rise to doubts as to its accuracy, it is conclusive.[1] 'Prima facie evidence' seems in this context to mean the same as sufficient evidence.[2] Where a party can challenge the sufficiency of a certificate as proof by requiring the granter to be called as a witness and that requirement is made, the uncorroborated testimony of the granter is not sufficient for proof of facts for which corroboration is required.[3] And where a certificate is said merely to be 'evidence' it is no more than a substitute for oral testimony and so requires corroboration in order to establish an essential fact at any rate where it is signed by only one person.[4]

An examination of the various statutes under which certificates may be received in evidence is outwith the scope of this book but notice may be taken of the provisions of the Criminal Justice (Scotland) Act 1980[5] for routine evidence by certificate. In any proceedings, whether summary or solemn, for certain offences under the Road Traffic Regulation Act 1967, the Misuse of Drugs 1971, the Immigration Act 1971, the Social Security Act 1975, the Child Benefit Act 1975 and the Supplementary Benefits Act 1976, a certificate which meets the specified requirements of the 1980 Act is sufficient evidence of the matter to

20 *Jameson v Dow* (1899) 2 F (J) 24; *Henderson v Wardrope* 1932 JC 18.
1 *Chalmers v McMeeking* 1921 JC 4.
2 *Bisset v Anderson* 1949 JC 106.
3 *Callan v MacFadyean* 1950 JC 82.
4 *Bisset v Anderson* above.
5 S 26.

which it relates and of the qualifications and authority of the person by whom it is signed. In any summary criminal proceedings a report purporting to be signed by two authorised forensic scientists is sufficient evidence of any fact or conclusion as to fact contained in the report and of the authority of the signatories. The Act lays down provisions for service of a copy report on the accused and for his giving notice of challenge.

PRIVATE DOCUMENTS

Private documents are those which do not have any of the public or official characteristics which have been described and which are used for the constitution or proof of private right or obligation. Many documents used by governmental and other public bodies are private documents in this sense (eg the documents by which they enter into contract or conveyances of land).

With the exception of probative deeds (ie deeds executed in accordance with the prescribed legal formalities and which as so executed prove their own authenticity) the authenticity of a private document requires to be established by evidence. The evidence should normally be that of the person who wrote or compiled the document but if his evidence should for good reason not be available the authenticity of a document may be established by those who saw it being written or compiled or by hand-writing evidence. The authenticity of a non-probative document may of course be challenged by any evidence tending to show that it is not what it appears to be. Holograph writings must be proved in the same way as other private documents.[6] The only special feature of holograph writings from the standpoint of the law of evidence is that holograph testamentary writings are presumed to be executed on the date they bear.[7] The same presumption applies to writs in *re mercatoria* (ie commercial documents) whether or not they are holograph.[8] The equivalence of holograph writings to probative deeds does not relate to their evidentiary character but is a feature of the law of wills and of the law relating to the constitution of certain contracts.

On principles already noticed the original of a private document is normally the only admissible evidence of its terms.[9] A private document is not evidence of any fact which it narrates unless it falls within one of the exceptions to the rule against hearsay.

6 *Harper v Green* 1938 SC 198.
7 Conveyancing (Scotland) Act 1874 s 40.
8 *McIntyre v National Bank of Scotland* 1910 SC 150.
9 Ch 5 above.

STAMPING

> 'An instrument executed in any part of the United Kingdom, or relating, wheresoever executed, to any property situate, or to any matter or thing done or to be done, in any part of the United Kingdom, shall not, except in criminal proceedings, be given in evidence, or be available for any purpose whatsoever, unless it is duly stamped in according with the law enforced at the time when it was first executed.'[10]

It is *pars judicis* to take the point[11] but where the deed can be legally stamped after execution the defect may be cured by after-stamping[12] and if an undertaking is given that that will be done and the penalties paid the deed may be conditionally admitted.[13] There is authority for the view that inadmissibility attaches only where the deed is tendered in proof of the right or obligation to which it relates and that it may be admitted unstamped in evidence of a fact foreign to the purpose for which it was executed.[14] That view expressed in relation to previous legislation can, however, scarcely be reconciled with the prohibition on the availability of the deed 'for any purpose whatsoever'.[15] A lost or destroyed document is presumed to have been stamped in the absence of evidence to the contrary[16] but if there is evidence that it was at any time unstamped the presumption is that it remained unstamped.[17]

REAL EVIDENCE

It is characteristic of real evidence that the object should be produced to the court for its direct inspection. The term is, however, sometimes extended to embrace objects or phenomena the significance of which is interpreted to the tribunal of fact by expert witnesses. Fingerprints, palmprints, dental impressions and other identifying features of similar kind, blood samples and the behaviour of tracker dogs can be regarded

10 Stamp Act 1891 s 14(4).
11 *Cowan v Stewart* (1872) 10 M 735.
12 Stamp Act 1891 s 14(1).
13 *Simpson's Trustees v Simpson* 1933 SC 128.
14 *Durie's Executors v Fielding* (1893) 20 R 295 per Lord Kinnear at 299.
15 See Walker and Walker *The Law of Evidence in Scotland* p 252, para 238.
16 This is an application of the presumption *omnia rite et solemniter esse acta* (*Dickson* para 1978). If the impossibility of producing the original be proved (*Cowan v Stewart* (1872) 10 M 735) secondary evidence is then admissible (ch 5 above).
17 This is an application of the presumption of continuance.

as real evidence in that sense.[18] The expert describes and interprets the phenomena to the tribunal of fact which, as it were, sees them through his eyes but comes to its own conclusion about the significance of what is thus seen. Expert evidence is in any event often required to interpret real evidence even when it is directly open to the jury's inspection. The significance of blood stains may often have to be interpreted by experts and although a jury may make use of its own observation of samples of handwriting it should not reach a conclusion on the comparisons without expert assistance or the testimony of persons familiar with the handwriting.[19] Even where an expert interpretation is not required real evidence is always partly dependent on testimony because without testimony the relation of the real evidence to the issues in the case cannot be understood. A witness must speak to where an allegedly incriminating object was found and to the provenance of samples of handwriting before they can have significance. The same is often true of documentary evidence. The contents of a probative deed or of a document whose authenticity has been established may sometimes themselves be immediately relevant to the issue or give rise to an inference which can be drawn on an inspection of their terms, but usually testimony will be required to link the document to the parties and the issues.

COMPUTERISED RECORDS

Evidence of computerised records is the subject of detailed statutory regulation.[20]

FOREIGN REGISTERS AND RECORDS

The rules discussed earlier in this chapter on evidence of public documents do not apply to the public records of countries outwith the

18 Sheriff ID MacPhail *Research Paper* para 13–01. *Cross on Evidence* (6th edn) pp 35–6 regards these as examples of retrospectant circumstantial evidence.

19 The older Scottish cases present a confusing pattern. In some cases the jury was allowed and even encouraged to make its decision on its own comparison. In others they were directed to decide on the evidence they had heard and in others again they were not even allowed to see the documents (see *Walker and Walker* p 436, para 414(c)). The jury is, however, entitled to see productions (*HM Advocate v Hayes* 1973 SLT 202 at 205) and it is submitted that the view expressed in the text accords with principle and modern practice. Cf *R v Tilley* [1961] 3 All ER 406, [1961] 1 WLR 1309; *R v Smith* (1968) 52 Cr App R 648; *R v O'Sullivan* [1969] 2 All ER 237, [1969] 1 WLR 497.

20 Law Reform (Miscellaneous Provisions) (Scotland) Act 1968 ss 13, 14 and 15. Acts of Sederunt (Computer Evidence in the Court of Session) 1969, (Computer Evidence in the Court of Session) (Amendment) 1970, (Computer Evidence in the Sheriff Court) 1969, (Computer Evidence in the Sheriff Court) (Amendment) 1970.

UK. Entries in the public registers of overseas countries and other similar matters of public record may, however, be proved under the Evidence (Foreign Dominion and Colonial Documents) Act 1933 wherever an order in council applying the Act has been made. A certificate under the Act affords evidence not only of the contents of the register but also of facts falling within their purview and so may be used for proof of foreign births, deaths and marriages.

FOREIGN LAW AS FACT

Where foreign law (including English law) forms under the relevant rules of international private law one of the issues in the case it is a matter of fact. Certain notorious matters of foreign law such as the legality of roulette at Monte Carlo may, however, be within judicial knowledge.[1] European Community law is within the knowledge of Scottish courts[2] and Northern Irish and English law as well as Scots law are within the knowledge of the House of Lords on Scottish appeals.[3] Under the Maintenance Orders Act 1950 the law with regard to maintenance orders in every part of the UK is within judicial knowledge.[4] Otherwise foreign law, as an issue in the case, must be proved.

COLONIAL STATUTES

Copies of Acts, ordinances and statutes passed by or under the authority of the legislature of any British possession are under the Evidence (Colonial Statutes) Act 1907 to be received in evidence by all courts of justice in the UK if purporting to be printed by the government printer and it has been held in England that such statutes may be construed without the aid of expert evidence in the colonial law.[5] With that possible exception, a Scottish court will not interpret a foreign statute without expert assistance.

PROOF OF FOREIGN LAW BY EXPERTS

Unless one of the alternative procedures indicated in the next paragraph is used the testimony of expert witnesses is necessary where foreign law

1 *Saxby v Fulton* [1909] 2 KB 208. Cf *Re Turner, Meyding v Hinchliff* [1906] WN 27.
2 European Communities Act 1972 s 3.
3 *Elliot v Joicey* 1935 SC (HL) 57.
4 S 22(2).
5 *Jasiewicz v Jasiewicz* [1962] 3 All ER 1017, [1962] 1 WLR 1426.

has to be proved as a matter of fact. There is no fixed rule on what is required to make a witness a suitable expert but an experienced practitioner in the foreign jurisdiction or a judge is undoubtedly suitably qualified. Other qualifications may, however, suffice. In England non-lawyers have been admitted where they had the requisite practical acquaintance with the legal provisions in question[6] but in modern conditions where suitably qualified witnesses are more readily available it may be preferable to insist on a legal qualification. The question, as with other expert witnesses, is whether the witness has sufficient qualifications, practical or academic,[7] to enable him to assist the court.

REMIT TO ASCERTAIN FOREIGN LAW

On consent of parties the court may remit any question of foreign law to foreign experts. If that is done the experts' opinion is binding[8] except that on appeal to the House of Lords the opinion may be disregarded if it is on English or Northern Irish law.[9] A further option available where the question at issue is one of the law of a Commonwealth country is a remit to a superior court of the country concerned.[10] The opinion of the foreign court is conclusive[11] except that if it is an English or Northern Irish court it may be reviewed by the House of Lords.[12] The court has a discretion whether or not to remit and may do so even if expert evidence has been led.[13]

6 *Van der Donckt v Thellusson* (1849) 8 CB 812 (businessman); *Re Dost Ali Khan's Goods* (1880) 6 PD 6 (Embassy official); *Cooper-King v Cooper-King* (1900) P 65 (Governor-General); *Ajami v Customs Controller* [1954] 1 WLR 1405 (banker).
7 *Brailey v Rhodesia Consolidated Ltd* [1910] 2 Ch 95 (Reader in Roman-Dutch law, to Council for Legal Education).
8 *Duchess of Buckingham v Winterbottom* (1851) 13 D 1129 at 1141; *Baird v Mitchell* (1854) 16 D 1088 at 1092.
9 *Macpherson v Macpherson* (1852) 1 Macq 243.
10 British Law Ascertainment Act 1859.
11 S 3.
12 S 4; *De Thoren v Wall* (1876) 3 R (HL) 28.
13 *MacDougall v Chitnavis* 1937 SC 390; *De Thoren v Wall* above.

CHAPTER 12

Requirements of proof: onus and presumptions

ONUS

> 'Whenever a litigation exists somebody must go on with it; the plaintiff is the person to begin; if he does nothing he fails; if he makes out a prima facie case, and nothing is done to answer it the defender fails.
>
> The test therefore as to the burden of proof or onus of proof, whichever term is used, is simply this—to ask one's self which party will be successful if no evidence is given, or if no more evidence is given than has been given at a particular point of the case; for it is obvious that as the controversy involved in the litigation travels on, the parties from moment to moment may reach points at which the onus of proof shifts and at which the tribunal will have to say that if the case stops there it must be decided in a particular manner.
>
> It is not a burden that goes on forever resting on the shoulders of the person upon whom it is first cast. As soon as he brings evidence which, until it is answered, rebuts the evidence against which he is contending, then the balance descends on the other side and the burden rolls over until there is evidence which once more turns the scales.
>
> The question of onus of proof is only a rule for deciding on whom the obligation of going further, if he wishes to win, rests. It is not a rule to enable the jury to decide on the value of conflicting evidence. So soon as a conflict of evidence arises it ceases to be a question of onus of proof.'[1]

The above quotation from Bowen LJ is the *locus classicus* on onus of proof as it was at one time understood in England and is the understanding generally reflected in Scottish practice. Its strong affirmation of the

1 *Abrath v North Eastern Railway Co* (1883) LR 11 QBD 440 per Bowen LJ at 456.

shifting character of the onus is, however, now controversial and requires further examination.

Legal and provisional burdens

In *Brown v Rolls Royce Ltd*[2] Lord Denning distinguished between the legal onus which is imposed by the law itself and the provisional onus which is raised by the state of the evidence. The legal onus in that case rested on the pursuer: ie he had to prove the defenders' negligence and that their negligence caused the disease in respect of which he claimed damages. Evidence prima facie sufficient to discharge that onus might, however, have the effect of provisionally placing an onus on the defenders and that provisional onus might shift many times as the case proceeded. That may appear to say little more than that the onus may (provisionally) shift but the point which the distinction seeks to make is that the party on whom the law affixes the onus of proof is never, as a matter of law, relieved of that onus until the proof is concluded and the issue decided in his favour. The onus can then be said to have been discharged. Although it may, at certain stages of the proof, be possible to say that an onus lies provisionally or tactically on the other party, it never rests on him as a matter of law. If, at the conclusion of the proof, the onus seems so to rest, that is but another way of saying that as a matter of fact the onus may have been discharged. The only direction in law to be given to the trier of fact is that the onus rests where it has always lain and that he has to determine whether, applying the appropriate standard of proof that onus has been discharged. On this view the legal burden never shifts. Rebuttable presumptions of law seem, however, to constitute an exception.

As the provisional onus never arises as a matter of law, it may be questioned whether it is necessary to use the term at all. Its incidence will vary infinitely from case to case according to the particular facts and can never be defined in legal terms. It may, however, be a convenient term for describing how the exigencies of proof present themselves to the litigants as the case progresses or how they may appear from time to time to the tribunal of fact.

Ultimate burden

Clarity is best served if onus of proof is regarded as arising separately in relation to each issue of fact, ie each *factum probandum*. There is, however, a tendency implicit in the quotation with which this chapter began to regard onus as spreading over the case as a whole. Modern terminology

2 1960 SC (HL) 22 at 27 and 28. For a fuller exposition see Denning 'Presumptions and Burdens' (1945) 61 LQR 379.

has sometimes sought to accommodate that usage by speaking of 'the ultimate burden'[3] or 'the burden on the case as a whole' and distinguishing that from the legal burden on each issue. It may happen that where there is more than one issue in a case, one party may bear the onus in respect of some of them and his opponent in respect of the others. A puruser may have the onus of establishing the facts essential to the contention on which his claim is based; the defender of proving the facts necessary for a specific defence. If, in such a situation, one postulates an onus in respect of the case as a whole, it is intelligible to speak of its shifting. It matters not, so far as the defender is concerned, whether or not he establishes his defence as long as the pursuer does not succeed in proof of the facts which he needs to prove, but if he does so succeed the onus on the defender is activated. In that way the onus 'on the whole case' or 'the ultimate burden' can be said to shift. This shifting of the ultimate burden may be what is meant by some dicta which speak simply of the shifting of the onus.

If the ultimate burden is a necessary concept it is one of law because it is concerned with the interrelation of legal burdens and itself arises from rules of law. It is, however, doubtful if it is necessary. It is sufficient to speak of an onus on each issue. When it has been ascertained whether or not each burden so conceived has been discharged the result for the decision of the case follows by the application of rules of law without the necessity of any further consideration of burdens of proof.

How legal burden ascertained

Alternative expressions used to describe the legal burden are 'formal', 'persuasive', 'probative', and 'fixed'. Its incidence in relation to each issue is usually said to be determined by the substantive law. A party who, by his fault, has caused injury to another is, generally speaking, liable in damages therefore. That is a rule of the substantive law. Because the liability arises only on proof of fault the onus of such proof and of the necessary causal connection with his injury rests on the pursuer. The move from the substantive law to the imposition of onus is, however, achieved by what seems to be properly a rule of adjectival law, the necessity for which is, no doubt, usually so obvious that it does not need to be stated, such as that he who asserts a right given to him by the law must prove the facts necessary to establish it. A similar rule puts the onus on the defender of establishing a substantive defence or exception or excuse to a ground of action which would otherwise be good against him. There are, however, cases in which it is doubtful how the onus lies.

3 Denning (1945) 61 LQR 379 at 380, *Cross on Evidence* (6th edn) p 131.

Affirmanti incumbit probatio is a maxim by which such doubts may seem to be resolved but practically any proposition can be adjusted so as to be expressed in either positive or negative terms. No doubt what, in common sense terms, amounts to 'proof of a negative' is often easy to recognise but even then *affirmanti incumbit probatio* is not an infallible guide. 'Whenever a person asserts affirmatively as part of his case that a certain state of facts is present *or is absent*, or that a particular thing is insufficient for a particular purpose, that is an averment which he is bound to prove positively.'[4] So a pursuer may have the burden of proving a negative as an essential part of his case.

Nor is the borderline always easy to draw between issues which pertain to the ground of action and those which form part of a substantive defence. Where the question arises on an interpretation of a statute, the fact that an issue is not cast in the form of an exception or defence is not a conclusive reason for putting the onus on the pursuer. In *Nimmo v Alexander Cowan & Sons*[5] where the statutory requirement was that 'every place at which any person has at any time to work shall so far as is reasonably practicable be made and kept safe for any person working there', the House of Lords held, by a majority of three to two, that although the onus was on the pursuer to prove that his working place was not made and kept safe, it was, if that were established, for the defenders to prove by way of exception that they had made their place safe so far as was reasonably practicable. There does not seem to be any general rule which can afford a solution to questions of difficulty. The incidence of the onus of proof is, at least in civil cases, to be determined by the particular rules applicable to particular issues. These rules, although often based on considerations of reasonableness, are to be ascertained by reference to precedents rather than by general principle. In criminal cases, propositions of a more general kind may be possible and these are discussed below.

Evidential burden

Not only the legal but also the evidential burden requires to be considered. The expression itself is unfortunate because all burdens are concerned in some way with evidence and so 'evidential' does not suggest any meaningful point of distinction. If, on the other hand, 'evidential' is intended to be in contrast with 'legal' and so distinguish the evidential burden from the legal burden, the point of contrast is false because both burdens are imposed by the law. Moreover, 'evidential'

4 *Abrath v North Eastern Railway Co* (1883) LR 11 QBD 440 at 457.
5 1967 SC (HL) 79.

has sometimes been confusingly applied to the provisional burden.[6] The term is, however, in common use and no alternative is readily available. By evidential burden, in the proper sense, is meant the burden of adducing such evidence as is necessary to enable an issue to be considered by the tribunal of fact.[7] It is in Wigmore's phrase the requirement of 'passing the judge' with evidence fit for the issue to go to the jury. The Scottish rule on corroboration brings the matter into sharper focus than in other jurisdictions. If, as is ordinarily the case, the party who bears the evidential burden also bears the legal burden, he will not discharge the former burden unless there is corroborated evidence of the matter to be proved because it is impossible that he could succeed on that issue unless he has such evidence and it would be absurd to allow an issue to go to the tribunal of fact on which success for the proponent was impossible. On the other hand, if there is corroborative evidence he will have discharged the evidential burden because it is of the nature of corroborated evidence that an issue so supported should be fit for consideration by the trier of fact. By no means, of course, does it follow that he will discharge the legal burden. The evidential burden is a burden of adducing evidence such as to make the issue fit for consideration; the legal burden is a burden of proof. Evidence sufficient for the former may fall short of proof necessary for the latter. A consideration of the evidential burden is, however, of importance mainly in the exceptional cases in which it falls on a party other than the party bearing the legal burden. The scope for that happening seems to lie mainly in criminal cases.

Onus in relation to mens rea

The legal burden of proof in a criminal trial rests on the prosecution. That is a consequence of the presumption of innocence. The burden extends to proof both of actus reus and mens rea and therefore generally to every aspect of the case. The institutional writers may seem to qualify that view to the effect that proof of the actus reus raises a presumption of mens rea which the accused must rebut.[8] It is thought, however, that no more is meant than that in most circumstances the prosecutor may, in proof of mens rea, rely on the presumption of intentionality, ie that the accused is to be taken to have intended the natural consequence of his

6 *Henderson v Henry E Jenkins & Sons* [1970] AC 282 per Lord Pearson at 301 where he speaks of an evidential burden in the sense in which Lord Denning had spoken of a provisional burden in *Brown v Rolls Royce*.

7 *Cross* pp 107 and 108.

8 Hume I 254, Alison I 49.

act. That presumption, although important and normally strong, is no more than a presumption of fact and need not be followed if in the circumstances of the case it would be inappropriate to do so. It does not, therefore, affect the incidence of the onus, although in the ordinary case it facilitates its discharge, and if any circumstances emerge which cast doubt on the accused's intention the onus is on the Crown to prove his criminal intent.[9] That will, it is submitted, be so whether the circumstances suggest error, inadvertence, accident or anything else inconsistent with intent. Similar considerations apply where the mens rea of the offence requires guilty knowledge. Such knowledge will normally be a matter of inference from the particular facts of the case and the onus will be on the Crown to prove facts from which that inference can be drawn, but in some cases the knowledge may be presumed without such proof (eg in cases of incest, knowledge of the relationship may be presumed on the basis that men commonly know with whom they are closely related). In all these cases the evidential, as well as the legal, burden is on the Crown but where, as in intentionality, an adverse inference can readily be drawn in the absence of any special feature, the practical position of the accused may be little different from the case where an evidential burden rests on him.

Onus in relation to special defence

It was at one time thought that the onus of establishing a special defence lay on the accused. In *Lambie v HM Advocate*[10] that view was, however, rejected for all special defences (alibi, self-defence, impeachment) other than insanity (with which must be taken diminished responsibility) and the onus of negativing these special defences now rests on the Crown. The result is that the tribunal of fact having regard to all the evidence including the evidence relating to the special defence, must, in order to justify a conviction, be satisfied of the accused's guilt beyond reasonable doubt and that the special defence is not a separate issue to be considered only if it is established by the accused. Nothing is said in *Lambie* about whether or not an evidential burden rests on the accused. The silence is consistent with the view that all the accused need do to cast the burden of rebuttal on the Crown is to give notice of his special defence. That might, however, lead to enormous consequences putting an impossible burden on the prosecutor of negativing fanciful or recondite grounds of defence. It is submitted, therefore, that an evidential burden does rest on the accused and that he must lead sufficient evidence to put the special defence fairly in issue before the

9 See Sheriff ID Macphail *Research Paper* para 22–11.
10 1973 JC 53, 1973 SLT 219.

tribunal of fact. The burden is not, however, a heavy one as no more is required than evidence which is capable of raising a reasonable doubt in the mind of the tribunal of fact and that can be done by the uncorroborated evidence of the accused or other single witness. Dicta that a defence of self-defence can succeed only where the accused himself gives evidence,[11] probably represent a counsel of prudence for the accused's advisers or a principle to guide decision in the ordinary case rather than a fixed rule of law.

Onus and presumption from possession of stolen goods

The doctrine that guilt of theft or reset can be inferred from the possession in incriminative circumstances of property recently stolen is sometimes cited as giving rise to an exception to the general rule that the legal burden rests on the Crown. There is, it is said, in these circumstances a presumption of guilt and the onus is on the accused to rebut that presumption by showing that his possession was innocent. There are fairly numerous dicta which are broadly to that effect.[12] They are, however, all made without any close analysis of the concept of onus and of the distinction between the legal and provisional burdens. The view that there is a legal burden on the accused can be maintained only if the doctrine of recent possession represents a presumption of law and not, as argued later, a presumption of fact. The true position, it is submitted, is that:

> 'the court as a judge of fact is not bound to draw any inference adverse to the accused from proof of the possession of stolen property or from the absence of any explanation of such possession by the accused, but it may draw an inference of theft if in its opinion such an inference is justified.'[13]

When courts speak of a burden on the accused in this context they are, it is thought, speaking of the provisional burden in the sense used by Lord Denning in *Brown v Rolls Royce Ltd*. The provisional burden is, however, dependent on the facts of each particular case and although it will, of course, fall similarly in similar circumstances no rule of law can be laid down about its incidence. Many of the problems in this and other contexts of the apparent imposition of a legal burden on the accused are eliminated if it is borne in mind that the rule that the legal burden rests throughout on the prosecution in no way excludes the view that the state

11 *Blair v HM Advocate* (1968) 32 J Crim L 48 per Lord Justice-Clerk Grant.

12 See *Fox v Patterson* 1948 JC 104; *Simpson v HM Advocate* 1950 JC 1; *Brannan v HM Advocate* 1954 JC 87; *Cryans v Nixon* 1955 JC 1; *Wightman v HM Advocate* 1959 JC 44; *Cameron v HM Advocate* 1959 JC 59.

13 *R v Nxumalo* [1939] AD 580 at 587. See Sheriff ID Macphail *Research Paper* para 22–13.

of the evidence may give rise to a provisional burden on the accused, or if other terminology is preferred, that the onus may shift provisionally to the accused; provided always it is recognised that the ultimate decision on the evidence must be whether the legal burden has been discharged and that burden always rests on the party on whom it is, at the outset, imposed by law.

Onus and facts within knowledge of accused

Another example often given of a burden resting on the accused is proof of facts peculiarly within the accused's own knowledge. One of the difficulties here is defining what facts fall within that category. The accused's state of mind is peculiarly within his own knowledge but it is for the Crown to prove facts and circumstances from which the state requisite for guilt can be inferred. Where the alleged crime is of a hidden character, knowledge of whether or not it was committed and by whom may often be in the possession of one person but that does not place an onus on him to exculpate himself. There are, however, cases in which one would expect it to be easy for the accused to prove the positive fact in his favour from information which he possesses or to which he alone can have ready access and in which 'it would be absurd and quite unworkable if one were to expect or require the Crown to prove the negative'.[14] The offence of using a motor vehicle without the insurance required by the Road Traffic Acts is a cogent example. The question is again one of the provisional burden. Proof of failure to produce evidence of insurance when requested is sufficient to put a provisional burden on the accused.[15] If he does nothing the legal burden on the Crown will almost certainly be taken to have been discharged and he will be convicted; if he adduces satisfactory evidence that he had the appropriate insurance, he will, of course, be acquitted. Because in that example it is difficult to conceive an intermediate position the distinction between the legal and provisional burden is of theoretical, rather than practical, importance; but in other instances of fact within his peculiar knowledge the accused may be able to shift the provisional burden by evidence short of proof of his innocence. The distinctive feature of cases in which the facts are peculiarly within the knowledge of the accused is that very little in the way of proof by the Crown is required in order to bring about a state of facts in which a provisonal burden on the accused arises. That consists with what was said by Lord Jamieson in *Cruickshank v Smith*: 'Where facts lie peculiarly within the knowledge of one of the

14 *Milne v Whalley* 1975 SLT (Notes) 95.
15 See *Milne v Whalley* above.

parties, very slight evidence may be sufficient to discharge the burden of proof resting on the opposite party'.[16]

Onus on accused

The only true examples in which a legal burden can be said to rest on the accused seem to be in cases of a defence of insanity or diminished responsibility and in certain cases in which the burden is imposed by statute.

Insanity and diminished responsibility

In *Lambie v HM Advocate* the defence of insanity at the time of the offence is expressly excluded from the rule there laid down in relation to other special defences.[17] The onus of proof of insanity rests on the accused and is discharged by proof on a balance of probabilities.[18] It is, therefore, a legal burden. That rule is based on the presumption of sanity but has been criticised as involving a conflict with the presumption of innocence. It requires, it is said, juries to convict although they entertain a reasonable doubt of the accused's sanity and so of his guilt.[19] But the present law, even if somewhat unsatisfactory in principle, may have a practical justification. To require the Crown to prove beyond reasonable doubt that the accused was sane might often be to impose an impossible burden and so lead to abuse. Indeed it is not clear what would be required to prove that someone is sane and no help could be obtained from the presumption of sanity because it would be inherent in the reform that that presumption should be displaced. What is required, on the other hand, to prove insanity is sometimes elusive but in most cases is relatively clear. Yet once a question of whether the accused may be insane is properly raised on the evidence nothing short of full proof of sanity will meet the theoretical objection. Diminished responsibility is governed by similar considerations to those applicable to insanity.

Effect of statute

There are fairly numerous instances in which statutes require certain matters to be proved by the accused in order to establish a defence. An examination in detail of these particular instances lies outwith the scope of this book. The question is always one of the construction of the particular statute. Such provisions are, however, generally construed as imposing on the accused a legal burden to be discharged by proof on a

16 1949 JC 134 at 152, quoting from *Taylor on Evidence*.
17 1973 JC at 58.
18 Hume I 43; *HM Advocate v Braithwaite* 1945 JC 55; *HM Advocate v Mitchell* 1951 JC 53.
19 See Sheriff ID Macphail *Research Paper* para 22–09, quoting *Davis v US* (1895) US 469.

balance of probability.[20] The objection can again be taken that the tribunal of fact is required to convict although it holds a reasonable doubt of the accused's guilt. As with insanity that consideration may sometimes have to be weighed against considerations of practicality but, subject to that, the argument is a powerful one for construing statutes, where express words do not otherwise require, in a sense which does not place a burden on the accused or, failing that, for construing them so as to impose only an evidential burden. Where, however, the words of the statute expressly require proof by the accused, it is submitted that seldom, if ever, can they be construed in a sense other than that of imposing a legal burden. The burden cannot be an evidential one because an evidential burden does not require proof. Nor can it be a provisional burden because, by its nature, a provisional burden is not imposed by law.

Proof of exemption, exception, etc

The only statutory rule of general application which places a burden on the accused is contained in the Criminal Procedure (Scotland) Act 1975 which provides:

> 'Any exception, exemption, proviso, excuse or qualification, whether it does or does not accompany in the same section the description of the offence in the statue or order creating the offence, may be proved by the accused, but need not be specified or negatived in the indictment, and no proof in relation to such exception exemption proviso excuse or qualification shall be required on behalf of the prosecution.'[1]

The burden so placed on the accused is a legal burden to be discharged by proof on a balance of probability.[2] The main problem is to determine what constitutes an exception, exemption, proviso, excuse or qualification and so must be proved by the accused on the one hand, and what goes to the substance of the offence and so must be proved by the prosecutor on the other. In *Archibald v Plean Colliery Co Ltd*[3] it was held that a clause of exception in regulations under the Coal Mines Act 1911 was a condition prerequisite to the offence with the result that the exception had to be negatived by the prosecutor but the case may turn on specialties of pleading and is no longer regarded as authority for any

20 *Neish v Stevenson* 1969 SLT 229.
1 Ss 66 and 312(v).
2 *Nimmo v Alexander Cowan & Sons* 1967 SC (HL) per Lord Pearson at 114. Cf *Gatland v Metropolitan Police Commissioner* [1968] 2 QB 279.
3 1924 JC 77.

principle of general application. In *McCluskey v Boyd*[4] where the accused was charged with trafficking in exciseable liquor without a certificate it was held that the accused must prove that he had a certificate and that there was no onus on the prosecutor to prove that he did not. That case, however, is difficult to reconcile with *Cruickshank v Smith*,[5] in which the onus was put on the prosecutor of proving the lack of right, or permission, to fish on a charge of fishing 'not having a legal right or permission from the proprietor' and is no longer authoritative. In *British Transport Commission v Dalgleish*[6] the onus was held to be on the prosecutor to prove publication of a notice where a statutory penalty was not recoverable unless the notice had been published, but in *Chalmers v Speedwell Wire Co Ltd*[7] on a prosecution under the Factories Act 1937 s 13(1) which made it an offence to fail to fence transmission machinery securely 'unless it is in such a position or of such construction as to be as safe . . . as it would be if securely fenced' it was held that the prosecutor did not require to libel and so did not require to negative the exception. On a prosecution of a parent in respect of a child's failure without reasonable excuse to attend school regularly there is no onus on the prosecutor to prove lack of reasonable excuse[8] but on a prosecution under the Road Traffic Act for failing to supply a specimen of blood or urine without reasonable excuse, the accused has only an evidential burden and if he adduces enough evidence to put the matter in issue the onus is on the prosecutor to negative reasonable excuse by proof beyond reasonable doubt.[9]

The only principle which, although imperfectly followed, can be extracted from the rather confusing pattern of authorities is that the onus of proving an exception, exemption, etc rests on the accused only where it is 'independent of the description of the offence itself'.[10] Onus on the accused therefore applies only where there is first of all a description of an offence and 'an exception which is something apart from that description'.[10] The question of the separability of the exception from the description remains one of some nicety but it seems that the exception can be separated if the description of the offence can stand on its own without the offence loosing intelligibility. So if an enactment prima facie requires a stated result to be achieved with penalties for

4 (1916) 7 Adam 742.
5 1949 JC 134.
6 1955 JC 80.
7 1942 JC 42.
8 *Kennedy v Clark* 1970 JC 55.
9 *R v Clarke* [1969] 1 WLR 1109.
10 *Muir v Grant & Co* 1948 JC 42 per Lord Carmont at 46.

failure, but, in addition, provides a possible excuse, it is for the accused to prove the facts by which he contends that he is excused.

Role of onus in relation to decision

To say that the onus lies on one party or another is to say that that party will fail if the evidence adduced is not sufficient to amount to proof of the matter in issue. Where there is an abundance of evidence, questions of onus do not arise but where the evidence is slender they may be critical. To decide a case on a question of onus is something of a last resort. In *Thomas v Thomas*[11] Lord Thankerton said that no question of burden of proof as a determining factor of the case arose on a concluded proof except insofar as the court is ultimately unable to come to a definite conclusion on the evidence or some part of it and a question arose as to which party had to suffer thereby. Cases which turn on onus do, however, occur. Every case which fails for lack of evidence sufficient in law is of that kind. And there are other examples. In *Harper v Green*[12] the pursuer had to establish the validity of a will by proof that it was holograph in face of a defence that it was forged. The evidence on both sides was inconclusive. The onus of setting up the holograph will was on the pursuer and of proving forgery on the defender. Essentially, however, the issue was whether or not the will was holograph of the testator; forgery merely added strength to denial. The pursuer failed because he could not discharge the onus incumbent on him. Similarly, in *Mitchell's Executor v Gordon's Factor*[13] proof failed because of inability to discharge an onus of proving who had died first in a common calamity. In criminal practice cases which turn on a failure to discharge the onus of proof rather than on a comparative weighing of evidence are, because of the enhanced standard of proof required of the prosecutor, even more common than in civil cases.

PRESUMPTIONS

> 'Presumptions are aids to reasoning and argumentation which assume the truth of certain matters for the purpose of some given enquiry. They may be grounded in general experience, or probability of any kind; or merely on policy or convenience. On whatever basis they rest, they operate in advance of argument or

11 1947 SC (HL) 45.
12 1938 SC 198.
13 1953 SC 176.

> evidence, or irrespective of it, by taking something for granted; by assuming its existence.'[14]

The common classification of presumption is into three kinds:
1 conclusive presumptions of law (presumptions *juris et de jure*);
2 rebuttable presumptions of law (presumptions *juris* or *juris tantum*); and
3 rebuttable presumptions of fact (presumptions *judicis* or *hominis* or *facti*).

Conclusive presumptions

Conclusive presumptions are not properly matters of the law of evidence. They are rather rules of substantive law expressed in the form of presumption. Without exception they can be made the subject of alternative formulations which do not use the language of presumption. It is, for example, sometimes said that there is a conclusive presumption that no child under the age of eight can be guilty of an offence. There are a number of other ways in which that can be put (eg no child under the age of eight can incur criminal liability or no proceedings in respect of a crime or offence can be taken against a child under eight). So too with other presumptions of the same kind (eg that a pupil is presumed to be incapable of consenting to a contract, or that a pregnant woman who does not reveal her condition or call for assistance at childbirth is presumed to be criminally indifferent to the life of her child). They can all be described in ways which make it unnecessary to speak of them as presumptions. Indeed, it is usually better to express so-called presumptions of this kind in an alternative form. The maxim *ignorantia juris neminem excusat*, is sometimes translated into the language of presumption by saying that there is a presumption that every man knows the law, but there is no such presumption. There is, however, a rule that no one can rely on ignorance of the law as an excuse, which is based on considerations of public policy such as the need to avoid the abuses which would otherwise accrue.

Character of rebuttable presumptions of law

The effect of a rebuttable presumption of law is that the facts to which it relates must be presumed until the contrary is proved by acceptable evidence. It is their obligatory character which marks the fundamental distinction between such presumptions and presumptions of fact. Other distinguishing features follow. Because the presumption, when appli-

14 Thayer *Evidence at Common Law* p 314.

cable, must be made, definite criteria are required for its operation. So, rebuttable presumptions of law apply in defined circumstances (ie when a defined question is put in issue or after certain well defined facts have been proved), and where they depend on proof of basic facts it will generally be found that these facts are easily ascertainable and of common occurrence.

Presumptions of fact

Presumption of fact when used in a legal context is something of a misnomer. Such presumptions are really ways of describing the operation of inferences based on circumstantial evidence. They apply in some of the more commonly recurring situations in which such inferences are drawn. The difference in principle between presumptions of fact and rebuttable presumptions of law is clear. Where a rebuttable presumption of law applies the presumption must be made. In the case of a presumption of fact, there is no such obligation. The point may be illustrated by reference to the presumption that someone who in criminative circumstances is in possession of goods which have recently been stolen is guilty of theft. It will turn very largely on the circumstances of each particular case whether or not as a matter of fact the inference that the possessor stole the goods should be drawn.[15] All that is involved is a state of facts from which it is reasonable to infer guilt. Whether or not it is reasonable to do so must vary from case to case. There is, therefore, no obligation on court or jury to draw the inference and that is so even if there is no evidence in rebuttal. Failure to draw the inference cannot, therefore, amount to an error in law. It would, of course, be otherwise in the case of a presumption of law.

It is sometimes said that because presumptions of fact raise no questions of law and because they cannot be sharply distinguished from the infinite variety of situations in which inferences may be drawn on the basis of circumstantial evidence, it would be best that they should not be called presumptions at all. It is largely a question of semantics whether one accepts that view or not. It is, however, wrong to exclude altogether presumptions of fact from a discussion of the law of evidence. They are rules of law at least in the sense in which they describe circumstances in which a court or jury may properly draw certain inferences. Thus, it is clear that it could not be argued that it was error for a court or jury ever to draw an inference of guilt of theft from the fact that the accused was in possession of goods which had recently been stolen. The fact that such an inference may, at least in many circum-

15 That, it is submitted, is clear from the requirement that there be criminate circumstances which necessarily involve a case by case analysis for which no rules of law can be laid down.

stances, be drawn has received repeated judicial recognition and to that extent is a matter of law. Moreover, these presumptions may be very important for proof and to exclude them from a discussion of the law of evidence would be to give such a discussion an air of artificiality.

The presumption from possession of stolen goods is an example of an important presumption of fact. The presumption of intentionality, that a man is presumed to intend the natural consequences of his act, is of even more fundamental importance. It is usually described as a presumption of fact, perhaps because what is to be considered the natural consequence of any given species of act may vary considerably according to circumstances, but comes close to being a rebuttable presumption of law. There are many circumstances in which it seems inescapable that, in the absence of evidence in rebuttal, the inference must be drawn. If, for example, a firearm is directed towards and deliberately discharged at someone, it would be perverse, in the absence of some speciality or of some evidence in rebuttal, to refuse to infer that the person who fired the gun had the manifest intention of killing or at least causing severe injury. On the other hand, the presumption of continuance illustrates a presumption of fact which is far removed from a presumption of law. By this presumption is meant that once a state of affairs, capable of continuance, is shown to have existed, it is presumed to have continued down to the time which is the subject of enquiry. Obviously, this presumption is almost infinitely variable according to circumstances and in many situations will be so weak or so outweighed by contrary presumptions that it can and sometimes should be ignored. On other occasions it may be comparatively strong. If it be shown that I entertained a malicious disposition to someone 30 years ago there can, at most, be an extremely weak presumption that I continue to harbour that disposition now. If, however, I evinced a malicious disposition towards someone last week, the presumption that I will entertain malicious feelings towards him today is quite strong. On no view, however, could one even begin to lay down rules about when the presumption of continuance *must* be applied.

Classification of rebuttable presumptions of law

Rebuttable presumption of law can be divided into two classes: 1 presumptions that do not depend on the proof of basic facts; and (2) presumptions which do so depend. Presumptions in the former class merely describe how the legal onus lies when questions to which they relate are put in issue, eg the presumption of sanity applies whenever a question of sanity arises. Presumptions in the latter class operate when the facts necessary to bring them into operation have been established (what are usually called 'the basic facts'). They represent what are probably the only occasions on which the legal onus can properly be said to shift from one party to another. An example is the presumption of legitimacy which, subject to some qualifications, applies when it is proved that the child whose legitimacy is in issue is the child of a married woman born during the subsistence of the marriage. The distinction between these two classes of rebuttable presumptions of law is not, however, for most purposes important and it is not always strict. Another distinction made in recent literature is between presumptions of law which cast only an evidential burden on the opponent and those which cast a legal burden. The point is not noticed in Scottish authorities but, implicitly, a transfer of the legal burden seems always to be contemplated.

Presumptions in criminal cases

The use of presumptions in criminal cases raises some specialties. As has been seen, the presumption of sanity operates so as to impose on the accused a legal burden of proving insanity on a balance of probabilities. It is thought, however, that that is an exceptional instance and that in general presumptions will not be used to impose a legal burden on the accused unless where that is authorised by statute. Moreover, a prosecutor may not be able to rely on a presumption even for the purpose of shifting an evidential burden to the accused, at least where the matter presumed is central to the commission of the offence. It has been held that in such matters there is no room for presumptions in favour of the Crown. So, on a charge against a policeman of negligently permitting the escape of prisoners who were lawfully within his custody there was no case to answer when the Crown failed to adduce any evidence, even of a formal kind, that the custody was lawful.[16] The presumption in favour of regularity could not be used.

Examples of rebuttable presumptions of law

Presumptions of law are numerous and to be found in practically every branch of the legal system. The following discussion covers a number of those of general importance.

(a) Presumptions in favour of life

At common law the presumption was strong and difficult to rebut. Under the Presumption of Death (Scotland) Act 1977[17] it may now, however, be rebutted on a balance of probabilities. Proof may take either of two forms: either evidence tending to show that the missing

16 *Dillon v R* [1982] AC 484, [1982] 1 All ER 1017.
17 S 2.

person has died; or evidence that he has not been known to be alive for a period of at least seven years,

(b) Presumptions in favour of morality

There is a general presumption in favour of innocence and freedom from fault whether in a moral or in a legal sense: *odiosa et inhonesta non sunt in lege praesumenda.* This general presumption is illustrated by a number of particular presumptions of which the presumption in favour of innocence is typical and perhaps the best known. The effect of that presumption—or another way of describing it—is that in criminal cases the onus rests on the Crown, with rare statutory exceptions, of proving the guilt of the accused person and that proof must, of course, be beyond reasonable doubt. The presumption also applies to civil cases in which crime is alleged and it has been said that in civil cases too, the presumption must be rebutted on the criminal standard (ie beyond reasonable doubt).[18] If that is so it can, however, be the rule only in the case of common law crimes. It is a matter of everyday practice that contravention of statute (eg the Road Traffic Acts and the Factory Acts) are proved where they are relevant to fault in a civil case on a balance of probabilities. Even in the case of common law crimes, the better view seems to be that now taken in England which is that proof on the criminal standard is not required in a civil case although the evidence to rebut the presumption must be such as is appropriate to the seriousness of the allegation and the circumstances to the case.[19] It has been held that once a criminal act has been proved or admitted its consequences can be proved on a balance of probabilities.[20]

The presumption in favour of morality (considered in this context as distinct from allegations of crime) is in general rebuttable by proof on a balance of probabilities and that is now true of proof of adultery in actions of divorce and of separation and aliment[1] where the standard had previously been proof beyond reasonable doubt. The presumption embodied in the maxim *pater est quem nuptiae demonstrant*, requires, however, to be rebutted by proof beyond reasonable doubt,[2] as does the general presumption against illegitimacy. Morality for this purpose

18 *Arnott v Burt* (1872) 11M 62 per Lord Neaves at 74. See also *Wink v Speirs* (1867) 6M 77 per Lord Justice-Clerk Patton at 80 and *Cullen's Trustees v Johnston* (1865) 3M 935.

19 *Hornal v Neuberger Products Ltd* [1957] 1 QB 247 especially per Denning LJ at 258 and Morris LJ at 266. The view there expressed is consistent with what is said in the Scottish authorities other than *Arnott v Burt* above. In *Lennon v Co-operative Insurance Society Ltd* 1986 SLT 98 the standard applied was 'somewhere halfway' between a balance of probabilities and reasonable doubt.

20 *Buick v Jaglar* 1973 SLT (Sh Ct) 6.

1 Divorce (Scotland) Act 1976 ss 1(6) and 4(1).

2 *Brown v Brown* 1972 SC 123.

extends to allegations of suicide. Thus, in *McDonald v Refuge Assurance Co* where an assured person was found drowned two months after taking out a policy of assurance against accident, it was held that, in the absence of evidence to the contrary, the assured must be held to have met his death accidentally.[3]

(c) Presumptions in favour of regularity and validity

In formal transactions, regularity and validity are presumed: *omina praesumuntur rite et solemniter acta*. The presumption has its typical application in the actings of public bodies and of persons acting in a public or official capacity but is also applicable to formal transactions between private individuals. It is particularly strong against attempts to disturb a state of affairs founded on apparent regularity which has persisted over a long number of years. Thus in *Presbytery of Stirling v Heritors of Larbert & Dunipace* it was presumed that two parishes had been united legally and were a competent body where the Crown and the Church had acted on that basis for nearly 300 years although no record of the union existed.[4] Applications of the presumption can also be seen in *Hill v Finlayson*[5] and *Marr v Stuart*[6] in which it was presumed that a procurator fiscal and an interim sheriff substitute respectively had been duly authorised and appointed. Regularity or lawfulness will not, however, be presumed where it is central to a criminal charge.[7]

In the sphere of private transactions there is a presumption that books kept in the ordinary course of business are accurate and that the ordinary practice of a business establishment has been followed.[8] There is also a presumption in favour of the validity of probative deeds and that they have been executed in accordance with the prescribed legal formalities. Thus, when the deed bears the signature of witnesses it is presumed, unless the contrary be proved, that they saw the grantor sign or heard him acknowledge his signature.[9] Holograph writings enjoy no such privilege and there is no presumption in favour of their genuineness. So, in *Harper v Green*[10] an argument was rejected that there was presumption that a will containing the words 'written by my own hand' and bearing to be signed by the grantor was in fact holograph of the person who purported to sign it. So too, at common law holograph

3 (1890) 17 R 955.
4 (1902) 4 F 1048.
5 (1883) 10 R (J) 66.
6 (1881) 4 Coup 407.
7 p 195 Above.
8 *Guthrie v Stewart* 1926 SC 743; *Dickson* para 114.
9 See *McBeath's Trustees v McBeath* 1935 SC 471 per Lord President Clyde at 476. If ex facie valid the deed can be impugned only by an action of reduction.
10 1938 SC 198.

writings do not prove their own date but there is a statutory presumption that holograph wills and bills of exchange are of the date which they bear to be.[11] Mercantile documents, as an exception to the common law rule, are presumed to be of the date they bear in any question arising in relation to the commercial purpose for which the document was granted, although perhaps not for other purposes.[12] In *Sutherland v Barbour* it was held that there was a presumption of due compliance with the requirements of a Feu Charter which provided for buildings to be erected in accordance with a common feuing plan and the plan could not be found.[13]

(d) Presumption from possession

In pari causa melior est conditio posseidentis. In relation to heritable property, presumptions from possession underlie the rules on the positive prescription, acquisition of rights of servitude and of public right of way and the law relating to possessory judgments. These rules fall outwith the scope of this work. But presumptions from possession also have an application in relation to moveable property and to writings. When a deed is in possession of the grantee it is presumed to have been delivered to him and when a document of debt is in the debtor's possesssion it is presumed to have been implemented or discharged.[14] The presumption is particularly strong in the case of documents which are commonly discharged by re-delivery.[15] On the other hand, the presumption may have no, or at the best a weak, application where the debt in question is of a kind which would normally be discharged only by a formal deed.

The presumption arising from the possession of writings can normally be rebutted by parole proof but where the contention is that the party in possession of the writing was acting as a trustee proof by writ or oath may be necessary.[16]

Since corporeal moveables are, in general, transferred without a written title, there is a strong presumption that the possessor is the owner.[17] To rebut the presumption, it must be shown not only that the moveables once belonged to the person claiming them but also that his possession came to an end in such a way that the subsequent possessor could not have acquired a valid title to them. The presumptions may

11 Conveyancing (Scotland) Act 1874 s 40, Bills of Exchange Act 1882 s 13(1).
12 Bell's Commentaries I, 343.
13 (1887) 15 R 62.
14 *Dickson* paras 936 and 173.
15 *Cumming v Hendrie* (1861) 23 D 1365.
16 Ch 13 below.
17 *Prangnell–O'Neill v Lady Skeffington* 1984 SLT 282.

also be displaced by proof of the relationship of the parties, eg that the possessor is an agent or carrier.[18]

(e) Presumption in favour of onerosity

It is an aspect of the recognition which the law gives to ordinary human conduct and experience, including the consistent practice and business habits of mankind, that there is a presumption in favour of onerosity (that obligations are undertaken for a consideration) and against donation. 'As mankind do not generally prejudice themselves to benefit others, a debt or transaction is held not to be a donation unless any other supposition regarding it is inadmissible according to the ordinary probabilities of conduct.'[19]

The maxim *donatio non praesumitur* puts the matter too weakly. It is not merely that there is no presumption in favour of donation: there is a positive presumption against it. Although the presumption is strong it may be overcome, not only by direct evidence *prout de jure* but also by contrary inference drawn from, among other things, the relative positions of the parties, the nature of the right and the circumstances attending the transaction. Indeed, in the case of certain relationships, of which the clearest is that of parent and child, the presumption will normally have no applications. Thus, unless there is evidence to the contrary, payments by parents to children will be regarded as gifts *ex pietate* and not as loans.[20] The presumption is strongest with regard to a deed or payment by a debtor to his creditor—*debitor non praesumitur donare*—on the view that someone is unlikely to make a present to another and continue to be under obligation to him.[1]

As with gifts of things, so with services; services are presumed to have been rendered and accepted in accordance with a contract, express or implied, for payment and not gratuitously. This presumption too may be displaced by circumstances including, in particular the relationship between the parties. A son or a daughter working in a family business will not be presumed to do so gratuitously but where the work done is domestic work at home it will be presumed that it is done either gratuitously or in return for board and lodgings.

(f) Apocha trium annorum

In all obligations which are prestable by termly payments such as rent, feuduties, interest on money, etc there is a presumption that if the

18 *Dickson* paras 149 and 150.
19 *Dickson* para 158.
20 *Dickson* para 159.
1 *Dickson* para 165.

creditor has granted three consecutive written discharges for three corresponding terms' payments all payments previously due have been settled.[2] The receipts need only be for three consecutive payments not for three full years as the latin title of the presumption might suggest.

(g) Presumption of sanity

There is a presumption that every person is sane and therefore capable of understanding the ordinary consequences of his acts and the meanings of his statements. The presumption does not apply where judicial proceedings have been taken to establish the insanity of the person in question (eg by his being cognosced or by a *curator bonis* having been appointed to him in respect of his unsoundness of mind) and indeed in such cases there is a presumption that insanity continues until the contrary can be demonstrated.[3]

(h) Presumption of procreative capacity

There is a presumption that every man is capable of begetting and every woman of bearing children although in the latter case a contrary presumption may arise from advancing age.[4]

(i) Res ipsa loquitur

There is a presumption against negligence or, to put the matter another way, there is a rule that he who alleges negligence must prove it. The types of evidence which may be used to establish negligence and so rebut the presumption are, however, infinitely various according to the circumstances of each case. Direct evidence is not necessary and it may be sufficient to prove facts and circumstances from which an inference of negligence can be drawn. In these cases it is always a question of fact for the court or jury whether or not to draw the inference. Where, however, circumstances of the case are the same as or closely resemble those which have already been the subject of judicial decision in superior courts as apt to give rise to an inference of negligence, the considerations pointing to the drawing of the inference come close to constituting a legal requirement.

Walker and Walker maintain that instances of res ipsa loquitur are properly regarded as examples of the drawing of an inference of fact and that it is unfortunate that the maxim has been used as if to suggest a distinct category of case.[5] Their solution is that cases of res ipsa loquitur

2 *Dickson* para 177.
3 Bell's Principles para 2103.
4 *G v G* 1936 SC 837.
5 Para 80, pp 72 and 73.

should merely be classed along with all other instances of an inference of negligence drawn from circumstances.[6] Dicta can be cited which tend to support that view but it seems reasonably clear from recent authority that res ipsa loquitur represents a presumption of law applicable in defined circumstances from which negligence is as a matter of law to be presumed unless sufficient evidence is adduced in rebuttal.[7] It accordingly becomes of importance to clarify the scope of the presumption and the circumstances in which it applies.

The *locus classicus* on res ipsa loquitur ('the thing itself speaks' or to translate more freely but perhaps more appropriately 'the event speaks for itself') is contained in what was said by Erle CJ in *Scott v London & St Katherine's Docks Co*:

> 'There must be reasonable evidence of negligence. But where the thing is shown to be under the management of the defendant or his servants, and the accident is such as in the ordinary course of affairs does not happen if those who have management use proper care, it affords evidence, in the absence of explanation by the defendants, that the accident arose from want of care.'[8]

In Scotland that definition was accepted in *Milliken v Glasgow Corpn*[9] and has been repeatedly followed. There are, therefore, two requirements for the operation of the presumption: 1 the thing whose behaviour caused the accident must have been under the management of the person against whom negligence is alleged or his servants; and 2 the event causing the damage must be such as in the ordinary course of affairs does not happen if those who have management use proper care. Where those requirements are met the presumption applies.

The facts of *Scott v London & St Katherine's Docks* are illustrative of the operation of the presumption. A customs officer was walking past a warehouse when some bags containing sugar fell from a height onto him. In those circumstances the conditions for operation of the presumption were held to be satisfied: the bags of sugar were under the control of the defendants or their servants and bags do not, in the ordinary course of affairs, fall from warehouses if those having the management of the bags use proper care. A modern Scottish example is

6 *Ballard v North British Railway Co* 1923 SC (HL) 43 per Lord Shaw of Dunfermline at 56; *O'Hara v Central SMT Co* 1941 SC 363 per Lord President Normand at 377.

7 *Devine v Colvilles Ltd* 1969 SC (HL) 67. The examination in that case of the circumstances necessary to give rise to the presumption and of the proof required for rebuttal is, it is submitted, inconsistent with anything other than a presumption of law.

8 *Scott v London and St Katherine's Docks Co* (1865) 4 H & C 596 at 601.

9 1918 SC 857 per Lord Salvesen at 867.

Devine v Colville's Ltd[10] in which the pursuer was injured when he jumped from a platform on which he was working as a result of a general panic caused by a violent explosion nearby.

The proof required for rebuttal varies according to whether or not the accident was immediately brought about by voluntary human action. Where it was so brought about, full legal proof is required of the defender in order to rebut the prima facie case of negligence established against him. But where the immediate connection with voluntary human action is lacking it suffices for the defender to show that there were conditions present which could have caused the accident without negligence on his part.[11] In the latter situation the defender does not have to prove the actual cause of the accident but he must go beyond mere speculation and prove conditions from which a plausible explanation of the occurrence may be inferred. He must also show that that explanation is consistent with the absence of negligence on his part.[12] That consistency is to be understood in the sense that if the facts which the explanation narrates were to be proved to be the true cause of the occurrence the defenders would be exculpated. Neutrality is not enough. An explanation which shows how the accident probably occurred but is silent on exculpation does not avail a defender.[13]

10 1969 SC (HL) 67.
11 Ibid per Lord Wheatley at 84.
12 Ibid at 85.
13 Ibid per Lord Justice-Clerk Grant at 82–83.

CHAPTER 13

Requirements of proof; sufficiency of evidence; corroboration; standard of proof; proof by writ or oath

PROOF

In determining whether or not the evidence led amounts to proof of any fact in issue, the following considerations, in addition to the competency and relevancy of the evidence and the onus of proof, require to be taken into account:

1 corroboration;
2 agreement or discrepancy between the evidence led and the facts averred in the pleading;
3 the coherence of the evidence;
4 the standard of proof; and
5 the weight and value of the evidence.

Of these, the last (weight and value of the evidence) is a question of fact to be determined by the jury or other tribunal of fact. The others all raise, or may riase, questions of law which have to be decided by the judge.

CORROBORATION

A requirement that proof proceed from the evidence of more than one witness is ancient[1] and was at one time widespread but Scots law is unusual among advanced legal systems in retaining it as a principle of general application. It is defended as a valuable safeguard against the

1 Balfour *Practicks* 373, Bisset I 200; Stair IV xliii 1 2. Stair puts the requirement on a biblical basis (Matt 18:16, 2 Cor 13, Deut 17:6, 19:15) but it also has its roots in the civil law.

fallibility[2] of testimony but is at odds with the rejection of other safeguards formerly employed and goes against the modern emphasis on the free assessment of evidence unencumbered by restrictive rules as well as the more ancient precept *testimonia ponderanda non numeranda sunt.*

Requirement of corroboration

Subject to certain statutory exceptions the oral testimony of one witness, however credible, is not full proof of any ground of action or defence either civil or criminal. If the only evidence in support of a case is the uncorroborated testimony of one witness, it is the duty of the judge to direct the jury that the proof is not sufficient in point of law.

> 'By the law of Scotland no person can be convicted of a crime or of a statutory offence, except where the legislature otherwise directs, unless there is evidence of at least two witnesses implicating the person accused or charged with the commission of the crime or offence with which he is charged.'[3]

The same is true of civil cases at common law but, whereas the statutory exceptions in criminal cases are, for the most part, fairly unimportant, there is in the realm of civil litigation the important exception created by the Law Reform (Miscellaneous Provisions) (Scotland) Act 1960 s 9, that corroboration is no longer required in actions of damages where the damages claimed consist of or include damages or *solatium* in respect of personal injuries. Even where that section applies uncorroborated testimony may not be sufficient for proof unless the absence of corroboration is explained.[4]

What requires to be corroborated

It is sometimes said that a case requires to be corroborated.[5] That is true only in a loose sense. It is with proof of facts not of cases that the law of evidence, of which the rule regarding corroboration forms part, is concerned. Once it has been ascertained what facts have been proved, it is a question of substantive law whether on those facts a case is made out. The matter is better put by saying that all facts essential to the case (sometimes called crucial or material facts) must be proved by corroborative testimony. Evidential facts (ie facts which are not in themselves essential but which, taken along with other facts, may lead to the

2 'Corroboration of Evidence in Scottish Criminal Law' 1958 SLT (News) 137 (Anon).
3 *Marton v HM Advocate* 1938 JC 50.
4 *Morrison v J Kelly & Sons Ltd* 1970 SC 65 per Lord President Clyde at 79. Cf *McGowan v Lord Advocate* 1972 SC 68, 1972 SLT 188; *McLaren v Caldwell's Paper Mill Co Ltd* 1973 SLT 158; *Mason v S L D Olding* 1982 SLT 385.
5 *Maitland v Glasgow Corpn* 1947 SC 20 per Lord President Normand at 25.

inference of an essential fact, eg items of circumstantial evidence) do not require to be corroborated, nor do procedural facts (ie facts which require to be proved but only for some incidental or procedural purpose). It should be possible to ascertain what constitutes the essential facts from the pleadings in a civil case and from the indictment or complaint in a criminal case. They are the facts which must be averred in order that the case may be held to be relevant. These are the *facta probanda* and it is for proof of these facts that corroborated testimony is required. In a criminal case the facts which require to be proved are that the crime was committed as set out in the indictment or complaint and that it was committed by the accused.[6] Corroboration of the identity of the accused as the person who committed the crime is essential.[7]

Forms of corroboration

Corroboration may take a variety of forms. It is necessary now to consider what evidence will amount to corroborated testimony sufficient for proof.

(a) *The direct testimony of two or more witnesses to the facts in issue*

Such testimony represents the simplest form of corroborated testimony. An admission made by the accused in the course of his evidence, of a crucial fact spoken to by a single witness for the prosecution is sufficient for this purpose.[8] But absence of cross-examination by the accused will not per se justify the prosecutor in failing to lead corroborative evidence.[9] Minor discrepancies in the evidence may be ignored, as no two witnesses ever get precisely the same impression of the same incident; but their testimony must correspond in essential parts.

(b) *The direct evidence of a single witness as to a fact in issue may be corroborated by evidence of surrounding facts and circumstances*

These facts and circumstances must come from a source other than the witness whom they corroborate. They may be deponed to by other witnesses, or they may consist of writings or real evidence.

> 'What the law is anxious to avoid is a man's being convicted by the testimony of one witness, and that is why the law insists on incriminating testimony from more than one source. So long as

6 Ch 1 above. See also ch 1 for definition of essential, evidential and procedural facts.
7 *Mitchell v Macdonald* 1959 SLT Note 74.
8 *MacArthur v Stewart* 1955 JC 71, 1955 SLT 434.
9 *Innes v HM Advocate* 1955 SLT (Notes) 69 per Lord Justice-Clerk Thomson at 70.

there are separate sources, each incriminating the accused person, it is unnecessary to have more than one witness to each source.'[9]

The classic test for sufficiency of evidence in cases of this kind was laid down by Lord President Normand in *O'Hara v Central SMT*:

> 'There is sufficient corroboration if the facts and circumstances proved are not only consistent with the evidence of the single witness [who requires to be corroborated] but more consistent with it than with any competing account of the events spoken to by him. Accordingly if the facts and circumstances proved by other witnesses fit into his narrative so as to make it the most probable account of the event, the requirements of legal proof are satisfied.'[10]

That is difficult to reconcile with the view expressed in *Maitland v Glasgow Corpn*[11] that probability cannot afford corroboration. A distinction is, perhaps, to be made between antecedent probability (ie an inference that an event was likely to occur drawn from facts obtaining before its occurrence) and an inference that the event did occur drawn as a matter of probability from facts and circumstances observed at the time of or after the occurrence. The former, it may be said, cannot but the latter can amount to corroboration.[12] That distinction is not, however, observed in *Cleisham v BTC*[13] from which it appears that antecedent probability may afford corroboration.

(c) *Evidence derived from facts and circumstances alone*

Such evidence may be sufficient in law but must be derived from two or more sources. The facts and circumstances proved must be such that from them as a whole a reasonable inference can be drawn of the existence of the facts[14] in issue but it is not necessary that each item should be established by two witnesses. The mutual interlacing and coincidence of the circumstances themselves form ample corroboration of the witnesses who depone to them.[15] A chain of circumstances may be established with only one witness to each link if the evidence is indicative

10 1941 SC 363 at 369.
11 1947 SC 20 per Lord President Normand at 25: 'The fact that the story told by the pursuer is probable may render it more easy to accept her evidence as truthful, but it is not corroboration of the pursuer'. Cf. *Spindlow v Glasgow Corpn* 1933 SC 580.
12 See W A Wilson 'Cleisham and Corroboration' 1964 SLT (News) 57.
13 1964 SC (HL) 8. Cf *Robertson v John White & Son* 1963 SC (HL) 22; *Ritchie v James McCaig & Sons* 1963 SC 527; *Ferguson v Western SMT Co Ltd* 1969 SLT 213.
14 *Hamilton v HM Advocate* 1934 JC 1 (fingerprints and accused's residence in the neighbourhood sufficient).
15 *Dickson* para 1811.

of correlation but the logic of the 'speed-trap'[16] cases, in which each of two witnesses spoke to separate events neither of which gave rise to any inference regarding the other, seems to be unsound.

(d) Mutual corroboration of a series of similar acts

Where a series of similar acts is alleged, and each is deponed to by one witness, they may afford mutual corroboration of each other, provided there is a close interrelation between these acts in time, nature and circumstances. If there is not that close interrelation, the evidence of one witness to an isolated act is not corroboration of another isolated act even if it is of a similar nature. The leading case is *Moorov v HMA*[17] which concerned a number of charges of simple and of indecent assault. The only direct evidence in each case was that of the woman assaulted. It was held that there was sufficient interrelation in time, place and circumstances between the indecent assaults to afford corroborated testimony of their commission. The principle laid down was that the series of offences 'must not only be the same in kind, committed under similar circumstances, or in a common locus, but must owe their source and development to some underlying circumstances or state of fact'.[18] In *Ogg v HMA* it was held that three sexual offences were not sufficiently interrelated in time, there being intervals of one year and 18 months between them.[19]

The *Moorov* doctrine was applied in *Burgh v HMA* although there were only two incidents where they took place in precisely the same locus, within a matter of minutes of each other and were of a peculiar nature.[20] And it is not confined to sexual offences. In *HM Advocate v McQuade* in which there were six charges of assault with a razor, between December and March; all within a relatively small district and apparently motiveless, it was held that the evidence in each charge might corroborate the evidence in the other charges.[1] and in *McCudden v HMA* where the

16 *Scott v Jameson* (1914) 7 Adam 529; *Gillespie v Macmillan* 1957 JC 31. These cases are analysed in 'Corroboration of Evidence in Scottish Criminal Law., 1958 SLT (News) 137 and W A Wilson 'The Logic of Corroboration' (1960) 76 Sc L Rev 101.

17 1930 JC 68. The principle is, however, ancient (*Lady Milton v Laird of Milton* (1667) Mor 12102 in which proof was allowed by the evidence of single witnesses to reiterated but connected acts of the same kind). For a full analysis of the Moorov doctrine, see P K Vandore '*The Moorov Doctrine*' 1974 Jur Rev 30 and 179.

18 Per Lord Justice-General Clyde at 74. See also *Tudhope v Hazelton* 1985 SLT 209.

19 1938 JC 152. But 15 months may not be too long an interval if the other factors, particularly those showing a course of similar conduct, are sufficiently strong (*HM Advocate v WB* 1969 JC 72).

20 1944 JC 77. But in *Tudhope v Hazelton* above where there was an interval of 15 months and insufficient indications of nexus the doctrine was not applied.

1 1951 JC 143.

accused offered bribes on two occasions to footballers to lose a match it was held that the evidence of one footballer could corroborate the other.[2] Although typically associated with proof of crime the doctrine is applicable to civil cases.[3]

Corroboration by contradiction

In affiliation cases proof may often be difficult because there may be only two witnesses (the pursuer and the defender) whose testimony bears at all closely on the principal fact in issue and they may contradict each other. Because of such difficulties, some relaxation in the strict requirements of corroboration has been allowed. If the defender denies some material fact and his denial can be shown to be false that false denial may be held as corroboration of the pursuer's evidence. This is what is known as corroboration by contradiction or corroboration by false denial. It has been said that it is only in affiliation cases that corroboration may be afforded in this way[4] but there are parallels in proof of adultery[5] and the rule, although it has been described as 'highly exceptional and not quite intelligible',[6] has a rationale capable of wider application.[7] That rationale is, simply, that the probabilities are that a false denial of a fact material for proof of an allegation against the person making the denial is motivated by fear based on awareness of guilt.

The rule is often said to have been first recognised in *Macpherson v Largue*,[8] but in that case the Lord Justice-Clerk said that if the defender's

2 1952 JC 86.

3 *Murray v Murray* (1847) 9 D 1556; *Whyte v Whyte* (1884) 11 R 710 especially per Lord Lee at 711; *Wilson v Wilson* 1955 SLT (Notes) 81 (all adultery); *Walker v Walker* 1953 SC 297; *Tullis v Tullis* 1953 SC 312 (cruelty); *Landales v Gray* (1816) 1 Mur 719; *Ramsay v Nairne* (1833) 11 S 1033 at 1046 (slander); *Lady Milton v Laird of Milton* (1667) Mor 12102.

4 *Davies v Hunter* 1933 SC 10.

5 *McInnes v McInnes* 1954 SC 396; *Hall v Hall* 1958 SC 206, but see comment on *McInnes* in *Burnett v Burnett* 1955 SC 183 per Lord Cormont at 188.

6 *Davies v Hunter* 1934 SC 10 per Lord Anderson.

7 In England the accused's lies whether told in the course of his testimony or out of court may constitute corroboration where that is required. It is, however, not enough that the accused should be disbelieved; there must be testimony from another witness showing his statement to be false. See *R v Lucas* [1981] 1 QB 720, [1981] 2 All ER 1008: 'to be capable of amounting to corroboration the lie told out of court must first of all be deliberate. Secondly, it must relate to a material issue. Thirdly, the motive for the lie must be a realisation of guilt and a fear of the truth. The jury should in appropriate cases be reminded that people sometimes lie for example in an attempt to bolster up a just cause, or out of shame or out of a wish to conceal disgraceful behaviour from their family. Fourthly, the statement must be clearly shown to be a lie by evidence other than that of the accomplice who is to be corroborated, that is to say by admission or by evidence from an independent witness'.

8 (1896) 23 R 785.

evidence was not to be believed it must be taken out of the case altogether and the case treated as if he had not been examined (a view which is inconsistent with rejection of the defender's evidence affording corroboration)[9] and Lord Trayner's view was that the false denial did not by itself afford corroboration but gave an incriminating complexion to other evidence which, in the absence of the false denial, might have borne the appearance of innocence and so enabled the evidence as a whole (if spoken to by two or more witnesses other than the defender) to amount to corroborated testimony.[10] Lord Trayner seems, moreover, to have thought that the mere fact that the defender was not believed was sufficient to enable his denial to be used in that way.

Dawson v McKenzie[11] reflected the view of the effect of the false denial taken in *Macpherson v Largue* except that it was made clear that the defender's denial must be proved to be false:

> 'Opportunity may have a complexion put upon it by statements made by the defender which are proved to be false. It is not that the false statement made by the defender proves that the pursuer's statements are true, but it may give to a proved opportunity a different complexion from what it would have borne had no such false statement been made.'

It is, however, now settled not only that a false denial affords corroboration but that it may itself supply evidence of opportunity as well as being relevant to the construction to be put upon such evidence. That is put beyond doubt by *Macpherson v Beaton*[12] in which it was held that the defender's false denials might be used as corroboration of the pursuer's evidence and might be so used in relation both to opportunity for sexual intercourse at the time of conception and to the occurrence of sexual intercourse following on the opportunity.

The fact denied need not be such that if it had not been denied it would afford corroboration. Where it is such, there is indeed in strictness no need to have resort to corroboration by false denial. It must be a fact which, if he admitted it, the defender would find difficulty in explaining consistently with the case he is putting forward.[13]

There is sheriff court authority for the view that no distinction is to be made between denials in evidence and denials on record[14] but it is not

9 At 790.
10 At 791.
11 1908 SC 648.
12 1955 SC 100 especially per Lord Patrick.
13 *Costley v Little* (1892) 30 SLR 87; *Lowdon v McConnachie* 1933 SC 574.
14 *Morrison v McArdle* 1967 SLT (ShCt) 58.

easy to reconcile that view with more recent authority on the distinction between pleadings and evidence.[15]

AGREEMENT WITH RECORD OR INDICTMENT (OR COMPLAINT)

If the party on whom the onus lies is to succeed he must discharge that onus by corroborated testimony which, moreover, is substantially in accord with the record or with the indictment or complaint. That does not mean, however, that a pursuer or prosecutor must prove all his averments. It is sufficient that the pursuer proves sufficient within the general scope of the averments which he has made to justify the remedy which he seeks[16] and similarly it is sufficient that the prosecutor, within the scope set by the averments in the indictment or complaint, proves sufficient to justify conviction. Problems may, however, arise where there are discrepancies between the evidence led and what has been averred. Normally it is sufficient that the party on whom the onus rests proves the substance of his averments and he will succeed despite discrepancies which do not detract from that substance. That, at least, is the general rule in civil cases.[17] In criminal cases a stricter view may be taken, subject to a certain latitude allowed in proof of time, place and quantity.[18] In both civil and criminal cases the court has power by allowing amendment of the pleadings, to cure serious discrepancies between evidence and averment but that power will be exercised only where the other party will not be prejudiced.

COHERENCE

The evidence must be reasonably coherent, ie it must not be self-contradictory or mutually destructive. The natural and common characteristics of truthful testimonies coming from different persons is consistency, while that of false evidence is discrepancy and generally speaking, the more numerous the circumstances over which the examination extends the more likly it is to bring out one or other of these qualities. The value of consistency should not, however, be pressed too far. Where evidence is generally consistent, there is some probability that it is true, while, where it is a mass of contradictions, it may be

15 *Lee v National Coal Board* 1955 SC 151; *Stewart v Glasgow Corpn* 1958 SC 28; *Wilson v Clyde Rigging & Boiling Scaling Co Ltd* 1959 SC 328.
16 *Gunn v Mcadam & Son* 1949 SC 31.
17 *Mcdonald v Duncan* 1933 SC 737.
18 Criminal Procedure (Scotland) Act 1975 ss 50, 51 and 312(f) and (g).

virtually impossible to decide what is the true version. Monolithic consistency is, however, suspect. Because of the difference of human powers of observation and recollection it is scarcely in accordance with human nature for two or more witnesses who are seeking to tell the truth to give exactly the same account of an event, at any rate where the facts are at all complex. Accordingly, where they do give absolutely identical accounts, the proper inference may be not that they are telling the truth, but that they have got together to concoct a story.

Generally speaking, the consistency of evidence, or the lack of it, is a question of fact to be taken into account by the jury or other tribunal of fact in weighting the evidence. Cases may, however, occur of evidence so riddled with inconsistency that one can say, as a matter of law, that the evidence cannot amount to proof.

STANDARD OF PROOF

The party on whom the onus rests must discharge that onus by corroborated testimony in substantial accord with the pleadings and reasonably self-consistent and he must, moreover, do so to the satisfaction of the jury or other tribunal of fact on the standard appropriate to the case. The standard appropriate to criminal cases is proof beyond reasonable doubt. In order to qualify as a reasonable doubt, there must be something more than a strained or fanciful acceptance of remote possibility.[19] The doubt must, in other words, be one which one might reasonably entertain in practical affairs. In England, there has been some dissatisfaction with the expression 'reasonable doubt' but attempts to find some other formulation have not shown any clear improvement[20] and in Scotland the practice still is, to use the expression 'reasonable doubt' with, perhaps, some explanation along the lines indicated above.[1]

The standard of proof in civil cases is not so high as in criminal cases. It is enough that the party on whom the onus lies shows that his version of the facts is the more probable. That has always been the general standard although the actual term 'balance of probabilities' is said to have been introduced from English practice by Lord Dunedin in *Simpson v LMS Railway Co*: 'There is no such thing as absolute certainty even where there is direct testimony so that if analysed strictly any conclusion is based on the balance of probabilities'.[2] So if more than one inference may be drawn from the proved facts, weighing them together, that will

19 *Irving v Minister of Pensions* 1945 SC 21 per Lord Justice-Clerk Cooper at 29.
20 *R v Hapwert & Fearnley* [1955] 2 QB 600.
1 See *Shaw v HM Advocate* 1953 JC 51 per Lord Justice-Clerk Thomson at 54.
2 1931 SC (HL) 15 at 20.

prevail which is the more probable. But if an inference pointing one way is equally consistent with one pointing the other, the matter is left in even scales and he on whom lies the onus of proof fails.[3]

Exceptionally, the standard of proof in civil cases may be higher than a balance of probabilities. As has already been noted, that was at one time true of actions of divorce or of separation and aliment on the ground of adultery, in which cases, proof beyond reasonable doubt was required; but that is no longer so.[4] Reference has also been made to the standard of proof which may be necessary to prove allegations of crime in a civil case.[4] The presumption arising under the maxim *pater est quem nuptiae demonstrant* must still be rebutted by proof beyond reasonable doubt and particularly strong evidence may be required to rebut the presumption against donation.[4] In other cases, particular circumstances may justify a higher than usual standard of proof.

WEIGHT OF EVIDENCE

Whether or not the onus of proof is discharged will, of course, depend on the weight and value which the tribunal of fact attaches to the evidence. Question of weight and value resolve themselves in the main into questions of the credibility and reliability of witnesses and strength of inferences from the facts. These are questions of fact on which no rules of law can be laid down and are entirely distinct from questions of sufficiency of evidence in law.

SUFFICIENCY OF EVIDENCE IN LAW

There is sufficient evidence in law if the party on whom the onus lies has adduced corroborated and consistent evidence in substantial accord with his pleadings. The questions of on whom the onus lies, whether there is corroboration and whether the evidence is consistent and in accord with the pleadings, are all questions of law. Accordingly, sufficiency in law is a matter to be decided by the court. The standard of proof applicable to the case is also a question of law (usually one to which the answer is clear) and is, therefore, a matter on which the jury, if there is a jury, must be directed by the judge. It is, however, for the jury or other tribunal of fact to decide, as a matter of fact, whether the evidence is of sufficient weight to satisfy the standard of proof. It is possible for evidence to be of sufficient weight to satisfy the tribunal of

3 *Hendry v Clan Line Steamers* 1949 SC 320 per Lord Jamieson.
4 Ch 12 above.

fact but not to be sufficient in law (eg because it is uncorroborated). Equally evidence may be sufficient in law but not carry sufficient weight with the tribunal of fact to satisfy the standard of proof.

CREDIBILITY ON REVIEW

Unless in the cases specified by statute where appeal is limited to questions of law an appeal court may review a decision on questions of fact as well as on questions of law. Where, however, the decision on fact turns, as is often the case, on questions of the weight of evidence and particularly of the credibility of witnesses an appeal court will be slow to interfere with the conclusion reached at first instance by the tribunal of fact. The principal reason is that questions of credibility of witnesses must turn very largely on the impression the witness made on those who saw him—something which an appeal court cannot assess for itself.

Because juries do not give reasons for their verdict, it is impossible to know whether any conclusion of fact they reach is based on an impression of the credibility of witnesses or on some other reason. A verdict of a jury which is unassailable on legal grounds (eg misdirection by the judge or insufficiency of evidence in law) will therefore be overturned on the facts only if it is such a verdict that no jury, properly instructed, could have reached. Where, however, a case is tried by a judge alone, reasons have to be given and it is easier to distinguish between questions of credibility of witnesses and other question of fact although the distinction may not always be sharp. Where questions of fact other than the credibility of witnesses are at issue there is little obstacle to review by the appeal court although weight should be given to the view formed by the judge of first instance. Thus in *Benmax v Austin Motor Co Ltd*[5] it was said that where there was no question of the credibility of witnesses and the sole question was the proper inference to be drawn from specific facts, an appellate court was in as good a position to evaluate the evidence as the trial judge and should form its own independent opinion though it would give weight to the opinion of the trial judge. Where, however, only questions of credibility of witnesses are at stake or where such questions are closely interrelated with other questions of fact, the scope for interference by the appeal court is much more limited. In *Clark v Edinburgh & District Tramways Co*[6] Lord Shaw of Dunfermline had questions of credibility in mind when he said in a famous passage:

5 [1955] AC 370.
6 1919 SC (HL) 35 at 37.

> 'Witnesses without any conscious bias towards the conclusion may have in their demeanour, in their manner, in their hesitation, in the nuance of their expression, and even the turns of the eyelid left an impression upon the man who saw and heard them that can never be reproduced on the printed page. Am I—who sit here without these advantages, sometimes broad and sometimes subtle, which are the privileges of the judge who heard and tried the case—in a position not having these privileges, to come to a clear conclusion that the judge who had them was plainly wrong? If I cannot be satisfied in my own mind that the judge with these privileges was plainly wrong, then it appears to me to be my duty to defer to his judgment.'

The whole question of review on fact is summarised in the speech of Lord Thankerton in *Thomas v Thomas*:[7]

1 Where a question of fact has been tried by a judge without a jury, and there is no question of misdirection of himself by the judge, an appellate court which is disposed to come to a different conclusion on the printed evidence should not do so unless it is satisfied that any advantage enjoyed by the trial judge, by reason of having seen and heard the witnesses, could not be sufficient to explain or justify the trial judge's conclusion.

2 The appellate court may take the view that without having seen or heard the witness it is not in a position to come to any satisfactory conclusion on the printed evidence. (In which case, of course, it cannot do other than adhere to the decision of the trial judge.)

3 The appellate court, either because the reasons given by the trial judge are not satisfactory, or because it unmistakenly so appears from the evidence, may be satisfied that he has not taken proper advantage of his having seen and heard the witnesses, and the matter will then become at large for the appellate court.

REFERENCE TO OATH

Before the Evidence Act 1853 parties were not competent witnesses. This meant that the people with the best knowledge of the facts of the case were often barred from giving evidence. As a result the party on whom the onus lay was often faced with the prospect of having insufficient evidence to establish his case. He could, however, refer the facts in

7 1947 SC (HL) 45 at 54. Cf *Islip Pedigree Breeding Centre and Others v Abercromby* 1959 SLT 161.

dispute to the oath of the other party. If he did that all other methods of proving these facts were excluded and the decision was, in effect, left to the conscience of his opponent. The underlying principle is that a party is not entitled to a judgment of the court unless his conscience is clear.

When competent

Since parties became competent witnesses, reference to oath has become much less frequent. It is, however, still a competent procedure and in some cases is still the only way in which a party can establish his case. It is a civil procedure and is not available in criminal cases. In consistorial cases, within the meaning of the Court of Session Act 1830, the whole case cannot be referred to oath but it seems that certain parts of such cases may be referred.[8] Apart from certain specialties of proof of irregular marriage (a question now obsolete or obsolescent), reference to oath is, however, of limited, if any, utility in consistorial cases. In practically all other civil actions, it is competent for one party to refer the whole or part of his case to the oath of the other party and, if he does so, the opponent's oath is then conclusive of the matters referred and all other evidence on those matters is excluded. In practice, however, references to oath are rarely encountered except in those instances where the only competent form of proof is by writ or oath and the writ of the appropriate party is not available. In cases where the difficulty is scantity of evidence it will usually now be preferable for the party faced with the onus of proof to seek to overcome that difficulty by calling his opponent as a witness rather than by referring to his oath.

The following points should be noted:

1 only questions of fact can be referred;
2 when writing is required by law as a solemnity essential to the constitution of a right or obligation, reference to oath cannot take the place of writing;
3 reference to oath is only competent in a relevant action. The case cannot be referred until the record is closed and all preliminary pleas have been disposed of. After that, reference is competent at any stage even after final judgment so long as the decree has not been extracted;
4 reference can only be made to a party who is the true debtor in the claim and who has the beneficial interest in opposing[9]; and
5 reference to oath is incompetent if the party seeking to refer has examined or cross-examined the opposite party as a witness, or if the parties have entered into a judicial reference. Where, however, a

8 *Ross v Macleod* (1861) 23 D 972; *Mackie v Mackie* 1917 SC 276; *Lindsay v Lindsay* 1927 SC 365.
9 *Craig & Rose v Lamarra* 1975 SC 316 (reference to oath of agent incompetent).

party is examined or cross-examined on only part of the case, the remaining part may be referred to his oath.[10]

Procedure

The procedure for reference to oath is that a minute of reference is signed by the party referring or by his counsel (or in the sheriff court, by the party's solicitor). The minute may refer either the whole cause or a defined part of it to the oath of the other party. The minute may be withdrawn before the oath is taken. After the minute has been lodged a diet is then fixed for the attendance of the other party to take the oath. He is put on oath and examined by the referring party as to the matters covered by the minute of reference. The party on oath must answer all competent questions put to him under penalty of being held as confessed should he fail or refuse to do so. His counsel or solicitor has, however, no right to examine him and will not be allowed to do so, although in order to clarify a matter which has been left obscure, he may propose questions to the judge. The judge may, of course, ask questions in order to elucidate any obscurity. The deposition of the party on oath is taken down in shorthand and authenticated by the judge who decides whether the matters to which the party has sworn are affirmative or negative of the reference. In coming to that decision, he is not concerned with any question of credibility. The question is not whether what the party has said is credible. The sole question is as to what he has sworn. Any admission made on oath must be taken subject to explanations or qualifications which are intrinsic to the admission but extrinsic qualifications may be separated and disregarded.[11]

PROOF BY WRIT OR OATH

By rules of law, probably now obsolescent, proof of certain matters is restricted to the writ or oath of the party who has an interest to deny the contention which it is sought to prove.

By oath is meant the party's oath on a minute of reference. The writ may be any document which is his. 'The writ may be of the most informal kind. Any writing, however informal, which can be held to be actually, or even constructively, the writ of the persons sought to be bound is competent evidence.'[12] An unsigned writing is sufficient, at any

10 *Dewar v Pearson* (1866) 4 M 493. See also *Hamilton v Hamilton's Executors* 1950 SC 39.

11 See *Thomson's Executor v Thomson* 1921 SC 109; *Cowbrough & Co v Robertson* (1879) 6 R 1301 at 1312.

12 *Paterson v Paterson* (1897) 25 R 144 per Lord Moncrieff at 168.

rate, if it is holograph.[13] A typed document, if signed, will be sufficient[14] but there is no authority on the status of unsigned typewritten papers or of messages transmitted and recorded by electronic means. The writ of an agent is the writ of his principal so far as it relates to matters within the agent's actual or ostensible authority.[15] A writ of one party may become constructively the writ of the other when it passes into his hands and he retains it for his own purposes.[16] Parole evidence is admissible to identify whose writ a document[17] is or to show the extent of an agent's authority.[18] The use of a party's writ in this way *in modum probationis* is to be distinguished from, and is entirely independent of, the requirement of writing for the constitution of *obligationes litteris*.

Obligations proveable only by writ or oath

The following are the obligations proof of which is restricted to writ or oath:

(a) Loan

An allegation that money has been lent can, in general, be proved only by the writ or oath of the alleged debtor.[19] The rule does not apply to loans of less than £100 Scots. The fact that the loan is outstanding must, if disputed, also be referred to the debtor's writ or oath.[20] The rule applies only in questions with the debtor at the instance of the creditor or his representatives[1] and it does not apply to the loan of corporeal moveables.[2] It was not applied to debit items which were said to take the form of advances in a current account between principal and agent,[3] but it seems that it is not excluded merely by the fact that the allged loan is part of a series of similar transactions between the parties.[4] A receipt in

13 *Storeys v Paxton* (1878) 6 R 293.
14 *Wink v Speirs* (1868) 6 M 657.
15 *Bryan v Butters Bros* (1892) 19 R 490; *Clark's Executors v Brown* 1935 110; *Fisher v Fisher's Trustees* 1952 SC 347. The agent's authority may be proved by parole evidence (*Smith v Smith* (1869) 8 M 239).
16 *Wood v Howden* (1843) 5 D 507; *Thomson v Lindsay* (1873) 1 R 65; *Campbell's Trustees v Hudson's Executor* (1895) 22 R 943.
17 *Christie's Trustees v Muirhead* (1870) 8 M 461; *Dunn's Trustee v Hardy* (1896) 23 R 621 at 633; *Borland v Macdonald* 1940 SC 124 at 137.
18 *Smith v Smith* (1869) 8 M 239.
19 Gloag *Contract* (2nd edn) pp 192 ff.
20 *Patrick v Patrick's Trustees, Walker v Garlick* 1940 SLT 208.
1 *McKie v Wilson* 1951 SC 15 per Lord President Cooper at 20.
2 *Scott v Fletcher* (1665) Mor 11616; *Geddes v Geddes* (1678) Mor 12730.
3 *Robb v Robb's Trustees* (1884) 11 R 881; *Boyd v Millar* 1933 SN 106, 1934 SN 7.
4 *McKie v Wilson* above; *Smith's Trustee v Smith* 1911 SC 653 at 659.

absolute terms is a writ affording sufficient proof of loan as also is an IOU.[5]

(b) Trust

By the Blank Bonds and Trusts Act 1696[6] trust may be proved in the circumstances to which the Act applies only by the writ or oath of the alleged trustee. The Act applies only in the following circumstances:

1 in actions between the truster and his representatives on the one hand, and the alleged trustee and his representatives on the other;[7]
2 where the alleged trustee has with the consent of the truster an ex facie absolute right of property including the *jus disponendi*. Lack of consent, as where there has been fraud[8] or failure to carry out instructions,[9] may therefore be proved by parole and the Act does not apply where the alleged trustee holds on a title which is less than an absolute right of property;[10] and
3 where the alleged trustee holds, under a deed or document of title, or, perhaps, under missives of sale.[11]

All three of the above conditions must be satisfied before the Act applies.[12] If trust is proved the terms of the trust may be established by evidence *prout de jure*.[13]

(c) Gratuitous obligations

The doctrine of consideration is no part of the law of Scotland and accordingly gratuitous obligations may be binding.[14] They may be proved, however, only by the writ or oath of the creditor.[15] The

5 *Christie's Trustees v Muirhead* (1870) 8 M 461; *Thiem's Trustees v Collie* (1899). 1 F764
6 C 25.
7 *Middleton v Rutherglen* (1861) 23 D 526; *Wink v Speirs* (1868) 6 M 657; *Wallace v Sharp* (1885) 12 R 687; *Hastie v Steel* (1886) 13 R 843.
8 *Marshall v Lyell* (1859) 21 D 514 at 521; *Wink v Speirs* abive; *Galloway v Galloway* 1929 SC 160 at 167 and 169.
9 *Mackay v Ambrose* (1829) 7 S 699 at 702; *Horne v Morrison* (1877) 4 R 977; *Dunn v Pratt* (1898) 25 R 461 at 468.
10 *Anderson v North of Scotland Bank* (1901) 4 F 49 at 54; *Cairns v Davidson* 1913 SC 1054; *Newton v Newton* 1923 SC 15 at 25; *Kennedy v Macrae* 1946 SC 118; *Weissenbruch v Weissenbruch* 1961 SC 340.
11 The Act was applied to missives of sale in *Dunn v Pratt* (1898) 25 R 461, but see the dissenting opinion of Lord Kinnear at 469. See also *Cairns v Davidson* 1913 SC 1054 at 1057; *McConnachie v Geddes* 1918 SC 391 at 399 and *Newton v Newton* 1923 SC 15 at 25.
12 *Duggan v Wight* (1797) Mor 12761; *Knox v Martins* (1850) 12 D 719; *Pant Mawr Quarry Co v Fleming* (1883) 10 R 457; *McNair's Executors v Litster* 1939 SC 72; *Pickard* 1963 SLT 56.
13 *Livingstone v Allan* (1900) 3 F 233 at 237.
14 Gloag *Contract* (2nd edn) p 50; *Hawick Heritable Investment Bank v Hoggan* (1902) 5 F 75 per Lord Kyllachy at 78.
15 *Millar v Tremamondo* 1771 Mor 12395; *Smith v Oliver* 1911 SC 103.

restriction on proof does not apply where the obligation is, on its face, unilateral and gratuitous but is, in fact, part of a bilateral and onerous contract.[16] Fulfilment by the person to whom a promise was made of a condition attached to the promise does not, however, change the character of the promise so as to make it an onerous contract.[17]

(d) *Obligations of relief*

In general, an obligation of relief can be proved only by the writ or oath of the party alleged to be obliged.[18] The rule does not, of course, apply where the right of relief is implied by law and there is some authority for the view that it does not apply where the obligation is an integral part of a transaction which can be proved by parole.[19]

(e) *Innominate and unusual contracts*

Where an alleged contract does not fall within a class known by a recognised and distinctive name (eg sale, agency) and is also unusual and anomalous proof of the contract is restricted to the writ or oath of the party disputing its existence.[20] There is no firm guide as to what makes a contract unusual and anomalous.[1]

(f) *Performance and discharge of obligations constituted or vouched by writing*

If an obligation has been constituted in writing or is vouched by a writ, its discharge or performance may be proved only by the writ or oath of the creditor.[2] The rule probably does not apply where the creditor has an interest to prove performance and seeks to do so (as, eg to establish *rei interventus*).[3] In general the rule applies only to performance by payment and not to obligations *ad factum praestandum*.[4] Even where performance is by payment, the rule does not apply if performance or discharge is a

16 *Hawick Heritable Investment Bank v Hoggan* above.
17 *Millar v Tremamondo*; *Smith v Oliver* above.
18 *Devlin v McKelvie* 1915 SC 180; *Woodrop v Speirs* 1906 SLT 319.
19 *Rhind v Mackenzie* 20 February 1916 FC; *Devlin v McKelvie* 1915 SC 180 per Lord Salvesen at 187 and Lord Guthrie at 189. In these circumstances proof by parole may, however, be competent only where the transaction in question relates only to movables (ibid).
20 *Forbes v Caird* (1887) 4 R 1141; *Garden v Earl of Aberdeen* (1893) 20 R 896; *Smith v Reekie* 1920 SC 188.
1 See Gloag *Contract* (2nd edn) p 196.
2 *Thiem's Trustees v Collie* (1899) 1 F 764.
3 *Foggo v Hill* (1840) 2 D 1322 per Lord Fullerton at 1334.
4 Stair IV 43 4; Erskine IV ii 21; Gloag *Contract* (2nd edn) p 720.

necessary inference from facts or circumstances.[5] The rule also does not apply where it is alleged that the party founding on a document of debt has no right to hold it (eg where it was granted for a particular purpose, the purpose has been fulfilled and the document should have been given up).[6]

(g) Payment under antecedent obligation

Where goods are sold on credit and in other instances where the matter at issue is payment under an antecedent obligation, proof of payment is limited to the writ or oath of the creditor even if the contract is verbal.[7] As in category (*f*) above, the rule does not apply if payment is a necessary inference from facts and circumstances.[8] It is uncertain whether it applies to proof of payment of wages and salaries.[9]

(h) Acceptilation

Where a right has been constituted in writing its gratuitous renunciation can be proved only by the writ or oath of the creditor.[10] The only exception is, again, where renunciation is a necessary inference from facts and circumstances.[11] It is uncertain whether proof of the renunciation of a right which was not constituted in writing is restricted to the writ or oath of the creditor.[12]

5 *Theim's Trustees v Collie* above; *Chrystal v Chrystal* (1900) 2 F 373 at 379; *Mackenzie's Executors v Morrison's Trustees* 1930 SC 830 at 836; Stair IV xlv 23.
6 *Bishop v Bryce* 1910 SC 426.
7 *Young v Thomson* 1909 SC 529; Gloag *Contract* (2nd edn) p 717.
8 *Couts v Couts* (1636) Mor 11423; *Irvine v Falconer* 1671 Mor 11424; *Lord Saltoun v Fraser* 1721 Mor 11425; *Wilson v Wilson* 1783 Mor 11646; *Stuart v Maconochie* (1836) 14 S 412; *Russell's Trustees v Russell* (1885).
9 *Brown v Mason* (1856) 19 D 137 at 138; *Annand's Trustees v Annand* (1869) 7 M 526 at 530.
10 *Reid v Gow* (1903) 10 SLT 606; *Keanie v Keanie* 1940 SC 549.
11 *Anderson's Trustees v Webster* (1883) 11 R 35; *Lavam v Gavin Aird & Co* 1919 SC 345 at 248; Gloag *Contract* (2nd edn) p 722.
12 Gloag ibid; Erskine III iv, 8; *sed contra Kilpatrick v Dunlop* (1909) 2 SLT 307; *Dickson* para 629; *Walker and Walker* p 131, para 128(b).

Index